Cypress Shade

Cypress Shade
A True Crime FBI Memoir

John W. Whiteside III

Copyright © 2015 John W. Whiteside III
All rights reserved.

ISBN 10: 1512172537
ISBN 13: 9781512172539
Library of Congress Control Number: 2015907678
CreateSpace Independent Publishing Platform
North Charleston, South Carolina

For my parents, who taught me to treat everyone with dignity and respect; to the special agents and professional support staff of the Jackson Division of the FBI who served from 1964 to the present time, for their dedicated efforts to ensure justice was served in Mississippi; and to all who suffered and died just because of the color of their skin, I dedicate this memoir.

Table of Contents

          Prologue ix
Chapter 1 Surprise 1
Chapter 2 Arrival 7
Chapter 3 White Bred 17
Chapter 4 G-Man 27
Chapter 5 Southern Comfort 35
Chapter 6 Road Trip 43
Chapter 7 Home 51
Chapter 8 Sharecroppers 61
Chapter 9 Lynchings 73
Chapter 10 High Times 87
Chapter 11 Racism and Slurs 97
Chapter 12 Delta Ways 107
Chapter 13 Race Riot 121
Chapter 14 Training 133
Chapter 15 SWAT 145
Chapter 16 Parchman 171
Chapter 17 The Blues 197
Chapter 18 Y'all Come Back 211
Chapter 19 The Big Apple 229
Chapter 20 Dixie Again 243
Chapter 21 Mississippi Musings 253
          Epilogue 265
          Author's Note 271
          Appendix 273
          About the Author 281

DISCLAIMER: The opinions expressed in this manuscript are those of the author and not those of the Federal Bureau of Investigation.

Prologue

Fidelity...Bravery...Integrity

—FBI motto

On this particular sticky summer evening, the muffled hum of an inboard engine drowned out the chirping nightly cacophony that I had grown accustomed to along the banks of the Mississippi River. The Delta's night sky was as black as ink, having no visible slice of moon to cast a shadow on the water. Lying down on the hard floor in the stern of a fiberglass fishing boat, along with two other Federal Bureau of Investigation (FBI) special agents, I tried to find a comfortable position to prevent my legs, arms, and other body parts from cramping up or falling asleep. That became a most difficult task, as the small space available to us meant our bodies were already intertwined as we struggled to keep our heads below the gunwale. The covert mission had begun just minutes prior, as darkness enveloped the mighty river. Already sweating profusely in our black neoprene wet suits, we concluded that comfort was the last thing we would be enjoying that night. As I stared at the white canvas bag unceremoniously packed with $1 million in ransom money, I began visualizing the task before me. The mission might go on for many hours, possibly until sunrise. Until then, we would just have to deal with our discomfort until the real action began.

As I lay in the boat, wondering if gunfire would be involved in our mission, my thoughts were drawn to friends in the US military who were deployed to the Vietnam War. Although Congress never declared a state of war against North Vietnam, I imagined that all of the dead, wounded, and debilitated patriots who fought in those jungles, including the still-missing US prisoners of war, would probably take issue with this semantic. My current predicament reminded me of secret Central Intelligence Agency (CIA) incursions into enemy territory, and Special Forces operations traversing furtively through jungle rivers and streams to engage the enemy. I wondered how my life would have been different had I enlisted in the military after high school, rather than going to college and eventually landing a position as an FBI special agent. Considering the circumstances, I suspected things would not have been too different from my current situation, as I forced myself to control my body and mind, focusing on the mission and waiting for the moment when events might explode into chaos and confusion.

Prologue

I was suddenly jolted from my thoughts as the boat came to an abrupt stop. Cursing, the pilot struggled to maneuver the boat as the stern swung around, the boat now facing the direction we had been traveling. "Dammit," he exclaimed with a whisper, "we've hit a sandbar. You divers will need to get out and push us off. Be careful of the river bottom as you go overboard. There are lots of underwater hazards out there, not to mention the water moccasins."

We left the uncomfortable, safe floor of the boat, slid over the gunwale, and began pushing the boat off the sandbar while wading in waist-deep water. We endeavored to dislodge the boat as quickly as possible, hoping the activity would not be noticed by anyone watching along the slippery riverbanks. After all, our presence in the boat was to be a great secret that would ultimately allow us the element of complete surprise. We were able to get the boat off the sandbar with some effort, and we quietly enjoyed cooling off in the muddy river water before climbing back into the boat to continue our mission. As the pilot got back underway, we repositioned ourselves on the floor once again, hoping we had not compromised our discreet presence on the Mississippi and would be able to continue unfettered until our task was complete.

CHAPTER 1
SURPRISE

Mr. Whiteside,
Your headquarters are changed for official reasons from
Akron, Ohio to Jackson, Mississippi.

— FBI TRANSFER LETTER DATED AUGUST 8, 1972

A white business envelope with a clear plastic window revealing my name and the address of the FBI's Cleveland Division arrived in the morning mail, delivered to the Akron, Ohio, Resident Agency of the FBI. Observing that it was sent from FBI headquarters, our clerical employee, Fred, waved the envelope in the air, announcing to all that Special Agent John Whiteside had just received his transfer orders. I was just finishing the remainder of some lukewarm coffee laced with milk and sugar and swallowed hard at the news. There was no surprise that a transfer was coming, as I'd been assigned to the Cleveland Division for thirteen months, and current FBI policy was to transfer agents to a second office of assignment after a year or so. The policy also meant that an agent might stay in his second office for the remainder of his career. It just depended on a lot of different factors and the "needs of the bureau." But this very possibly could be a permanent assignment for the rest of my career as a special agent of the FBI. I truly hoped it would be a good one.

"It looks like it's finally here, John," Fred bellowed to all in the office. "Where do you think you're headed?"

Laughter broke out among those agents sitting at their gray metal desks. "Someplace wonderful, no doubt," Bink shouted out. "How about Butte, Montana!" Everyone laughed, as it was no secret that Director J. Edgar Hoover used the Montana FBI field office assignment as a disciplinary transfer for those agents who in some manner ran afoul of FBI rules and regulations. Even though Director Hoover had passed away in May, his policies still remained at the core of the FBI. "My bet is that it will be somewhere hot, dusty, and deserted, like El Paso, Texas," Mick chimed in. It was all in good fun, and all eagerly anticipated the answer as I fumbled with the envelope seal.

This moment reminded all the agents of a similar time during training school when they received their first office assignment. Bets were placed then as to where everyone would be assigned. Few, if any, ever guessed correctly. All of the agents in the Akron Resident Agency were in their second office of assignment and would not likely be transferred again, unless they opted for administrative advancement or a special assignment of some sort. Akron was a great place to work in the FBI, and there was little reason for anyone to want to leave, other than perhaps to get closer to home. They had all experienced this second office transfer and simply enjoyed me getting to share something they'd all been through before.

A resident agency assignment was different from an assignment to a field office. Akron, Ohio, was a resident agency attached to the Cleveland Division of the FBI. It was a satellite office, like others including Toledo, Lima, Painesville, and Sandusky, Ohio. Resident agencies, more commonly referred to as RAs, were a way to spread FBI offices evenly through the territory assigned to the larger field office. The RA method allowed the response time for crime and other incidents to be much quicker in a particular geographic area. Unlike a field office where large squads of special agents were more specialized in selected investigations, special agents assigned to RAs were required to work all types of investigations handled by the FBI.

My initial shock was pretty visible to my colleagues as I quickly scanned the letter and announced my transfer to Jackson, Mississippi. Bink, a country boy who was from east Tennessee, thought the transfer was a good one. Mick, a Texan, didn't act like it was a bad thing either. Hudie immediately broke into song, singing Nancy Sinatra's recent hit "Jackson." All I could think about at that moment was the civil rights movement, the assassination of Rev. Martin Luther King Jr. in 1968, the race riots that followed his assassination, and all that had transpired in the Deep South in recent years. I had never worked any civil rights cases in my brief, one-year FBI career in Ohio, with the exception of assisting on a few leads pertaining to the shootings at Kent State University by the Ohio National Guard in 1970. But then another thought struck me like a thunderbolt. What would my fiancée think about this assignment? We were planning a wedding for early September, and while we knew a transfer was in the wind, I didn't think we ever gave a thought to a post in Mississippi. Who would?

We'd both figured on a transfer to a big office like New York City or Washington, DC, or perhaps even Los Angeles. My fiancée was an Ohio girl, born and bred. She had traveled a bit after graduation from high school, so I hoped she wouldn't be too offended at a long-distance transfer. She attended college in Minnesota for a year before signing up with the FBI and relocating to Washington, DC, where she worked as a fingerprint clerk in the Identification Division. A subsequent transfer that she personally requested brought her back home to work as the National Crime Information Center (NCIC) specialist at the Cleveland office. What would she think about a transfer to Jackson, Mississippi? How would it affect our wedding and honeymoon plans? Would she even want to go with me on this distant, southern assignment?

I was temporarily brought back to earth with continued, good-natured ribbing from my colleagues, and their best wishes as well. I knew I had to call my fiancée, who was working in the Cleveland FBI field office that morning, but wanted to wait a bit until I let the transfer news sink in. How would she take the news? What would our families think about a transfer so far from home? My fiancée's siblings, with the exception of her older brother, and all my siblings, still resided with our parents and lived at home. My stomach churned as I knew I had to make the call, and I got no privacy from my buddies in the office. They all wanted to see the reaction I would get.

I sat down at my desk and reached for the receiver and asked to be connected to my fiancée, Donna, at the Cleveland office. My heart was in my throat. Think about something wonderful to say about Mississippi, I mused, as I waited for her to pick up the telephone. I couldn't think of anything, funny or otherwise, to start the conversation. Silence was all I heard in my office as all watched me squirm with the impending news. I didn't know a damn thing about Mississippi, except for all the racial trouble down there.

"Hello…hi, Donna…it's me," I said.

"Oh, hi, sweetie. How's your morning going? Did you hear the latest office news?" she asked.

"No, fill me in," I said—anything for a break in the unnerving stress I was experiencing at the moment.

"I just heard that Wayne and John were both transferred to Jackson, Mississippi, of all places. Seems kind of strange that an office that small is getting two transfers from Cleveland at the same time."

I nodded my head. "Yes, I agree," I mumbled slightly.

She continued, "I think Wayne is pleased, as he is from Memphis, and I think John is from Florida or Texas, somewhere down south, so he's probably pleased too."

I was very friendly with Wayne Tichenor, as we both lived in the same apartment complex when I worked in Cleveland, prior to my transfer to Akron. We often double-dated and ate our frozen Swanson TV dinners together when we had nothing better to do. Wayne was also engaged to an office stenographer and was getting married before Donna and me. Wayne was in the FBI new agents' class one week before my class started, and John was in the class that followed mine by a month.

It was about time to fess up. I finally found my opening words. "Isn't it something that a guy a class ahead of me and a guy a class behind me were both transferred to Jackson. What do you think that means for me?"

After a moment of dreaded silence, Donna said, "Are you trying to tell me something?"

I answered, "Yes, I am. Looks like the FBI needs *three* new guys in Jackson!"

A long pause, then, "Oh my gosh, are we really going to Jackson too?"

A few short days after receiving my transfer letter to Jackson, Donna and I had another shock. Fred opened the daily mail and found another surprise for me. "Hey, John, looks like you got a second letter from the director. What'd you do wrong this time?" He brought the letter to my desk as I was completely baffled as to what it might be. I opened the letter, only to see yet another transfer order. The letter rescinded my transfer to Jackson, Mississippi, and transferred me instead to the Greenville, Mississippi, resident agency.

"Where the hell is that?" I wondered aloud. None of the other agents in the office were familiar with the place. I could only surmise that since I had resident agency experience in Akron, Ohio, the FBI felt I was the best fit of the three Jackson transferees to serve in another resident agency. Akron had been a fantastic assignment, and I only hoped that Greenville would be equally as much fun. I needed to call my fiancée soon and break the news yet again. I knew she was looking forward to socializing with Wayne's wife, Joy, in Jackson, as she was a fellow Ohioan. Once again, our plans and expectations changed before we ever left Ohio.

"You aren't going to believe this," I said to Donna as she picked up the telephone. "My orders have been rescinded, and I'm being sent to the Greenville, Mississippi, Resident Agency."

"Well, you like resident agency life, so that isn't too bad, is it?" she replied. I was glad she didn't seem to be bothered by the change of plans. We'd simply have to give it a try and see how it would all work out. It was really our only option.

CHAPTER 2
Arrival

There is no fear in love,
but perfect love casts out fear

— 1 John 4:18

"Please return your tray tables to their upright positions and ensure that your seatbelts are securely fastened for landing. Please extinguish all smoking materials. The captain has advised we will be arriving in Greenville, Mississippi, in ten minutes," said the sweet, southern-accented voice of a Southern Airways flight attendant over the intercom. Flight attendants, dressed in brown hot pants and white leather boots, 1970s style, paced up and down the cabin floor to ready the aircraft for landing. It had been a short hop of no more than a half hour from the Memphis airport to Greenville.

My wife and I were exhausted from our two-week honeymoon to the Hawaiian Islands, followed by several days' stay in San Francisco. The flight from San Francisco was a long one, yet the anticipation of arrival in Mississippi prevented any quality rest during the flight. Soon it would be time to pick up our luggage, find a way to get to our hotel, and begin our new lives together in what was known as the Mississippi Delta.

The plane landed smoothly on the cracked and pitted tarmac. It was mid-September 1972 and about ten thirty at night. In other words, it was pitch black outside. As the plane taxied to what I hoped would be a typical exit ramp into the airport terminal, I could see nothing outside the window. When the plane slowly came to a halt, a few of the passengers, predominantly black, retrieved their overhead luggage and packages of all manner and form and began to deplane. Many passengers remained on board for a continuing flight to New Orleans. As we waited to deplane, the first wave of humidity entered the fuselage from the open cabin door. When we arrived at the cabin door, I realized we would be exiting by portable steps that had been wheeled up to the aircraft. As we walked carefully down the steps, the full force of the windless Mississippi Delta heat and humidity greeted us.

Perspiration formed immediately on all parts of our bodies. And then there was the sound, unlike any I'd ever heard before. Bullfrogs, crickets, and insects of unknown species joined their wistful songs together, chirping and croaking happily in the eerie darkness of the Delta. But there was something else too, a peculiar scent to the air. It was difficult to describe, as it was mixed in with the thick Delta humidity and exhaust fumes from the airplane. There was a decaying characteristic to the odor, an earthy smell unfamiliar to me from the city streets of Philadelphia. It turned out that it was the scent of the Mississippi Delta, its noxious bayous and festering swampland. I briefly wondered if the peculiar scent was common to the entire town, or only in the vicinity of the airport.

My wife asked me where we should go to pick up our luggage, as those who had deplaned were simply standing around near the aircraft. Not realizing why they were waiting, and being the astute FBI man and new husband, I suggested we walk to the nearby terminal building. I noted we were the only two walking to the building with a small, hand-painted sign above the door reading Welcome to Greenville illuminated poorly with two small lights. We entered through the door, and to my great surprise, saw only two small car rental kiosks, one for Avis and one for Hertz, separated from each other by a Coke machine. Only one of the rental desks was open and being serviced by a young lady. I approached her and asked where we pick up our luggage, expecting to be directed to another part of the building (that I couldn't see at the moment). In a soft Mississippi accent she replied, "Out on the lawn, sir." My wife asked me what she said, as the accent was a bit difficult to decipher, and I simply replied, "Let's go back outside."

As we exited the building, we observed the same worker who had directed the airplane to a stop and placed the stair steps into position now towing by hand a luggage cart filled with suitcases. He let the cart handle drop, and the deplaned passengers mingled around the cart in the darkness, selecting their personal items. Now I realized why the passengers were all standing around the airplane. They'd been through this before. Welcome to Greenville, I thought!

We found our luggage and then realized we needed to find a way to get to our hotel. It was one of the few details I had forgotten to do before leaving Ohio. We had no map of the city and no idea where our hotel, the Downtowner, was located. I thought about going back inside the terminal building to rent a car, when my wife saw a man sitting in a car. "You folks need a ride?" he called out. There were no markings on the car and no meter suggesting it was a taxicab. I asked him about the cost for a trip to the Downtowner hotel. Once we settled on a price—US dollars, not Confederate script—we placed our bags in the trunk and entered the limo. Fortunately for us, we couldn't have run into a nicer guy.

He knew immediately we were, at the very least, visitors coming in by air with luggage and unusual Yankee and midwestern accents. He asked how long we would be in Greenville, and I replied a bit sarcastically, "Possibly forever." He asked if we had some time to spare, and when I replied that we did, he took us for a tour through town, before taking us to the hotel. He was pleased to point out that two new shopping malls had just been completed, the only two in Greenville. That was some comforting news for both of us, because from the looks of things, there wasn't much around.

He took us past the large, concrete levee protecting the town from river flooding. He pointed out a few different hotels and restaurants, inquiring if we liked southern food. I didn't want to tell him I had no idea what southern food was like. My wife asked a few questions about shops, medical facilities, and churches. He took us past both of the hospitals in town, and past the county courthouse. He showed me the location of the federal building where I would begin work on Monday, just a short walk from our hotel. We finally arrived at our destination, and I tipped him well, as his tour was invaluable. We got our luggage and bid our new friend a fond farewell. The front desk clerk at the Downtowner hotel was ready for us as we walked into the lobby.

"Welcome to Greenville. You must be the Whitesides," another young girl with that same soft, sweet accent said. "We've been waiting for y'all. We have a restaurant here on the first floor, and tomorrow we have a Sunday buffet from noon until three. Hope you can make it, and enjoy your stay with us."

We checked in, got our room key, and took the elevator to the third floor. Both of us were looking forward to a good night's sleep. It had been a really long day, accompanied by annoying jet lag as well.

Arrival

The room appeared adequate for our needs until we would be able to locate more permanent housing in town. As I was unpacking, my wife suddenly shouted that there was a cricket in the room. I found the cricket for her and removed him from the premises. What a hero! That was the first cricket I'd ever found in any hotel room I'd stayed in. I was hoping there would be no other insects or problems to contend with that night. But my hopes were dashed rather quickly when my wife exclaimed, "This room is disgusting; the toilet bowl hasn't even been cleaned. Come in here and look at it."

I did as I was requested, as a dutiful new husband, entering the bathroom and looking into the toilet bowl at a brownish-colored water. "The housekeeper probably forgot to flush the toilet when she was finished cleaning the room. Here, just flush it again and all will be okay." I pushed down on the handle and watched as the toilet bowl slowly filled up with the same brown-tinted water. "What is going on here?" I wondered aloud. Yet another flush brought the same results. "Try running the water in the sink," I said to my wife. At first the water seemed normal, but after placing the stopper in the drain, the water formed the same brown color in the white porcelain sink as it did in the toilet bowl. We both wondered what was wrong with the water supply in the hotel.

"This place is filthy and terrible," my wife exclaimed. "We'd better find more suitable housing as soon as we can."

"Tomorrow is Sunday, so it isn't likely anyone will be working in the realtor offices. We'll just have to wait until Monday morning when I can get a car, and we can start looking for an apartment. We'll survive here another day or two," I replied hopefully, assuming we didn't get poisoned by the water supply. "Let's just get to bed and get some sleep."

The room was very quiet, and we slept in until eleven o'clock or so. We decided to get ready and then go downstairs for the Sunday brunch, as we didn't have any transportation or any knowledge of other places to eat. Perhaps after brunch, we'd take a walk around and have our first daytime look at Greenville. Taking a shower was another major event, as the water was so soft it seemed impossible to rinse the shampoo out of our hair and get the soap off our bodies. We were also careful not to ingest any of the vile, brown water. Was everything going to be this difficult here?

My wife dressed in a halter top and a pair of short shorts and sandals; after all, we were just back from the Hawaiian Islands, and the summer heat was even greater in Mississippi. I wore a pair of shorts and a blue Primo Beer tee shirt that I purchased in Hawaii. We went downstairs at about twelve thirty for brunch and walked into the restaurant to be seated. We both immediately knew something was not right as every head turned, and every eye in the place looked at us. The hostess was gracious to us and without any fanfare took us to a table for two. As we walked behind her, we both noticed that everyone else in the restaurant was dressed in their Sunday best clothing. Here we were looking like a couple of low-class heathens.

"How come everyone is so dressed up?" I whispered to our waitress as she came by for our drink order.

"Everyone is here after church," was her response. "Everybody goes to church on Sunday here. I guess you're both new in Greenville," she said. "Welcome to our little southern town. You'll find that no one honks their car horns on Sunday, and even the tennis courts are closed. You're in the Bible Belt now. Everything is closed on Sundays, except for some restaurants."

We both ordered sweet tea, although I didn't know if it was like iced tea at home. We didn't want to order water after seeing what it looked like in the room. I couldn't imagine drinking the brown stuff.

We left our table to go to the buffet table. There was a wonderful spread of food from one end of a long table to the other end. Most of the food was unfamiliar to us, with the exceptions of the ham, fried chicken, and roast beef. None of the vegetables looked like anything I'd ever eaten. We slowly made our selections and returned to our table. I wasn't sure what we picked, but everything was delicious, especially the fried chicken. I also enjoyed something that looked like spinach, which I later learned was collard greens. The water might be dreadful, but the food was outstanding. And the sweet tea seemed to be so simply southern. I began looking forward to learning more about the famous southern cuisine and consuming lots of it.

After eating, we decided to take a walk around the area near our hotel. We thought about changing into some more conservative attire for the walk, but we really didn't have those items with us. They were being shipped along with the rest of the few household goods we had accumulated before we left Ohio. My car was being driven to Greenville from Ohio by a car transport company. We were hopeful that all would arrive intact as scheduled. As we left the front door of the hotel, it was like stepping into a humid blast furnace. The brilliant sun beating down on bleached-white sidewalks blinded us until we could find our sunglasses. The humidity was simply oppressive; it was hard to believe that people could tolerate this heat and humidity on a daily basis. Here it was, mid-September, with summer almost over, and no relief in sight.

We decided to walk in a westerly direction as we could see the river levee from the hotel. I was curious about the mighty Mississippi River and was looking forward to seeing the grand sight. A short walk brought us to the levee that was capped in concrete, which I assumed had been poured over an original earthen levee. Climbing to the top, I readied myself for an incredible vista of the mighty Mississippi of lore. Imagine my surprise to see a small body of water in which some barges of different sizes were docked at the water's edge. Was this the Mississippi, I wondered? I would later learn that this was Lake Ferguson, and that the Mississippi River was west of this lake, not visible from this location. Somewhat disappointed with the view and what I thought was the once mighty river, we walked back toward the hotel, taking a different road. We walked for a few blocks, out Main Street and past the post office/government building that housed the local FBI office on the second floor. I'd be checking in there tomorrow and, hopefully, picking up a government car.

We continued our walk past closed storefronts, some of which had been constructed in the mid- to late 1870s, after the Civil War had destroyed most of the original section of town. The buildings looked tired, needing paint in many cases, and with nothing open on Sunday, the place seemed to be deserted, something akin to a ghost town. Many of the shops had false fronts, seeming larger than the single story they actually were. After a few blocks, the sticky humidity and heat were making the walk very unpleasant. We turned north and walked to Washington Street, where we headed west back to the hotel. This street contained yet more business establishments, but nothing that made us look forward to patronizing them at a future date.

Arriving back at our hotel, we reflected on our first day in the Delta. I wondered about my first immersion into the FBI life in Greenville, Mississippi, and hoped it would be similar to our life in Akron. My wife's plans were to begin reaching out to realtors in order to find a suitable apartment. We decided we would rent a place for one year, and if we couldn't adjust to or didn't like life in the Delta, I would ask for a transfer to New York City. Those transfers were automatic during those years: anyone crazy enough to want to work in New York City and endure the expense, miserable commute, taxes, and high cost of real estate was welcome in Gotham. That was the plan anyway, and we'd just have to wait and see how things transpired. Tomorrow, Monday, would be a big day for both of us.

Greenville Municipal Airport, 1972

Arrival

Cypress brake southwest of Greenville, MS.

CHAPTER 3
WHITE BRED

All that I am, or hope to be, I owe to my angel mother.

—ABRAHAM LINCOLN

I was born in the late 1940s and raised in Philadelphia, Pennsylvania, also known somewhat ironically as the City of Brotherly Love. Just check the current crime statistics, and you'll see what I mean. I started my young life in the Logan section of the city, living close to Broad Street, which for years was the showplace of the city. Located near the Reading Railroad line and nestled between two subway stops, the Logan neighborhood reflected a post–World War I atmosphere of well-built row homes complete with front porches and small lawns. Many of the narrow side streets were still paved with cobblestones dating back to colonial days. Shops and restaurants abounded along the entire length of Broad Street, which ran in a north-south direction down the middle of the city.

My grandparents lived in that area, and the family Logan Methodist Church was there as well. Both of my parents were born and raised in that section of the city. The once opulent homes on Broad Street still stood, but the wealthy families who owned them had long since moved to the suburbs, leaving in droves in the late 1920s when the city decided to build a subway system underground along the entire length of Broad Street. While having a wonderful mode of transportation through the shining spot of the city was a great idea, the homeowners did not accept the dirt, dust, vibration, and noise of underground subway construction.

There was little crime in Logan at the time I lived there, and it was always safe to play outside, at least through the early 1960s. In my early youth, I remember hearing the distinct clip-clop of a solitary horse pulling an ice wagon through the neighborhood. Homes were heated at the time by coal-fired boilers. Noisy coal dump trucks roamed the streets, eventually backing up to small front-basement windows where a load of coal would be sent down a metal chute into a coal bin built in every basement. While the male population went off to work, many women would be seen pushing their post–World War II babies in strollers along the paved sidewalks of the neighborhood. When my parents acquired enough money for a down payment on a home in early 1950, we left my grandparents' house in Logan and moved into a typical brick-style row home in the West Oak Lane section of Philadelphia, about fifteen minutes northwest from

Logan. Like Logan, the neighborhood was all white, and rarely, if ever, did I see any black residents.

My father, a World War II veteran and B-24 bomber pilot, was unable to find a job as a commercial pilot after the war, due to the glut of returning pilots. He eventually became a salesman for the Gibson greeting-card company. His sales territory in the 1950s was in the region of north Philadelphia. He would make sales calls on what were then called variety shops or mom-and-pop stores, which sold all sorts of items ranging from greeting cards to toys, over-the-counter medicines, gifts, notions (small, useful items), cigars, cigarettes, and candy. All of the shops were owned by whites, or white immigrants, it seemed to me. On one occasion, my father asked me to accompany him on a short trip to see one of his customers so he could retrieve his greeting-card sample case. We proceeded down Twelfth Street into Philadelphia, only two short blocks east of Broad Street. I was shocked at first to see the neighborhoods were completely filled with black residents. I had never seen a community like this before. He pointed out a billboard advertising cigarettes, with a black couple pictured on the ad. It was the first time I had witnessed any media featuring black people. I was taken aback somewhat, as I never realized that this section of the city existed, and I was amazed at how it seemed to stay compacted into this small, isolated area.

We always enjoyed going to see the Phillies play baseball at Connie Mack Stadium. The stadium was located at Twenty-First and Lehigh Avenues, in north Philadelphia, west of Broad Street. Dad would usually park his car and briefly call on Mrs. Novia, an elderly Italian lady who owned a variety store and was always delighted to see me and squeeze my cheek. We'd usually leave her store with a lemon Italian water ice. As soon as we would reach the street and proceed to the ballpark, a young black youth would approach my dad and offer to watch his car for a quarter. Dad would always accept his offer, and usually gave the boy several quarters. At my young age, I never knew that he would continue to hustle others who were parking for the game. However, our car was always there after the game, and in the same condition as when we left it, so I always figured the kid did a good job.

Our next-door neighbor in West Oak Lane, Al Baker, was a successful businessman. He owned a Jewish delicatessen in the area on Wadsworth Avenue, just a few blocks from his residence. He had two sons, David and Billy, with whom I was friendly and who were part of the group of guys I played stickball and other games with growing up. This family was the only family I knew who had a black maid at their home on a daily basis. Her name was Cora; I have no idea what her last name was. Every time I was in the Baker home and saw Cora, she was dressed in a faded cotton-print, wraparound housedress tied with a matching strip of cotton fabric around her waist. Her hair was always fully covered in a colorful do-rag worn tightly against her head. She kept the house in order and, I presume, cooked meals on occasion. She was very soft-spoken and seemed to go about her business without interruption. Her silky smooth, medium-complexion skin and pleasant countenance belied any past hurt or pain she might have felt about her life situation. Whenever I was at their home, I always spoke to her, calling her "Aunt Cora." We treated each other with the respect any youth in the 1950s would have for an elder, regardless of color. I always thought the family must have been quite wealthy to afford to have someone like Aunt Cora working for them. I know the two boys treated her with the utmost respect as well. She was like a mother to them.

This was the extent of my contact with the black population in Philadelphia as I was growing up, until I went to high school and then to college at Temple University, also located on Broad Street in north Philadelphia, a few miles south of Logan. There were a handful of black students at Cheltenham High School where I attended from 1962 to 1965, the most notable being future baseball star Reggie Jackson. One of my more memorable moments with him was the time he asked me to play on his softball team in gym class. Quite an honor to be selected by a future baseball Hall of Famer. He knew I could hit the ball pretty well. The truth was, I usually swung late and only succeeded by hitting the ball where it was least expected to go. Two other notable students attending my high school at the same time were Benjamin and Jonathan Netanyahu. They were just two boys from Israel at the time, and no one expected them to attain the status they have earned today. Jonathan became a commando in the Israeli army and as a major, was killed leading a raid to free hostages at Entebbe Airport, Uganda, Africa, in 1976. His brother Benjamin is currently serving as Israel's prime minister.

I still remember the time when, shortly after I matriculated at Temple, the television show called *I Spy* debuted. For the first time I could recall, a black man named Bill Cosby had a starring role. There simply hadn't been other blacks with leading roles on television before that time that I knew of. I enjoyed the show as Cosby was a Temple alumnus who often wore a Temple sweatshirt during the show, making me very proud of my college. Yet the true significance of the show was the introduction to the television screen of notable blacks, sometimes from other genres like the music world, who were to become guest stars on the program. Lena Horne and Eartha Kitt were two ladies who appeared on more than one occasion. Little did I know at the time, this show would eventually lead me to a career interest in counterintelligence with the FBI. But that interest was still a long way off.

Temple University in 1965 had a higher percentage of black students than I had ever been associated with in my past. Still, the percentage was small, maybe 12–15 percent, given that the campus was located in the middle of an all-black population in the city. That population was friendly but mostly reserved. They were generally from lower-income families who kept to themselves and didn't mingle with the university students too often. There didn't seem to be any racial problems between the neighborhood residents and the students for the most part. Our fraternity had a frat house on Allegheny Avenue in an all-black neighborhood, and we never experienced any serious problems, despite the house being located in a high-crime area. As college students, we would patronize neighborhood bars, which were all frequented by the local residents. Again, there were no racial problems encountered whenever we partied. In fact, quite the opposite was true. Every time three or four of us went out for a few beers, sooner or later a black patron sitting alone at the bar would buy us a round of drinks. We always returned the favor and would strike up a conversation if the patron wanted to talk with us.

It wasn't until April 1968 that things got a bit ugly in the Temple neighborhood. When Martin Luther King Jr. was assassinated in Memphis, Tennessee, the black neighborhoods were understandably upset and angered. Arsons and riots were occurring in various parts of the United States, and it was feared the same would be true for Philadelphia. The police commissioner at the time, Frank Rizzo, sent three buses filled with riot police to the Temple neighborhood to prevent rioting and looting. Whether due to the police presence, or simply to the decency of the folks in the neighborhood, or some of both, Philadelphia remained calm during a dangerous time of potential civil unrest. By my senior year at college, there were no obvious lingering problems in the community, and things seemed back to normal in the area.

Following graduation in 1969, I began working as a physical education teacher in a predominantly white area known as Fort Washington, Pennsylvania. I taught classes from kindergarten through sixth grade, and two special education classes as well. For the most part, the faculty was very young, with most of us recently graduated from college. The school had just been built, so we got to enjoy wonderful working conditions, coupled with lots of after-work socialization. While I enjoyed parts of the teaching assignment, my other working experience was pulling me away from a career in the teaching profession.

I was extremely fortunate to have spent every summer of my life at Stone Harbor, New Jersey, a small seashore community located on a barrier island on the Atlantic Ocean in Cape May County. For the most part, this town had an all-white population. There were some black folks living on one or two streets at the northern part of the island, who were year-round residents. Several worked as lifeguards for the beach patrol during the early 1950s and taught school at the local high school in Wildwood, New Jersey. My grandparents had the use of part of a home where I stayed as a youngster. My parents built their own home in 1954, and it was there

I spent every summer day until 1971. I mowed lawns as a boy to earn some spending money. During my teenage years, I worked in the hardware department of the local five-and-ten. It was there I met Major Ruch, who was the Stone Harbor superintendent of police. He would come in to the lunch counter almost every day, and I'd strike up a conversation with him. My desire was to be hired as a seasonal police officer, better known at the shore as a "summer cop." He promised me that once I turned twenty-one, he would give me a job.

In June 1968, I commenced work as a Stone Harbor summer police officer. Major Ruch had fulfilled his promise to me. We did not carry revolvers at the beginning of the summer; only nightsticks for any necessary self-defense. However, we were able to eventually convince the major and his lieutenant, Bill Donohue, that we were mature enough and capable enough to train and carry revolvers. The town council agreed, and we soon found ourselves on the shooting range, qualifying to carry .38-caliber Colt revolvers. Major crime was not a factor in Stone Harbor; the biggest problems were underage drinking and teenage runaways who did not want to return home after a quick summer love affair, usually with a local lifeguard. On occasion, however, there was a serious traffic accident, a sick-person call sometimes involving a death, a bar fight, or stolen surfboards and bicycles; just enough action to keep the job interesting.

For the first time in my life, I actually got to work with a black man. Arthur Anderson, a sergeant at the police department, was a year-round resident of Stone Harbor and the only black man on the force. He was a soft-spoken, gentle man who tried his best to resolve police matters in a civil, nonthreatening manner. He was a great role model for anyone considering a profession in law enforcement. When he invited me and another summer cop to his home, I realized this was the first time I had ever been inside a black-owned residence. It seemed strange to me at first, realizing that I had been so isolated from a group of people who made up not only a large percentage of the population, but who had been such a unique part of American history. Looking back, I regret never having any conversations with Art about his personal feelings on the civil rights protests and marches occurring in the Deep South at the time.

I went back to the job in the summers of 1969 and 1970. Having taught for a full year, I knew my future was to be in law enforcement. I simply enjoyed it more than teaching. I had applied to the FBI in October 1969 after only one month of teaching but was told by a representative of the FBI that they were not hiring. He suggested I write a letter to the FBI in Philadelphia, expressing my continued desire to be considered for a special agent position. If anything changed, he said he would give me a call. As luck would have it, I received a telephone call from the FBI in October 1970, just one year later, asking if I was still interested in the special agent position. Without hesitation, I told him I was ready to go. By November, I'd taken and passed a physical examination. I also took the required written tests at the Philadelphia office of the FBI and had a personal interview with the assistant special agent in charge, Ted Gunderson. All I had to do was wait for an appointment letter from the FBI. That was a wait that seemed endless.

Two months later, in January 1971, I returned home at the end of my school workday. My mother was at the house, and as I walked in the door, she handed me two large envelopes that had both arrived for me that day in the mail. She said nothing as I began to open the letters, although she knew where they were from and was clearly interested in what my reaction would be. One had a return address of Temple University, Graduate School Department, and the other was from the Federal Bureau of Investigation, US Department of Justice. I opened the letter from the FBI first, of course. It contained a signed letter from Director J. Edgar Hoover offering me an appointment as a special agent in the FBI. I was to report to training school on April 12, 1971. I was thrilled—no, more than thrilled—but held my emotions in check as I opened the second letter. This was equally good news, a letter offering me entrance to a master of education program at Temple University.

My mother couldn't take the stress any longer. "Which one do you think you'll accept?" she asked. I knew immediately what I would do.

"Mother," I said, "I can always go on to graduate school, but I'll never get another chance to join the FBI. I am going to become a special agent."

I think she was very proud but would likely have preferred me to get my master's degree and stay in the area. We were a close family, and no one had ever ventured very far from the Philadelphia area. I was about to begin the most marvelous career I could ever have dreamed about.

I submitted my resignation to the elementary school staff and enjoyed my final day with the students on April 9, 1971. The faculty threw me a nice going-away party in my honor after school ended for the day. I spent the weekend getting my clothes and belongings together for the trip to Washington, DC, and said good-bye to friends and family. My departure was an emotional one as my family gathered to wave good-bye, standing together on the driveway as I drove away. I could only wonder what they thought would become of me and my new career. I had those same thoughts about myself that Sunday evening as I drove to Washington and lodged for the night at the Harrington Hotel, just a block or so from the US Justice Department building, where I was to report for duty in the morning. After a rather sleepless night due to my eager anticipation of the next day, I awoke, showered and dressed, ate breakfast, and walked to the Justice Department building on Pennsylvania Avenue. I was fingerprinted at the entrance to confirm my identity as a new agent and was directed to a nearby classroom. My FBI career had begun at last.

John Whiteside, Stone Harbor Police Officer, 1970

CHAPTER 4
G-MAN

As a regularly appointed Special Agent of the Federal Bureau of Investigation, United States Department of Justice, and as such is charged with the duty of investigating violations of the laws of the United States, collecting evidence in cases in which the United States is or may be a party in interest, and performing other duties imposed upon him by law.

—FBI CREDENTIALS

Upon entering the classroom, I found my assigned seat, identified by a small name tag. On the writing arm of the classroom chair was a shiny, new, gold FBI badge encased in a tan leather holder. A black notebook was also there for taking notes along with two sharpened yellow wooden number-two pencils. After the classroom eventually filled and all seats were taken, our class counselors arrived and introduced themselves to us. These were two experienced special agents who had entered the advancement ranks of the FBI and were fulfilling a requirement at the time of being new-agent counselors. They would be the point of contact for us for the next fourteen and a half weeks of training school. The morning started with a deputy assistant director having the class stand, hold our FBI badges up in our left hands while raising our right hands, and take the oath of office. What a proud moment it was! We were now sworn FBI special agents, assigned to the FBI Training Division until we completed training school.

My new agents' training class, known officially as NAC-23, was totally composed of white males. In 1971, females were not permitted to serve as special agents. That policy would change after the death of FBI Director J. Edgar Hoover in 1972. There were no other minority agents in our class either, although there were some minority agents already serving as special agents in the FBI. I never gave it any thought at the time. Only having just turned twenty-four years old, I was the second youngest in the class of forty-five new agents. After filling out insurance papers and completing other miscellaneous paper work, we were informed that we would be transported by bus to the FBI training facility at Quantico, Virginia, in the morning. We would not be permitted to take our own vehicles with us and would need to make arrangements to leave them somewhere for the next three weeks. Fortunately, I was able to leave my car at the home of a relative of one of the new agents I had just met in class. Our FBI training experience had truly begun.

The next day, we packed our suitcases into the blue FBI bus that took us on an hour's trip to Quantico, Virginia. We were all dressed in white shirts, sincere ties, tied shoes, and conservative-style suits, standard attire for all FBI agents at the time. Our bus entered the marine corps base at Quantico and drove to the FBI Academy barracks, a three-story, brick, rectangular-shaped building with a basement containing a long, narrow gymnasium. We were assigned to rooms with eight cots in each. Since I was second from the end in the alphabet, there were only three of us assigned to my room, which made for a much quieter abode. Beds were to be made every morning, and the rooms left in clean and orderly condition. Clean bed linen was provided and was changed weekly by each of us. We shared a large locker with other agents, located in the hallway. All of our clothing and personal possessions were kept in these "lockers," even though they didn't actually lock. This was an honor system; there were no locks. And I'm thankful and proud to say, there was never any theft from any locker, even though there were up to three classes of agents in the academy at any given time.

Staff prepared and served delicious meals at the academy. A large dining room complete with linen table settings and napkins made the home-style eating experience a warm one. We were required to pay room and board while at the academy, something that is not done today. The new FBI Academy that currently exists was being constructed as I went through the old academy. We would see the progress on it as we went to the firearms ranges, already located on the new academy premises. During the first three weeks at the FBI Academy, we had a lot of legal training, including constitutional and statute law, search and seizure laws, and rules of evidence. We learned defensive tactics in the gym and worked on disarming techniques to learn how to take a weapon safely away from an armed subject of an investigation or arrest. We began to practice with the .38-caliber Smith & Wesson Model 10 revolvers we were assigned, needing to memorize our individual gun serial number. We also practiced with the Model 870 Remington pump-action shotgun and Remington pump-action rifle, which was used by the FBI at the time.

After three weeks passed, we returned to Washington, DC, (called the Seat of Government by Director Hoover) for additional classroom instruction. We were required to find temporary housing for the next twelve weeks, and all of us went scurrying about the city to find some cheap rooms and roommates to help share in the cost. Classroom training included interviewing techniques, informant development, courtroom testimony, and photography. We spent a full week learning the science of fingerprinting, including how to take fingerprints, how to lift latent prints from a crime scene, and how to photograph latent prints. It was a section of the training class that I personally enjoyed. On occasion, we would return to Quantico to the FBI Academy for more firearms training and defensive-tactics sessions.

Part of the training course involved some specialized training in the "volume cases" that made up the preponderance of the FBI's work at the time, including bank robberies, fugitives, deserters (from the Vietnam conflict), interstate crimes like stolen motor vehicles, thefts from interstate shipments, thefts of government property, and stolen property. There were some lessons on gambling and the La Cosa Nostra mafia organization, and a lengthy block of time was devoted to the Communist Party and its activities in the United States. There was no specific training on civil rights cases per se, including the recently passed Civil Rights Act of 1964 and the Voting Rights Act of 1965. However, we were introduced to extensive handbooks and manuals of instruction that detailed procedures for working all of the almost two hundred different types of investigations we were charged with conducting and enforcing.

During my training, it was a difficult time for the United States as a whole. The conflict in Vietnam was not going well at all, and war protestors decided to have marches and rallies along the National Mall in Washington, DC. At times during classroom sessions in May, we could smell the tear gas used to dispel the protestors as they tried without success to breach some government buildings. As a further outcrop of the war protest, new radical groups of students, some known as the Students for a Democratic Society (SDS), were creating havoc on college campuses around the country. Several were placed on the FBI's Ten Most Wanted Fugitives list, wanted for crimes that had killed innocent people. The list now numbered sixteen fugitives. It seemed that the country was ill prepared to deal with the social unrest that had developed so quickly and with such intensity. The racial situation and unrest in the Deep South had not improved much either, even with the passage of the Civil Rights Act and Voting Rights Act. And several weeks before I entered the FBI, in March 1971, there had been a burglary of an FBI office in Media, Pennsylvania, by suspects believed to have radical motives. The entire country seemed to be on the edge of revolution and destruction at this time.

A few weeks prior to the end of training, we received our orders for our first field office assignment. I drew a transfer to Cleveland, Ohio, along with another classmate. It was only about a seven-hour drive from my home in Cheltenham, and I was pleased that I wasn't sent too far away. On our last day of training, we were issued our service revolvers and FBI credentials, we bid a fond farewell to fellow classmates, and we happily headed out to our new assignments.

Upon my arrival in Cleveland, I found an apartment and began to settle in to my new life. I started dating my future wife-to-be, who was already employed in the Cleveland FBI office. No sooner had our relationship become somewhat meaningful than I received transfer orders to the Akron Resident Agency. I suspected I was sent there because I was single, thus making it a cheaper relocation transfer for the FBI. I reported there in October 1971 after only ten weeks or so serving in Cleveland.

The territory covered by the Akron FBI office included three counties: Summit, Medina, and Kent. I soon learned the office territorial responsibilities were divided up by both county location as well as federal judicial districts. Interestingly enough, the infamous Kent State University shootings had occurred on campus just about sixteen months earlier, and several agents in the office were continuing to work that civil rights matter. It was the first and only civil rights case I knew about, and it had nothing to do with any racial-type incidents. My own work concentrated mostly on locating and arresting deserters from the military and working closely with the Akron Police Department's Auto Theft Unit regarding the interstate transportation of stolen motor vehicles. I also helped out the other agents on bank robbery cases and in arresting fugitives wanted for unlawful flight to avoid prosecution. The agents in the Akron Resident Agency and their families were very close with each other and socialized together often. Donna and I were always included in their social activities. It was here in Akron that I quickly learned of the bond we all shared with each other in the FBI. During my assignment in Akron, which lasted through August 1972, I was so fortunate to work with a great group of professionals and socialize with an even better group of friends.

They were all invited to and attended our wedding in Lorain, Ohio, on that warm, humid Saturday afternoon in September, as we started our lives together and bade our closest group of friends farewell. We both looked forward to our next assignment despite it being some twelve hundred miles away from our family and friends. There would be an FBI family in Mississippi as well, and we had no reason to suspect it would be much different from this one.

FBI's "16" Most Wanted List flyer, February 1972

CHAPTER 5
Southern Comfort

*Delta sunsets and cypress brakes,
Cotton plantations and juke joints,
Catfish and kudzu.*

—Anonymous

After a quick breakfast of scrambled eggs, grits, country ham, fresh-baked southern-style biscuits with honey and melted butter, and a cup or two of a rather strange-tasting coffee made with chicory, I bade Donna good-bye as I was off to my first day in the Greenville office. Donna planned to return to the room and look up a few realtors so as to get moving on finding an apartment in town. The telephone book for Greenville was noticeably thin, and it included other local small towns in the county, like Hollandale and Leland. The "yellow pages" section did supply her with enough information to get started, and she was eager to explore.

"I'll meet you back at the hotel sometime after five o'clock, or whenever I can get away. Here is my office telephone number," I said, handing her a small slip of paper. "You can always call me from the room. If you get a chance, stop by the office, and I'll give you a tour."

"Have a good day," she said with a smile as we kissed good-bye. I began my short walk to the federal building located on Main Street. It was seven thirty in the morning, and the heat and humidity were already getting oppressive. I could only wonder how much more uncomfortable it might possibly become. I entered the cool, air-conditioned lobby of the federal building and took the elevator to the second floor. Located directly across from a small canteen shop that sold coffee and candy was a door marked Federal Bureau of Investigation. It was locked, so I knocked and waited to be let in.

The senior resident agent opened the door and introduced himself as John Neelley. We shook hands as I introduced myself and entered the office space, which comprised four average-sized rooms. John had an office in the rear of the space by himself, one of the perks for serving as the boss. Directly outside of his office was another room, which he explained was used as an interview room when needed, although it was currently occupied by Ray Mislock, a first-office agent recently assigned here from training school. The next room held three desks, and John pointed out where I would be sitting, with Ron Ott and Joe Lattus. A fourth room, larger than the others, held another agent desk used by

Chuck Wilmore, and it was also a repository for equipment and supplies used by the office.

While we chatted, John told me he was originally from Tennessee, and that he'd been in the FBI since 1955. He explained that the Greenville Resident Agency was responsible for regional coverage of six counties, all located in the Mississippi Delta. I would be the sixth agent assigned to the office. As we talked, other FBI agents arrived for work. John introduced me to Chuck Wilmore, who was assigned to work cases in Bolivar County, north of Greenville. Greenville was located in Washington County, and John and Joe handled most cases there. Ron Ott subsequently entered the office. It was good to see him, as he was one of the agents I went through training school with just a year and a half ago. He was working in Sunflower County, the county east of Washington County, and had been previously assigned the counties I was getting. John advised me that I was being assigned to work the three southernmost counties in the office territory: Issaquena, Sharkey, and Humphreys. As Ray arrived on the scene, John introduced us and said that Ray was working with him, but he was available to assist any of the other agents in the office as needed.

John took me outside to the rear parking lot of the building, where we had parking space for the FBI vehicles. He handed me the keys and pointed to a pale yellow 1965 Chevrolet Bel Air sitting in the lot. "There's your assigned car, John. It's in good running condition despite a lot of mileage on it. There's no air conditioning in it, and no AM/FM radio. It has an FBI two-way radio as well as a Mississippi Highway Patrol two-way radio in it. The large whip antenna along the side of the car can be raised if you want to, but we usually leave them hooked in a lower position as the radio seems to work just as well." As we returned upstairs after inspecting the car, I could only wonder, No air conditioning…are you kidding me? The temperature was already close to ninety degrees, and it wasn't even nine in the morning yet!

After meeting everyone and listening to the good-natured stories designed to scare the new guy, I settled in and tried to get my desk in order. My work box and other FBI-related items had been shipped from the Akron office and had arrived in Greenville before I did. I wondered how my wife was doing in her apartment search, but I had no way to contact her. I tried calling the hotel room, but she did not answer. It was getting close to lunchtime, and John invited me to go with him to a local restaurant called Jim's Café on Washington Street. It was a little hole-in-the-wall, but the food was strictly southern style, home cooked, and allegedly very good. After a short walk to the café, John ordered a poke salad, actually made from pokeweed leaves. I ordered a hamburger; I wasn't ready for so radical a change in diet just yet. During lunch, John told me about some local restaurants and the cuisine they were noted for. This was very helpful as I knew Donna and I would be growing tired of the Downtowner hotel food real soon. During lunch, it seemed that many of the patrons knew John, and a few stopped by to say hello. It was an extremely friendly place where everyone seemed to know each other. Maybe this would be a good place to be assigned after all.

Following lunch, John walked me over to the local police department and introduced me to the chief, Tom Nance, and several of the officers. The chief explained to me that the city of Greenville and its outskirts had a population of close to fifty thousand residents and was the third-largest city in the state. Its nickname was the "Queen City of the Delta." Greenville itself was about 76 percent black, although most of the blacks lived in a small geographic area of the city around Nelson Street and Clay Street, and north of Highway 82 that crossed east and west through town. Most of the crime in town was against black citizens, perpetrated by black criminals, and some of it was pretty violent. He also took me to the records section of the police department and introduced me to the all-female staff employees, as I would have a lot of contacts with the ladies working there. As John and I departed from the police department, I noticed there were several black police officers employed in the department.

Meanwhile, Donna had become very busy. Reading through the local newspaper, the *Delta Democrat-Times*, she was unable to locate any apartments listed for rent. The newspaper was thin in size, maybe only six to eight pages in length, and she had no luck finding anything. Then she saw an advertisement for housing and contacted a realtor named Bob Jones, who worked for the Greenville Lumber Company. Bob listened to her story and then drove to the hotel to pick her up for a grand tour around the city. He showed her all there was to see in Greenville, including public and private schools, more restaurants, all of the shopping districts, and the different neighborhoods where there were homes for sale. He was unable to find any apartments for rent, which he indicated were mostly for lower-income families.

Eventually Bob took her to the Roman Gardens East section of Greenville, located off of South Main Street toward the south end of town. There just happened to be a house for sale on Lisa Drive, built by the Greenville Lumber Company. The house was nearly completed, needing only a few finishing touches. It was a three-bedroom ranch, built on a concrete slab as the water table was too high for basements in the area. She thought it was something we could afford and asked Bob to meet with both of us the next day. She had plenty to talk about that evening over dinner.

Before the work day ended, John drove me to the office of the Washington County sheriff, Harvey Tackett. On the way to the courthouse building where the office was located, he explained that the sheriff in Mississippi was the premier law enforcement officer in each respective county. In fact, the sheriff was referred to as the "high sheriff," and his deputies were simply called "sheriffs." John had developed a good working relationship with both the Greenville Police Department and the Washington County Sheriff's Office. He considered both of these leaders to be good friends of the FBI and rock-solid law enforcement people. We entered the sheriff's office and Harvey Tackett rose to meet us. John said, "Let me introduce our newest FBI agent to you, Harve. Meet John Whiteside."

"Nice to meet you, Sheriff," I said as we shook hands.

Tackett was a stocky man and built strong as an ox. He immediately detected my northeast accent. "So, you brought down another Yankee to work with us, did you, John?" he asked with a smile. "I hope I can understand this one," he continued with his strong Mississippi accent. "We here in Miss-sippi sure have a hard time understanding these northern boys." I was thinking the same thing about these southern boys, but kept quiet at the time. "Welcome to Miss-sippi. Feel free to call on us for anything you need. John is a good friend of ours, and I'm sure you'll work out just fine." Sheriff Tackett then introduced me to his deputies, George Martin and Billy Wagner, who happened to enter the office at the time. A few more good-natured Yankee jokes continued before John and I left to return to the FBI office.

"You'll find the sheriff and chief of police to be real fine law enforcement people who will be willing to help you in spite of their kidding with you," John said as we drove back to the federal building. "Don't be afraid to trust them or to call upon them for help. They know everything that goes on around here and throughout the county." I did not notice any black employees at the sheriff's office during my visit.

Upon returning to the FBI office, I had a message from my wife. I called her at the hotel, and she told me to plan on taking a couple of hours off the following day to look at a house she found. She sounded excited about the prospect, although I couldn't imagine owning a house at this time in my young life. I put in for a couple of hours leave for the next day, cleaned up my desk, and left work, looking forward to hearing about my wife's day.

I drove my newly assigned car to the hotel as I wanted to test it out. It seemed to perform okay, but I wondered how much life it had left in it. I went up to the room and met my wife. "I had a great day, and I think I've found a house for us," she enthusiastically exclaimed. "There is simply nothing available for rent that either of us would be willing to live in. The realtor will pick us up in the morning and take us to see the house again. I'm so excited!"

Talk about an information overload my first day on the job.

We went out for dinner that evening to a small, family-owned Italian restaurant called the Venetian Café, recommended to Donna by realtor Bob Jones. It was a BYOB restaurant, and we had yet to find a liquor or beer store. I again had to order sweet iced tea to avoid what I thought was bad water. While the restaurant was small and simply furnished, all the dishes, including the pasta, were homemade and delicious. It became one of our favorite places to eat during our tour of duty in Greenville.

The following day, we were met by Bob Jones and driven to our potential new home. After walking through it and listening to the price, financing, and closing costs, I began to grow apprehensive. While I'd rented apartments in the past, actually buying a house was becoming a bit unnerving to me. I knew lawyers would need to be involved, along with bank loans, possible collateral, down payments, and who knew what else. As I walked through the house, my thoughts were more focused on the impossibility and difficulty of an actual purchase, rather than seeing the house for what it was worth. However, Donna seemed very pleased with it, and we did want to get settled as soon as possible. I shared my financial concerns with the realtor, and he quickly reassured me that I had sufficient funds for a down payment, and that I would be able to afford the mortgage payments. I told him I did not know any bankers in town, and for that matter, any real estate lawyers. I think I was trying to avoid a real estate purchase at the time.

With that, Bob Jones said everything was handled. He asked me if I was happy with the home, its location, and style. Knowing that my wife seemed to be happy with the property, I told him I was as well. With that, he offered me his hand, and I shook it. As I did, he congratulated us and told us we were new homeowners. All we would need to do was sign a couple of papers in a day or two. All else was handled, or soon would be. And that was all there was to it. The sale was settled with a handshake with Bob Jones. It was the first and only time that a home purchase for us was that simple. It seemed that there was total trust between folks in this area. In a few days, the subsequent closing was uneventful and only took a few minutes. Just like that, we were new home owners in Greenville, Mississippi.

We went out and purchased a sofa bed so we would have both a place to sit and a place to sleep. What few other household goods we had accumulated were to be delivered in a few days. My personal car was en route and was expected in another day or so. We would continue to eat at local restaurants until we could settle into our new home. Fortunately, there was a Sears store and a new Kmart in town, so I could purchase all the lawn equipment I didn't think I would need in apartment life. We learned that my FBI classmate Ron Ott lived around the corner from us, so Donna made plans to meet up with his wife the following day to learn more about the town. I was itching to do some real FBI work for a change and was hoping to get out into my newly assigned territory the following day.

CHAPTER 6
Road Trip

A man's heart devises his ways,
But the Lord establishes his steps.

—Proverbs 16:9

It was time for me to explore the three counties I had been assigned responsibility for in the resident agency. I spoke with Ron, who had previously worked the counties. He hadn't been in Greenville all that long prior to my arrival, but he seemed quite relieved to pass on his counties to me and take on a new assignment. I was curious and asked him why. "You will never find three more rural and boring places than Issaquena, Sharkey, and Humphreys Counties," he replied. "There is very little industry, and all are predominantly farming counties. By the way, they aren't called farms around here, they're called plantations. And the locals don't even pronounce the word 'plantation': It sounds more like 'plan-ation,' dropping the 't.' You will see miles and miles of cotton, soybeans, and rice. And lots of 'shotgun shacks,' the decrepit wooden shacks where the black plantation workers live. Their accents are as difficult as the local white folks', so good luck trying to understand them. Issaquena doesn't even have one bank in the entire county, so you will never have to respond to a bank robbery there. There are only about seven hundred people living in the entire rural county."

I was beginning to wonder what kind of cases I'd even have in a place like this. As we talked, Ron handed me three assignment cards and folders containing three investigative matters he was transferring to me. There was one case in each of the three counties I was just assigned to take over from him. And all the cases were the same thing. They involved obtaining voter-registration statistics on a monthly basis from each of the three county courthouses. Ron explained that this had been an ongoing project for the Department of Justice, Civil Rights Unit, since the passage of the Voting Rights Act of 1965. Each county in the state was required to identify, on a monthly basis, the number of new voters registered, by race, and the number of voters purged from the records, by race as well. These statistics would be collected and forwarded to Washington, DC, to assist in ensuring compliance with the new federal laws and to help ensure racial equality at the polls. It sounded like a pretty simple investigative assignment to me. Ron provided the names of the county clerks who would provide the information and the addresses of the courthouses in the three counties.

Ron also explained all of the towns in the three county areas that were served by a local police department. I would be responsible for FBI liaison with each of these departments. They ranged in size from about ten police officers in Belzoni to only one police officer in some towns like Louise and Isola, all towns in Humphreys County. Tiny hamlets and unincorporated villages without any local law enforcement were covered by the county sheriff. He provided me with a list of names of all my new law enforcement contacts. He identified several officers whom he worked well with, and who seemed to respect him and the job he was there to do. He opined that many of the contacts were somewhat distrustful of the FBI and any federal intervention into their local affairs.

Ron was somewhat fussy in his dress and in his choice of food and restaurants. He cautioned me about the "eat places" in my three new counties, saying there were very few good choices. There were no fast-food chain restaurants in any of the three counties at the time. Even a McDonald's restaurant hadn't made an appearance in Greenville yet, although it was rumored that one was arriving. There was no place to eat in Issaquena County, and only a small café or two in both Sharkey and Humphreys Counties. He said, "No matter where you go to eat, everyone in the restaurant will know that you are an FBI agent, simply by your dress and from the fact that you aren't from around those parts. It will usually get quiet as no one will trust what is said in your presence. Welcome to the Delta!"

Point taken, I thought. I gathered my briefcase and notebook and several county maps and headed out the door, en route to my first visit to all three of the counties assigned to me. I was excited to get my first glimpse of the Mississippi Delta countryside and to see all it had to offer. As I traveled down Route 1, due south toward Mayersville, county seat of Issaquena, I marveled at the flatness of the terrain and the vast acreage of cotton, soybean, and rice fields. Tiny towns appeared along the route, with nothing to show but a few dilapidated homes and an old, unused cotton gin. Despite being early autumn, the weather was very muggy and hot. Open windows in my FBI car did little to ease the heat, and the small transistor radio I placed on the dashboard was unable to pick up any AM broadcast signals.

Arriving at Mayersville after nearly an hour's drive, I passed a historical marker advising that Issaquena County was created in 1844 and the seat of government was established at Mayersville in 1872. David Mayer donated this historic river port to the county for the founding of the town in 1871. The main road led to the county courthouse, a relatively new structure built out of brick and metal siding in 1957. I entered the building and found the clerk's office. After identifying myself as a special agent of the FBI, I asked for the voter-registration statistics for the past month. The clerk advised that there were none at all; no one had registered to vote in the county, and there were no purges of the voter records. I then thought it wise to meet the sheriff, since I was in the area, and begin a good liaison with him, and I inquired as to the location of his office. The clerk advised that the sheriff was the owner of the only grocery store in Mayersville, and she said I could catch up with him there, providing me with directions to his store.

I drove several blocks to the country store, owned and operated by the sheriff of Issaquena County. I entered the store and waited at the end of the line by the cash register, waiting for the customers, mostly black folks, to make their purchases. The cashier, I noticed, was wearing a sheriff's badge on his short-sleeved, casual-print cotton shirt. Everyone seemed friendly, and all the customers spoke with the sheriff as they made their way with their purchases. After the small line ended, I approached the cashier/sheriff and introduced myself as the new FBI agent who would be working in his territory. He said I could always find him at the store if I needed him, although there was little if any crime in the county, which had the smallest population of all Mississippi counties. Nonetheless, he pledged his cooperation and assistance whenever needed. He seemed to be a very friendly sort of person. We parted company as a line was beginning to form again behind me, and I returned to my car. As I drove away, I marveled at the simple life people in this area seemed to live, and at their apparent contentment with that low-key lifestyle.

I headed due east on Route 14 en route to Rolling Fork, the county seat of Sharkey. The twelve-mile trip took about fifteen minutes. This town was considerably larger than Mayersville, and I had to search a little harder for the courthouse. It was easy to find, however, located directly in the middle of the town square on Locust Street. It was an old building, styled in a similar fashion to the Washington County courthouse in Greenville. The big difference between this county and the neighboring Issaquena County was in its population. Sharkey had seven times the residents that Issaquena had. I parked the car and entered the courthouse, finding the clerk's office. I rang a small metal bell on the counter for assistance.

A gruff-looking, short, and stocky elderly white man appeared from a back room and asked my business. Exhibiting my FBI credentials to him, I introduced myself and told him I was here to obtain voter-registration statistics for the past month. He muttered, "Take a seat," and disappeared into a back room. I sat down and waited…and waited. A half hour passed and still no results. I began to think he had either forgotten about me or had amassed a large number of statistics that he was trying to obtain by hand. There were simply no computers in use at this time. After another fifteen minutes had passed, I got up and rang the bell again. The clerk appeared and said he'd be right with me. I sat down again and waited. While I waited, I fumed a bit, as I wanted to meet with the sheriff and get over to Humphreys County to complete my journey for the day. After almost a full hour had passed, the clerk reappeared. "Two white, two black, no purges," he grunted as he walked away and back into his inner sanctum. A whole hour for that? I wondered. Perhaps he should invest in a better system of record keeping, I thought to myself.

I was getting hungry and wanted to get to Belzoni, the county seat in Humphreys, so I left without meeting the sheriff, Maurice Phillips. I decided I'd do that the next time.

Belzoni was almost fifty miles northeast of Rolling Fork, about another hour-long drive. After reaching the courthouse there, I needed to use the restroom, so I thought I'd go to the sheriff's office, make my introductions, and use their facility. The sheriff's office was on an upper floor of the courthouse. Upon entering, I met Deputy Jack Dalton, who I was told by Ron was a friend of the FBI. I introduced myself, and we chatted a bit before he introduced me to the high sheriff, J. L. Huffstickler. This man was a true Mississippi country boy whose accent was difficult to decipher. He didn't seem too pleased to meet me, and the conversation was very brief. After he returned to his office, I asked Jack where their restroom was located. He told me it was back on the first floor in the main lobby. Somewhat puzzled, I said nothing, thanked him for his information and told him I'd keep in touch, and headed back downstairs to find the restroom.

It turned out to be a public restroom, one that looked as if it had never been cleaned or serviced. A disgusting collection of foul-looking liquid floated about two inches deep across the restroom floor, unable to seep through a debris-covered drain that badly needed to be cleared. I actually had to grip my trouser legs to keep the cuffs from touching the raw sewage on the floor. I was out of there as quickly as possible, irritated in knowing full well that there must have been a clean bathroom in the sheriff's office that wasn't accessible to both a Yankee and a federal agent like me. Payback is hell, I thought.

I left the courthouse and stopped in at the police department in Belzoni. This town was the largest in my entire three-county territory, and the chief of police, Toby Woods, was a younger, better-educated man than I expected. We hit it off well, and I was glad I had met someone I could trust in this county, and who seemed to respect me as well.

Hunger was getting to me, and it was getting late. As I made my way out toward Highway 61 for the trip back to the office, I saw a restaurant called the Pig Stand on the outskirts of town, one of the few places Ron had suggested to me. I stopped in for a quick barbeque pork sandwich and a Dr. Pepper. Ron was right…the place seemed rather quiet while I sat there and finished my lunch. I was the only person wearing a suit and tie, and I'm sure everyone in the place knew exactly who I was. It was good to get back safely on the road.

My first day canvassing my new territory was both tiring and intriguing. I would have to give this place more time before making any judgments about it. I had nothing against the people in Mississippi, and there was no reason they should have anything against me. I was there to investigate federal crimes, whenever and wherever they would occur. Other than that, I, too, was a resident of the Magnolia State, just like them…or so I thought at the time.

That evening, it being a Friday night, Donna and I ate dinner at the local Holiday Inn. We were told they had a good seafood buffet, and it was well worth the price. The spread of food was truly fantastic, with lots of local seafood delicacies I had never tried. There was steamed crayfish Cajun style, deep-fried frogs' legs, grouper, and cornmeal-battered deep-fried catfish. There was lots of steamed shrimp (pronounced "srimp" by the locals), fried chicken, cornbread, and plenty of macaroni and cheese. It was some of the best food I had ever eaten. After dinner, with nothing better to do, we returned to the hotel. We heard music playing and learned there was a Friday evening dance each week at the hotel. My wife and I had been raised on music by black artists from Motown, like the Supremes, the Four Tops, the Temptations, the Miracles, and Stevie Wonder. I was also accustomed to the doo-wop Philly sound from the late 1950s and early 1960s. She enjoyed the Beatles and Three Dog Night, and I liked Elvis Presley. We were not going to hear any of that music anytime soon, with the possible exception of Elvis Presley, a Tupelo, Mississippi, boy himself.

We stopped into the dance hall and ordered a drink. We then listened to artists like Anne Murray, Porter Wagoner (singing with some new artist named Dolly Parton), Waylon Jennings, Tammy Wynette, and other country-western performers singing their greatest hits, while the locals danced to the two-step style current at the time. When Conway Twitty's "Hello Darlin'" played, every single couple got up to slow dance. We simply watched, listened, and tried to take in a new culture so unfamiliar to us from up north. I had never heard any of this music before. I'm not sure if Philadelphia, Pennsylvania, even had a country-western radio station, and if it did, I'd never heard about it or listened in on it. About all I knew of country-western music at the time was the music sung by my childhood cowboy heroes, Roy Rogers and Dale Evans, and Gene Autry. After an hour or two of listening to something completely new to us, we returned to the room for the night, once again absorbing a bit of new Delta culture. It had been a very unique day for both of us.

Special Agent Whiteside at the Belzoni,
MS police department, 1973

Special Agent Whiteside visiting the
Isola, MS police department, 1973

CHAPTER 7
HOME

Where we love is home—
Home that our feet may leave,
But not our hearts.

—OLIVER WENDELL HOLMES SR.

During our last week at FBI training school, each of the new special agents was required to have a personal one-on-one interview with either the assistant director of the Training Division, Mr. Casper, or his number-one man, Mr. Jenkins. The title "number-one man" referred to the closest assistant of the primary supervisory employee. I suspect this personal interview was a final chance to reject any problem employee brought to their attention or to raise the level of tension and place the fear of God into each of us before sending us forth to do the director's bidding.

I was scheduled to meet with Mr. Jenkins, and at the appointed time, wearing my best, most conservative suit, tie, white shirt, and tied black shoes, I walked cautiously into his office, not sure what to expect. We shook hands firmly—as was expected—and he offered me a seat. We chatted a bit about my background and his as well. When he learned I was single, he replied, "So, I suppose anywhere you hang your hat will be home." I certainly agreed, though I wanted to tell him my home would always be in Pennsylvania. The interview was thankfully rather brief and ended amicably. I suspected I passed as required. At least I hoped I did.

Greenville, like so many other towns throughout this great nation, had a unique history of its own. Louise Eskridge Crump, a former writer and columnist for the *Delta Democrat-Times* newspaper, put together a brief history of the city around 1952. That story was acquired from the Greenville History Museum. Crump determined that there were two other Greenvilles in Mississippi prior to the one in which we currently lived. The first was located near present-day Natchez, Mississippi, about two and a half hours south of today's Greenville. That first town disappeared shortly after the American Revolution. Crump did not provide a reason for the town's eventual disappearance. The next Greenville was located about three miles from Greenville's present location. It was named after General Nathaniel Greene, a Revolutionary War hero and close friend of George Washington, for whom the county is named. The town was thriving prior to the Civil War. However, during the Union army's siege of Vicksburg, a Yankee gunboat landed at Greenville, and when its troops were fired upon from the town, the Yankee troops burned down the entire place. When the war ended, returning Mississippi troops found their homes destroyed and their families scattered throughout the state. The indomitable southern spirit persisted, and Greenville was constructed yet again, for a third and final time. The land chosen this time was the highest elevation in the Delta, located between Memphis and Natchez. Landowners Roach and Blanton owned a large portion of the land. And Harriet Blanton Theobald, who owned the largest tract of land, donated land for the construction of schools, churches, and public buildings. Her generosity gave her the name "Mother of Greenville."

Planning and responsibility for layout of the new Greenville fell to former Confederate major Richard O'Hea. He was responsible for the fortifications at Vicksburg that worked so well in holding back General Grant for a long time. Following the destruction of homes and businesses, the policy of Reconstruction after the Civil War stalled the growth progress and led to continued heartache for the people of Greenville. And, just as soon as Reconstruction efforts eased, the town suffered another disaster in 1877 with a deadly plague of yellow fever. Not a single family in Greenville was spared from the epidemic's tragedy. Then, by 1886, the city petitioned for and acquired its first charter. Two years later, a group of cotton buyers, merchants, and planters formed the cotton exchange, beginning the first real step to economic development for the area.

Floods were always a problem for the town, the first one hitting in 1890 and leaving half the city covered in water from the Mississippi River. The old business district, located on the bank of the river, was demolished by sliding down caving riverbanks. In 1927, the worst flood to ever hit Greenville came with a vengeance, breaking through the protective levee and covering every part of the town, lasting for almost three months. Shortly after this devastating flood, the federal government established more adequate flood control.

In 1952, Greenville was identified as the Mississippi River's largest river port. At the same time, Greenville was shown to be eight square miles in geographic size. By the time we arrived in 1972, I suspect the geographic size of Greenville had substantially grown, as new housing developments seemed to be extending south and east of the city. Thanks to the research regarding Greenville, we did understand a bit of the difficult history of our little Delta town, a proud history of folks who suffered, both black and white, during the life and growth of our nation. And Greenville's history was still being made, with many changes in its future yet to come.

I had yet to see the Mississippi River, being so busy familiarizing myself with my three counties of responsibility and seeking a place to live. Ron mentioned that the river could best be seen at a place south of town known as Warfield Point. One evening after work, Donna and I decided to take a short ride to Warfield Point to get our first sight of the mighty Mississippi. Thoughts raced through my mind during the short drive as to what the historic and life-giving river would actually look like. We arrived at Warfield Point in about fifteen minutes and drove to the edge of the riverbank. And there it was, in all its majesty and glory. Strong and powerful, very wide from bank to bank, yet moving as quietly as the evening hush over it, the Mississippi River was revealed in all its storied grandeur.

The setting sun and lengthening evening shadows cast an even muddier complexion across the gently rippled surface of the water. There were no boats to be seen floating along the river at this moment. It seemed as though the river was nothing more than a quiet sentinel to the geologic forming of our planet, and a giver of life to a land blessed with rich, loamy soil produced from generations of river floods. We stood in reverent silence for a few minutes, staring at the mighty river that had been such a force in the growth of our nation. And still, after all these past generations, the river continued to provide sustenance to many Americans and to the American economy. It was quite a moment to finally observe the great natural monument of the Magnolia State.

Home was now Greenville, Mississippi, in a ranch-style house on Lisa Drive. We moved into our home with our household goods, which were delivered by a small moving van. My car also arrived as hoped for, none the worse for wear. My wife paid the fellow who drove the car to Greenville and dropped him off at the local bus depot. We had our first guests a few weeks later, Donna's parents, who arrived from Elyria, Ohio. We took them on a drive around the area and showed off the few tourist sites we knew about. Since her dad farmed nine acres in Ohio, he had some interest in the cotton, soybean, and rice fields in the Delta, and the high quality of the local soil. There were also some Choctaw Indian burial mounds in the area that we visited. We did some shopping at Sears, and Donna's parents purchased a washing machine for us. I picked up the tab for a new dryer, so there would be no more trips to the Laundromat. While the house was still somewhat sparsely furnished, we had all we needed at the time. To our disappointment, our household water had the same brown tint as that water we first experienced in the Downtowner hotel.

I began to question the quality of the local water supply. But apparently, it had been a long-standing problem, as Mark Twain writes in his book *Life on the Mississippi*:

> What is a person to do here when he wants a drink of water—drink this slush? Can't you drink it? I could if I had some other water to wash it with. Here was a thing, which had not changed; a score of years had not affected this water's mulatto complexion in the least; a score of centuries would succeed no better, perhaps. It comes out of the turbulent, bank-caving Missouri, and every tumbler full of it holds nearly an acre of land in solution. I got this fact from the bishop of the diocese. If you will let your glass stand half an hour, you can separate the land from the water as easy as Genesis; and then you will find them both good: the one good to eat, the other good to drink. The land is very nourishing; the water is thoroughly wholesome. The one appeases hunger; the other, thirst. But the natives do not take them separately, but

together, as nature mixed them. When they find an inch of mud in the bottom of a glass, they stir it up, and then take the draught as they would gruel. It is difficult for a stranger to get used to this batter, but once used to it, he will prefer it to water. This is really the case. It is good for steamboating, and good to drink; but it is worthless for all other purposes, except baptizing.

We later learned that due to the silt in the Mississippi River, the lack of natural rock filtration prevented the water from appearing sparkling clean. The water was safe to drink, however, and we finally, but reluctantly, grew accustomed to it.

Living room furniture would have to wait to accent the piano Donna had sent from Ohio. Our stereo system sat on the boxes it had been packed in from the store. We set up one bedroom as a den, with our black-and-white television set and the sofa bed we recently purchased. Another wicker chair filled the room, and the piano bench served as a makeshift coffee table. We were only able to get one television channel using the rabbit-ear antenna on the television set. The local Greenville news was broadcast on ABC at the time, as was *The Porter Wagoner Show* with a young starlet named Dolly Parton. We could also watch *Hee Haw* episodes and *The Mac Davis Show*. Quite a change from what we were both used to watching at home. Fortunately, there was a television cable service eventually made available to us, which allowed us to get five or six channels clearly. It was a welcomed upgrade to our new lifestyle.

Our neighbors, also all new to Greenville, were a well-mixed collection of people from different states and personal backgrounds. We befriended a couple and their two small children from Alabama. Tom Brock was in the insurance business, and Linda was a public school teacher. One of our neighbors was in the military and was away most of the time, leaving his wife and their Doberman home alone. Our other neighbor was an inspector of tanks located on towboats, checking for gaseous, dangerous fumes. Another neighbor was an accountant originally from the Pennsylvania area. We would spend our first Thanksgiving Day dinner together with these neighbors, who two months earlier had never met each other. Home, indeed, was where we hung our hats.

We slowly became accustomed to our surroundings in Greenville. They still had a drive-in movie theater, which we attended on occasion. We learned about more of the good restaurants in the area. One of our favorites, the Marina, was a seafood restaurant located on the other side of the levee. It was erected on a barge and floated on Lake Ferguson, next to the Greenville Yacht Club, which was also built on a barge. Doe's Eat Place, a well-known fixture in the Delta, was one of the most famous steak houses in the country. Located in a small wooden-frame store, the tables covered with oilcloth in lieu of linen table coverings, the restaurant served up enormous steaks brought to the table by a waitress for approval prior to cooking. They also specialized in fried shrimp and in hot tamales wrapped in corn shucks. The unforgettable dining experience was topped by having to walk through the kitchen to get into the dingy dining area.

On occasion, we would cross a nearby Mississippi River bridge into Lake Village, Arkansas, which was about fifteen minutes or so from Greenville. There we would dine at the Cow Pen, also known for its steaks, as well as its Mexican food and fried catfish. On the return trip back to Greenville, a bridge inspector would stop all cars traveling into Mississippi and inquire as to whether the occupants were bringing any plants into the state. I believe this was an effort to protect the cotton crop from boll weevils and other damaging insect diseases. He never really seemed to inspect anything; he just asked the question and motioned you along and let the cars pass by. So much for a careful agriculture inspection process.

While we met a lot of folks who were not originally from Mississippi, we did not get to know too many locals. Perhaps it was a basic distrust of people from other regions of the country. However, once we joined the Greenville Presbyterian Church, we finally began to get to know the local residents. The church was predominately white, although there were some black staffers who helped with child care, maintenance, and cooking duties. My wife joined the choir, and I became an assistant scoutmaster for the church-sponsored Boy Scout Troop 43. It quickly became evident that being active in the church was one's primary social activity in a town like Greenville. From then on, we were included in more activities held by Greenville residents, and we became friends with more of the locals.

Work continued to be interesting, yet the cases were quite different from the ones I worked in Akron, Ohio. It seemed that the slower pace of southern living somehow slowed down the pace of crime in the Delta. Racial tension still simmered in many areas of Mississippi, but not so much in the Delta. It was apparent that the plantation owners still depended on black labor to take care of the cotton and other field crops, as well as the catfish farms, which meant continued employment for the blacks who wanted to work. The Greenville economy seemed to be as delicate as a magnolia flower, caught somewhere in the middle of trying to decide whether to grow or to begin a slow decline. As new companies arrived, others would close their doors and move away. Life seemed to be at a stalemate in the Delta during the 1970s.

A month or two after my arrival in Greenville, another agent was transferred in from Washington, DC. Ken White-Spunner was an experienced agent, having entered on duty with the FBI in 1961. Following postings in Seattle, Washington, and at Monterey, California, where he attended language school, Ken was transferred to the Washington, DC, field office. There, he was assigned to work foreign counterintelligence matters. His transfer to Greenville was a voluntary one to work a sensitive counterintelligence investigation. Ken sat with Chuck until an office space could be created for him. He was a likeable guy, and we all relied upon him for his FBI expertise as needed. His transfer to the Greenville Resident Agency brought our complement of agents up to seven, which was a good-sized office for the territory we managed and the population we served.

My wife eventually found a job working as a bank teller for Planters Bank and Trust in Greenville. Located in the business section of the city, this job would help her to meet more of the local population and provide an additional income for us. We still weren't sure that we would remain in Greenville forever.

One evening during supper, she related an incident to me that occurred at the bank earlier that day. She said that the bank employed a black man named Lee Tucker. He did odds and ends for the bank employees and served as a courier when needed. He tidied up the place and performed some janitorial duties. He was the only black person employed at the bank. That morning, Donna needed him for something and said to him, "Mr. Tucker, can you please bring me some deposit tickets from the storeroom when you get a chance?" He was happy to do so and quickly brought her the requested items. When he left the bank later on an errand, the head teller, a white lady, reprimanded Donna saying, "Don't you ever call him Mr. Tucker. His name is Lee!" My wife was shocked to hear this, and so was I. It was our first experience in observing some of the disrespect that still existed between the races in the area. Perhaps it was even hatred. It was hard to explain just what the anger seemed to be all about. Sadly, we would sense this underlying current of bigotry and hate more often the longer we stayed in the area and became more familiar with the residents. My wife relented to the pressure and called him "Lee" after the incident, always feeling uneasy about it and addressing him that way as little as possible.

She later related a second, more humorous incident that occurred in February 1973. Abraham Lincoln's birthday was fast approaching, and she wondered if the bank would be closed that day. "Is the bank shutting down for Lincoln's birthday next week?" she asked the senior teller. "Are you kidding me?" the teller exclaimed. "We don't celebrate *that* man's birthday, we celebrate Lee-Jackson Day!" We then knew for sure that we'd arrived in the Deep South.

As the winter of 1973 continued, we learned to our great surprise that Mississippi, despite the unrelenting heat and humidity of spring, summer, and fall, did have a fairly cold winter. While the temperature did not usually drop too far below freezing, the dampness and humidity from the rivers and swamps added to the winter chill. There was rarely any snow, and what might fall would only last a few hours. More dangerous and disruptive were the ice storms that coated power lines and trees with heavy ice and caused multiple power outages from snapped limbs and broken wires. Then, shortly after the year started, Donna learned to our surprise that she was pregnant with our first child. Once the initial shock wore off, it was time to make plans to settle in even more and get a bedroom ready for the little one. Greenville was fast becoming home for both of us.

Doe's Eat Place, Greenville, MS, 1973

CHAPTER 8
SHARECROPPERS

*These men ask for just the same thing,
fairness, and fairness only.
This, so far as in my power, they,
and all others, shall have.*

—ABRAHAM LINCOLN

On December 6, 1865, the Thirteenth Amendment to the Constitution of the United States was ratified, thus ending slavery in the United States forever. Even though President Lincoln's Emancipation Proclamation in January 1863 freed the slaves in the Confederate states, slavery was not abolished in the states that remained part of the Union. As strange a day as it might have been for the slave, achieving his or her permanent freedom, it still came with a mighty cost. The Civil War had destroyed the southern economy, where most former slaves still dwelt. Jobs in industry and on the plantations had vanished. The Reconstruction period that followed the war did little to improve the lot of former slaves. Primarily, continued racism failed to integrate the slaves into southern society. Political leaders in the North had no real plan for restoring the defeated and decimated southern cities and towns. In many cases, there was as much hunger, hurt, and intolerance as there had been prior to the war and the Thirteenth Amendment. The abject failure of the national Reconstruction program was to blame for leaving the black man in a status nearly identical to the one he thought he'd escaped following the end of the Civil War.

One of the ways that former slaves found a means of survival after the war was through sharecropping. This system began shortly after the end of the Civil War, but may have existed in some areas of the South prior to the war. Just slightly removed from the old slavery system, the sharecropping method provided a labor force for the landowner and an income from the crop, usually cotton, that was produced. For the sharecropper and his family, housing and a meager income were provided by the landowner in exchange for the labor needed to plant, grow, and reap the crop. A slight variation in method of payment sometimes existed between the landowner and the sharecropper. Some sharecroppers may have received free housing in exchange for their labor and their purchase of seed and supplies. Others may have paid rent for housing and equipment used, but in turn got a better share of the profits from the cotton crop. In either case, the sharecropper, usually a former slave, was barely able to make ends meet, no matter the system under which he worked on the plantation. Sharecropper wives were also hired by plantation owners as nannies and wet nurses for the children of the owners. They, too, would receive a small stipend or perhaps something in barter or trade for their tiresome efforts.

Most sharecroppers and their families lived in wooden shacks made of cypress wood, constructed before and after the Civil War. These simple homes, usually containing only one room, were often equipped with a gas or wood stove for heating and cooking. Water was usually available from a nearby creek or from a well. Toilet facilities comprised an outhouse a short walk from the shack. Sharecropper shacks became known as "shotgun shacks," as one could reportedly "fire a shotgun through the front door, with the buckshot leaving out the back door, hitting nothing in between." The outside grounds surrounding the shacks were often filled with discarded farm equipment, tools, and other farming implements that had long since given up their usefulness and were left to rot where they lay. Many of the shotgun shacks still standing throughout the Delta, some dating from the days of Reconstruction, still had small plots of ground where the sharecropper could grow his or her own vegetable patch and try to augment whatever limited resources they had to feed themselves and their family.

The shotgun shacks weren't limited to the Delta countryside. The city of Greenville itself boasted numerous shack structures in the older, predominantly black sections of town. This was clearly the cheapest and preferred way for lower-income folks to get a roof over their heads. Any skilled or unskilled laborer would be able to erect one of these shacks in very little time. And they did all that was required of them, providing shelter and a home at a low cost.

Upon my arrival in Greenville, and in my subsequent early travels throughout the Delta, my most poignant moments included the sights of the shotgun shacks, still standing as sentinels to a bygone era of Civil War and Reconstruction. It was hard to believe that the shacks had been occupied, and even more surprising to see that, in fact, they still were. Some of the more fortunate folks had a single strand of electric wire running to their home. Smoke from a chimney—likely never inspected for adherence to a fire code—at times rose from a home on a winter day, although most shacks were heated by a natural-gas ceramic-style heater. Almost every single shack exhibited photographs of Martin Luther King Jr. and President John F. Kennedy, pasted to the inside wall of the home. It was a rare sight to see any occupant of one of these shacks not sitting outside on the small porch. This was the Mississippi Delta, in all of its questionable glory. I wondered if I would ever get to see the inside of one of these shacks and meet the folks who lived in them.

One day I was working with my partner, Ray Mislock, helping him out on a case. He was seeking information about a man who was wanted for unlawful flight to avoid prosecution. This man in question was a fugitive from the law and was believed to be hiding out in Chicago. Ray's lead on the case was to locate and interview a relative of the fugitive and try to get her cooperation, so as to assist in locating him. We always paired up on these types of cases as we were never sure if the fugitive might actually be at the relative's home. Ray and I drove to the house, which turned out to be a shotgun shack right in the middle of Greenville. We exited the car and cautiously approached the porch. I noticed a strong, offensive odor emanating from the house as Ray knocked on the door. An elderly gray-haired woman—who was white, to my surprise—opened the door, and after being shown our FBI credentials, she invited us in. There must have been at least seventy-five cats of various sizes and breeds running free. The place reeked of cat urine, so much so that I began to breathe through my mouth, so as not to smell the pungent air. A ceramic wall heater turned on full blast and the heat it produced exacerbated the stench of animal waste. Ray was quick to get the information he needed, and we left as soon as humanly possible. The smell had been so foul that I never really got a good look around. It was all I could do to keep from stepping in cat feces on the floor. We only hoped that the dry cleaner would be able to get rid of the odor from our suits.

Sometime later, I was assigned to an impersonation case in Arcola, Mississippi. Twenty miles away from Greenville, down Highway 61 on the way toward Humphreys County, Arcola was a very small town, built strictly around agriculture. The address we were seeking was far removed from the town limits, located somewhere in a remote, rural area. Impersonation cases were fairly common in the Delta. They usually involved some sort of scam by criminals impersonating a US government official in an effort to steal something from the victim. In this particular case, the sheriff's office reported the incident to us, and since the impersonators used some type of federal documentation, it became a matter for the FBI to investigate. All the sheriff was able to tell us was that there were two white male impersonators who were able to abscond with the entire savings that an unlucky local couple maintained in their home. I asked Ray to accompany me on this investigation as we got along well with each other, and our wives had become close friends. At the time, Ray had recently purchased a new camera, and he was eager to take photographs of as many different sights as possible. As new agents in training school, we had been trained in photography using the infamous Speed Graphic camera.

In its day, the Speed Graphic was probably the finest camera around. It had many different capabilities suitable for law enforcement purposes. But it was large and unwieldy, and if the user forgot to remove the dark slide before taking a photograph, there wouldn't be any photograph. Picture a group of people from the press in the 1940s and 1950s, holding cameras and burning flashbulbs at a news event, and you'll have some idea about the looks of the Speed Graphic. A heavy camera requiring two hands to hold it steady, the Speed Graphic was the Mercedes of cameras in its time. An accordion-type bellows fit between the lens and the back of the camera, allowing the lens to move forward and back to adjust for depth of field. A large, round, shiny metal reflector close to six inches in diameter surrounded the electrical port for a single flashbulb, attached to a lengthy tube running along the entire side of the camera unit. The carrying case alone measured the size of a medium valise and contained all sorts of attachments for the camera.

Ray had purchased a new Canon single lens-reflex camera with more capability than the Speed Graphic and built into a sleeker unit. He was going around taking pictures of everything, enjoying his new toy. He brought it with him whenever he went out on a case. On this day, preparing to go to Arcola, he had his new camera with him. After stopping at several shotgun shacks along the highway in an effort to locate the victims' residence, we finally found the correct location. The shotgun shack was the poster child for shotgun shacks in the Delta. The front land area of the shack was littered with tree stumps, fifty-five-gallon oil drums in various stages of decay, an old washing machine, a sink, and an automobile that had long since been of any value. The shack itself seemed to have permanent sag in it, making it appear that it might just collapse upon itself at any time. The scene exuded poverty at the highest level. It was hard to believe that the occupants of the shack would have had anything remotely worth stealing, harder yet to believe that a house in this condition would have drawn the attention of thieves looking for a big score.

Ray and I approached the shack, and I knocked on the door. Simultaneously, as Ray snapped my photograph at the door, a large dog that was chained outside somewhere startled us with vicious snarling and barking. Looking over the edge of the porch, I saw a large German shepherd spewing saliva from his fierce jaws as he lurched against the small, rusty chain holding him in place. Had he escaped and come after us, I would have had no choice but to shoot him. That was something I was glad I didn't have to do as I am a true dog lover. I had learned earlier from a sheriff's deputy to simply honk the car horn prior to exiting the car whenever approaching a house that had dogs visible in the yard, and some occupant would come outside and take control of the dogs. A small but important tip to working cases safely in the Delta. However, this dog was not visible, and it quickly heightened our senses after scaring us half to death.

An elderly black man answered the door and said he was the owner of the house. He invited Ray and me in, and we stood inside the door in a large room. There were bowls of what looked like dog kibble sitting in several places on the floor. At least, I was hoping it was dog food. An elderly black woman, seriously overweight and suffering from some obvious health ailments, lay upon some dirty cotton bedding sitting on the floor. There were piles of clothing scattered throughout the room, making it look as though it had just been ransacked. The sight was simply incredible, like nothing I had ever seen. I stood close to the elderly man, as there was little room to move around in the shack and no visible place to sit. Ray stood across from him and me, his camera slung across his shoulder. We both exhibited our FBI credentials, and I advised him that we were there to investigate the two men who stole his money a few weeks ago. I opened my notebook and began taking notes of the event as told by the soft-spoken victim. During the interview, it dawned upon me that Ray would love to have photographs of the interior of this shack. I knew I would like them as well. I looked up at Ray and asked him to take a few pictures of the crime scene. He didn't answer, so I prodded him again. "Ray, why don't you go take some photographs of this crime scene? We might need them for evidentiary purposes."

He answered authoritatively, "That won't be necessary, John." Somewhat baffled by his response, I asked him a third time. This time, he responded more firmly, "They won't be needed, John." I thought to myself, to hell with him then. If he didn't want photographs, so be it.

I completed the interview, realizing there was little to go on in trying to identify the perpetrators of the theft, as the man and his wife could not provide much in the way of detail or description of the impersonators. They had been asked to go outside and walk around to the back of the house with one of the impersonator's, while the other impersonator went through the shack and stole all the cash he could quickly find. The impersonators were described only as two white males, and little other description was furnished. I thanked the victims for their time and wished them well. I told the couple that if we identified any suspects, I would return with photographs of them for their identification as the thieves. Then Ray and I departed from the home.

Halfway to the car, I turned to Ray and said, "What the hell is wrong with you? What a fantastic opportunity to get some photographs of that place. Didn't you see what I meant for you to do?"

Ray looked at me and smiled. "John, I know you don't know this, since you were standing close to the victim and had your notebook open, writing down notes. You obviously didn't see that he was holding a gun in his pocket, pointed at you the whole time. I kind of knew you couldn't see his hand on his gun as your open notebook blocked your vision. And I suppose you didn't see that I had my hand on my Magnum as well."

I was dumbstruck! I had no idea of any danger present during the interview, and I certainly didn't expect any. After all, they were victims, and we were there to help them. No wonder Ray wouldn't leave my side to get his camera. He may have just saved my life. "Thanks, pal. I'm glad you stayed there. Good catch—I never noticed a thing."

As we drove away, Ray managed to capture some quality photographs of the shotgun shack from the outside.

Before returning to the office, we stopped at the Sunflower County Sheriff's Office in Indianola, Mississippi, as Ray had to check a criminal record. He introduced me to High Sheriff C. O. "Jack" Sessums. Jack was a gregarious fellow and liked to talk. While Ray was checking on the record, I related to Jack what had happened to us during our interview earlier in the day. "You damn feds," he unloaded on me with a grin on his lips. "When are you going to understand how to relate to these local folks out in the county? Most of them cannot read or write. Then you highfalutin federal boys show up at their doorstep, and the first thing you do is show them your credentials, which they cannot even read or understand. If you want to be the law in these parts, here's what you have to do. Leave that fancy suit coat and your FBI credentials in the car, pin your gold badge to your shirt pocket like so, so that it pulls your pocket down a bit, and let the folks see that big ol' Magnum sittin' on your hip...then they'll understand that you're the law. That's how it works here in Miss-sippi!" Then he laughed and reminded me that his message was the best and safest way to operate as a law enforcement agent in the rural areas of the Delta. That was advice well taken, although I knew it wouldn't sit well with the powers that be in the FBI Hoover Building in Washington, DC. Regulations were very firm about appropriate dress for FBI agents, and this advice, while most beneficial, certainly was far from the expected dress of a special agent working in the field.

Ray and I would subsequently conduct many more interviews in shotgun shacks throughout the counties, but we never encountered one quite like the one in Arcola. I recall another interview where we were looking to locate a relative of a woman who lived in a shotgun shack. We knocked on the door, and a very tiny, elderly black woman answered. We told her who we were and why we were there. She invited us into her home. This was totally unlike the place in Arcola. The place was as neat as a pin, and the floor was carefully swept. Everything was put in its place. We took seats across from her as she slowly lowered her withered, arthritic body into her wooden rocking chair. She began slowly rocking back and forth as Ray began asking her questions about our person of interest. I could barely understand any of her responses. She seemed to be at least ninety years old, but I really had no way of knowing her true age. She may have been older, I guessed, as she seemed barely able to mumble her answers. As I strained to hear her responses, Ray continued his interview.

Suddenly, without breaking stride, she pitched forward in her chair, so far forward that I thought she was collapsing out of the chair. As I began to reach forward to catch her, I noticed a stream of foul-looking black liquid shooting out of her mouth, aimed directly into a rusty coffee can sitting on the floor at her feet between her legs, which I had not observed earlier. Initially, I thought she was hemorrhaging, as I had seen a death like that as a policeman in Stone Harbor. I almost felt sick to my stomach as she finished emptying her mouth into the coffee can and slowly returned to her erect sitting position. She was simply chewing tobacco, something I had never seen before. Once she spat her saliva out, her answers were much clearer. I was astounded that such a tiny, old woman would be chewing tobacco. It was always something new and different when out working in the Delta.

Cypress Shade

Abandoned sharecropper shack, Washington County, MS, 1973

Special Agent Whiteside at sharecropper shack near Arcola, MS, 1973

Sharecroppers

Arcola town jail, Arcola, MS, 1973

CHAPTER 9
Lynchings

*It may be true that the law cannot make a man love me,
but it can keep him from lynching me,
and I think that's pretty important.*

—Martin Luther King Jr.

About six weeks after my initial rural road trip, it was time to return to my southernmost counties and pick up voter-registration statistics again. Prior to making my next trip, I was curious to know a bit more about these rural Mississippi counties that appeared so delightfully peaceful and quiet. The green, lush cotton fields stretched for miles, and it seemed as though the existing populace, small as it was, played a major role in the life of these verdant fields. Red-and-green-painted farm equipment splattered with mud sat in nearly every scattered field and property. Tired-looking, rusted-metal cotton gins stood as reminders to a troubled past in each tiny town and village, the only obvious means of income for the local population. There simply were no other manufacturing plants, business office parks, or other means of economic support for these unincorporated areas except for agriculture.

However, there was more to learn about these deceivingly quiet towns. I knew about the murders of the three civil rights workers in Philadelphia, Mississippi, back in June 1964, as the event was splashed all over the news media at the time. Andrew Goodman, James Chaney, and Michael Schwerner were brutally executed by members of the Ku Klux Klan, and their bodies were buried under what would later become an earthen dam. Far from the geographic area of the Delta where I was assigned, it was this singular atrocious event that led President Lyndon Johnson to ask J. Edgar Hoover to establish a greater FBI presence in Mississippi, which led to the opening of the Jackson Division in 1964. It was not until October 1967, though, that Deputy Sheriff Cecil Price, from Neshoba County, and six other Klansmen would be found guilty of federal civil rights violations in connection with these murders. Their sentences ranged from three to ten years. The high sheriff of Neshoba County, Lawrence Rainey, was acquitted of all charges, as were two other suspects. Three other defendants were freed as a result of an all-white hung jury.

While I was living in Pennsylvania, the television news and print media made me aware of all the freedom marches and protests by blacks throughout the Deep South during the 1960s. These difficulties seemed remote to me at the time as we were not experiencing this blatant discrimination in the northeast parts of the United States. I simply didn't see any local protests by the black population in our area and didn't see any anger and hatred toward blacks by whites as was occurring in Selma and Montgomery, Alabama. At least that was what I was always led to believe. I was left to wonder if the counties in the Mississippi Delta had similar problems. I did some research to check on the counties where I would be working, to get a better feel for the folks who lived there as well as to try to better understand the attitudes of local law enforcement personnel. I was very disappointed to learn that members of the Neshoba County Sheriff's Office had participated in the deaths of the three civil rights workers.

It didn't take long to find out that lynchings of innocent blacks did in fact occur in Humphreys and Sunflower Counties. Although the word "lynching" usually evokes images of people being hanged by the neck and dangling from a tree, the word actually pertains to any manner of death of a black citizen by a white hate extremist group. Targeted blacks were usually outspoken advocates of the right to vote or those who encouraged all blacks to register. Many of the lynchings I read about involved a black man who became an active member or officer of the National Association for the Advancement of Colored People (NAACP). Based upon the large percentage of blacks in the community, a solid black vote would likely oust many white politicians from office. This certainly was not acceptable to many office holders, and they began to target those blacks who created the biggest stir. Lynchings weren't always politically motivated either. For some, it was simply a cruel pleasure to go out and kill an innocent black man, for no reason whatsoever but the color of his skin. This was the case in one incident I learned about in Humphreys County, Mississippi.

Rainey Pool was a fifty-four-year-old black farmhand with one arm who was believed to have lived in Midnight, Mississippi, an unincorporated town near Sharkey County. Allegedly, he had a bit of a reputation as a troublemaker, especially when he had been drinking. On the night of April 12, 1970, Rainey apparently attempted to enter what was known to be an all-white restaurant called McMerchants Cafe in Louise, Mississippi. A differing account from those involved in the crime was that he was observed attempting to steal something from a pickup truck parked outside of the tavern. He was severely beaten into unconsciousness for his actions. Then he was thrown into the back of a pickup truck and taken to the banks of the Sunflower River at some point along Highway 14. There the men threw him into the cold, muddy river. His body was eventually recovered from the river several days later, after his wife had reported him missing on Sunday. Rainey was not known to have been involved in any of the local civil rights activities. The pathologist noted that Pool had a fractured vertebrae and larynx. He later testified in court that Pool's cause of death was drowning, even though his other injuries would have eventually caused death as well.

Humphreys County Sheriff J. L. Huffstickler—one of my new law enforcement contacts—announced on April 15, 1970, that two local men had been arrested and charged with Rainey's murder. Harold Crimm, a fertilizer salesman from Yazoo, and Doc Caston, a mechanic from Louise, were arrested and charged with murder. Subsequently, two additional men were charged with murder in the case, and one allegedly confessed.

However, court records revealed that the charges were dropped. According to the record, after a defense attorney for defendant Joe Oliver Watson made a motion to suppress a statement given by Watson to the highway patrol, the motion was granted by Judge B. B. Wilkes. Judge Wilkes agreed that the statement had been obtained in such a manner as to completely violate Watson's rights. As a result, District Attorney George Everett asked the judge for a nolle prosequi, a legal action in which the prosecutor drops the charges against the defendants, as he did not think he could convict the defendants without the use of Watson's statement to the highway patrol. He told the judge that the statement was "the last evidence we had to get a murder conviction with." Despite the fact that there were several other witnesses to the crime, the state was unable to get them to testify in court.[1]

---

1. *Delta Democrat-Times,* July 30, 1970.

In 1999, at the behest of the Pool family, the case was again brought to trial. Joe Oliver Watson pled guilty to manslaughter and testified against the other three men. James "Doc" Caston, age sixty-six, his brother Charles Ernie Caston, age sixty-four, and his half brother Hal Spivey Crimm, age fifty, were convicted of manslaughter by a state jury and sentenced to twenty years in prison. A fifth accomplice, Dennis Newton, was acquitted.

I was kind of shocked that this type of killing had taken place only two years or so prior to my arrival in Greenville. But the Rainey murder wasn't the only one.

The Reverend George Lee was the pastor of a Baptist church in Belzoni, Humphreys County. Lee also operated a local printing press and was a known black activist in the community. It is alleged that he was the first black who registered to vote in the county. He was heavily involved in local voter-registration drives and had been reported responsible for getting ninety-two black voters to enroll. With a close friend, Gus Courts, Lee founded a local chapter of the NAACP in Belzoni. This in turn angered the white population who organized a white citizens council. They circulated the names of the new black voters to their white employers, who retaliated by firing them from their jobs, denying them credit, and raising their rents. Both Lee and Courts knew they were marked men.

On the Saturday before Mother's Day, May 1955, Reverend Lee was driving home when he was hit by gunfire from a passing car. With half his face blown away, he got out of his car and sought help at a nearby cab stand. Two black cab drivers took him to the hospital where he died. A subsequent investigation by the sheriff determined Reverend Lee was killed in an automobile accident and that the lead pellets removed from his face were likely dental fillings. A coroner's jury later determined that he died of unknown causes. Six months later, Gus Courts was also hit by shots from a passing car, but he survived his injuries. He finally abandoned his voter-registration efforts, in effect saving his life, and moved with his family to Chicago.[2]

The Lee lynching was some time ago, but really only seventeen years prior to my arrival in the Delta. It was hard to comprehend that this sort of violence took place in the very counties I was now working in, trying to enforce federal laws.

Another incident in Sunflower County was equally as disturbing as all those I read about. On May 25, 1971, an eighteen-year-old black girl named Joetha Collier was walking home from her commencement activities the night of her graduation from Drew High School. She was standing with a group of friends when she was shot in the head from a passing car. She was killed on the spot. Shortly after the shooting, based upon witness statements, three white men were arrested by the Cleveland, Mississippi, police department. One suspect, Thomas Allen Wilkerson, age nineteen, was a recent graduate at the same high school attended by the victim. The other two suspects, uncles of Wilkerson, were identified as Wayne Parks, age twenty-five, of Drew, and Wesley Parks, age twenty-six, of Memphis. At the time of their arrest, the police found a .22-caliber revolver believed to be the murder weapon, along with a sawed-off shotgun, a .22-caliber automatic rifle, and a knife in their car. The suspected murder weapon belonged to Wesley Parks. The chief of police, J. D. Fleming, commented that all three suspects had been drinking heavily prior to the shooting. No motive was ever ascertained or reason given for the shooting.

Subsequent marches two days later by members of the black community in Drew and Ruleville protesting racial violence ended with the arrest of thirty-seven marchers. There had also been some rock-throwing incidents in Drew during the night and on the day following Collier's murder. The marchers were protesting the murder and wanted five other grievances met in the town. They wanted blacks to be appointed to the school

---

2. *Free at Last, Teaching Tolerance* (The Southern Poverty Law Center, 1989).

board and to the town council. They wanted the town swimming pool to be reopened to the general public and better streets and drainage in the black sections of town. Lastly, they wanted the reinstatement of black teachers who had lost their jobs as a result of going to court against the school board.[3]

On Friday, March 3, 1972, just six months prior to my arrival in Greenville, murder charges against two of the three murder suspects, Thomas Allen Wilkerson and Wayne Parks, were dismissed. Wesley Parks was found guilty of the lesser charge of manslaughter on October 29, 1971, and sentenced to twenty years at the Mississippi State Penitentiary in Parchman. However, he was released on an appeal bond of $10,000.[4] The Mississippi Supreme Court refused Wesley's appeal in October 1972, and he was remanded into custody of the Mississippi State Penitentiary to serve his twenty-year sentence.

These cases barely scratched the surface of all the atrocities that occurred in Mississippi during the 1950s and 1960s when the FBI had its hands full with lynchings throughout the state. The high-profile lynching of Emmett Till, age fourteen, in Greenwood in 1955; the murder of Medgar Evers, age thirty-eight, in Jackson in 1963; and the murder of Vernon Dahmer, age fifty-eight, in Hattiesburg, in 1966 were but a few of the lynchings that exemplified the sorrowful state our nation was in during the tense days of the civil rights movement.

Thrust into the Deep South, I was now responsible, in part, to ensure racial equality and enforce the Civil Rights Act of 1964 and the Voting Rights Act of 1965, as well as all of the other federal laws assigned to the FBI at this time.

The Jackson Division had a powerful history of its own in the civil rights era. In May 1941, the FBI first opened the Jackson, Mississippi, field office. Its opening was prompted by the outbreak of war in Europe. Investigative responsibilities of the FBI increased as a result of the war, especially in the area of sabotage and counterespionage investigations.

---

3. George LeMaistre, Jr., Staff Writer, *Delta Democrat-Times*, May 27, 1971.
4. Bill Rose, State Editor, *Delta Democrat-Times*, March 5, 1972.

However, immediately following the end of World War II, the overall criminal caseload in the Jackson field office began a steady decline, and it became unfeasible to continue its operations. It was shut down in 1946, and all subsequent FBI cases in Mississippi were handled from the field offices located in Memphis or New Orleans.

During the 1950s, a growing number of high-profile civil rights cases that drew national attention occurred in Mississippi. In 1963, the Mississippi field secretary of the NAACP, Medgar Evers, was shot and killed by a sniper with a high-powered rifle, as he entered his home. That crime was followed up by an even more brutal murder of the three civil rights workers in Philadelphia, Mississippi. Shortly thereafter, President Lyndon Johnson requested that J. Edgar Hoover increase FBI presence in Mississippi. In accordance with the president's wishes, on July 10, 1964, the Jackson Division was reopened as an FBI field office. This opening, attended by Mr. Hoover himself, demonstrated the FBI's commitment to civil rights and other investigations in the state.[5]

Immediately, cases were opened on white supremacist organizations and the Ku Klux Klan, as well as the members in those organizations and the illegal activities connected to them. Soon the office was handling over 1,500 cases, including dozens of agents working on the case involving missing civil rights workers Goodman, Chaney, and Schwerner. Racially motivated church bombings and burnings, shootings, and personal attacks were other investigations conducted by the Jackson office and its resident agencies. Voter intimidation cases and other white extremist matters caused more FBI agent transfers to Mississippi. The FBI also supported federal peacekeeping efforts at civil demonstrations throughout the state.[6]

I was now assigned to the Greenville Resident Agency just eight years after a rash of lynchings, murders, riots, protest marches, and civil unrest descended upon the Magnolia State with a vengeance. And the Delta area had its own share of the problems. No wonder I felt so alone whenever I

---

5. www.fbi.gov/jackson/about-us/history.
6. www.fbi.gov/jackson/about-us/history.

was out by myself conducting investigations. I wasn't sure that the black population trusted me, a white man, and for that matter, I wasn't even sure I was trusted by local and county law enforcement personnel as a Yankee and, worst of all, a federal agent. The only things I knew for sure I could depend upon in time of personal trouble or danger were the Smith & Wesson .357 combat Magnum strapped to my hip and my own wits. It wasn't always possible to have another FBI agent accompany me on all my cases as so much of the work in the rural areas had to be done alone.

As I worked my way to Mayersville to obtain voter-registration statistics, I noticed an occasional abandoned building bearing faded, painted signs reading White and Colored over separate doors. To my knowledge, there were no current business locations or public places that continued to discriminate on the basis of race in that particular manner. But still being able to see the signs of the recent past was a clear indication that I was not driving through friendly territory. Whoever painted those signs were surely not friends of the federal government and its perceived intervention into their personal affairs.

I arrived in Mayersville at the courthouse and picked up the voter-registration statistics. Then I stopped by the town grocery store and met briefly with the sheriff, just to reintroduce myself and offer my assistance whenever needed. He seemed like a decent man who appeared to be very popular with the local town folk, someone who could be trusted.

I left Mayersville heading to Rolling Fork in Sharkey County to meet Sheriff Phillips and get my voter-registration statistics. Since everything was located in the courthouse, I stopped in to meet the sheriff first. Maurice Phillips seemed like a professional law enforcement person. He had a deep Mississippi accent and took his personal appearance very seriously, dressed in a military-pressed, tailored uniform shirt. He explained that the racial situation in the county was under control and that there had been no real problems between blacks and whites in recent years. I wasn't sure how much of that statement to believe, but I offered my assistance whenever it was needed. He did not make any comments about my Yankee background, although I knew he was keenly aware from whence I came.

I left the sheriff after a short visit and entered the Sharkey County clerk's office. I rang the small bell on the wooden desktop and awaited assistance. Déjà vu! The same small, gruff clerk I dealt with the last time appeared at the desk, looking as disheveled and miserable as he did the last time we met. I showed him my credentials and requested the voter-registration statistics for the last period. He again mumbled, "Take a seat," and disappeared into a back room.

I sat and waited about five minutes. Sitting there, I began to seethe a bit as I recalled my past effort to get the voter-registration statistics. I wasn't going to let this old curmudgeon take advantage of me again. Several more minutes passed, more than sufficient time for the clerk to obtain the voter statistics based upon the small number provided to me before. I stood back up and rang the bell for the clerk. He came through the door and approached the counter, his face ruddier than ever. I reached out over the counter and grabbed him by the wide lapels of his cheap, pilled polyester sport coat. I looked him squarely in the eyes and said, "You have five minutes to obtain the voter-registration statistics, or I'll arrest you for obstruction of justice." I let go of his lapels, and he scurried back behind closed doors, his face now flushed red with rage. Within two minutes, he returned with the requested statistics, again no more than one or two blacks and whites who registered during the period, and no purges. Interestingly enough, I never had another problem obtaining the voter-registration statistics from the Sharkey County clerk again.

I completed my run for the day by driving through Louise en route to Belzoni, where I planned to get the voter-registration statistics for Humphreys County. As I passed the place that Rainey Pool had been slain, I sensed I was in hostile territory. I knew that hatred existed between the races here but did not know to what extent. I only had the past to rely upon for my guide, and that past indicated there were serious problems.

After arriving in Belzoni, I obtained my voter-registration stats and stopped in at the sheriff's office to say hello to Deputy Dalton. We chatted for a bit, and I again offered my services whenever they were needed. I did not get to see Sheriff Huffstickler. I left the sheriff's office and used the still dank and repulsive public restroom on the first floor of the courthouse. I thought to myself that there should have been a sign reading Colored over the door. I figured the clean White restrooms were all behind closed county office doors.

I stopped in the middle of town to get lunch at the Belzoni Café. Much like at the Pig Stand where I had eaten before, there were only a few patrons in the small café. I sat at the counter and ordered a hamburger and Coke. While the old woman who waited on me and cooked my order was friendly enough, she had little to say. I could have heard a pin drop while I ate my lunch, as all conversation between the white patrons stopped from the moment I walked through the door. They knew who I was, and as a federal agent, I simply wasn't welcomed in their town. It was hostile territory indeed. I finished my sandwich as quickly as possible and headed out for a brief stop at the Belzoni Police Department. I sat with Chief Toby Woods for a bit and discussed the crime issues in town. He gave me a black leather slapjack to keep with me in the car, telling me it was a great weapon to have in the event of a fight. I accepted his gift enthusiastically so as not to offend him. I thought those leather-covered, lead-filled saps were illegal, but after all, he was the law in this part of the country.

I returned to the office and was pleased to tell Ron how I dealt with the Sharkey County records clerk. He laughed and told me he didn't want to tell me about dealing with the guy when I first planned to meet him. Ron wanted me to enjoy the surprise of the response from the clerk. I think I surprised him more with my follow-up response. Had I actually arrested the clerk for obstruction of justice, I'm sure there would have been a number of upset government prosecutors who would have had to get involved. Yet calling his bluff seemed to work out just fine and all was well. It seemed there was peace in the valley for the moment.

FBI Director J. Edgar Hoover arrives at
Jackson, MS airport, July 10, 1964

Hoover and Deputy Director Clyde
Tolson deplane, July 10, 1964

Lynchings

Director Hoover meeting local dignitaries, July 10, 1964

Director leaving airport en route Jackson
FBI building, July 10, 1964

Hoover preparing to open the Jackson FBI Division, July 10, 1964

Director Hoover meeting with local dignitaries in office, July 10, 1964

CHAPTER 10
High Times

Everything is funny, as long as it's happening to someone else.

—Will Rogers

Not every moment of the day was spent in dangerous activity or racially tense environments. There were a lot of lighter moments in connection with the work in the Delta, notwithstanding that all of the work was important. For some reason, it seemed that Ray and I couldn't escape having a few funny experiences and embarrassing ones along the way.

One day, we were working together and had traveled to the vicinity of Hollandale, Mississippi, looking to find a Selective Service violator. Even though the Vietnam conflict was winding down, there was a federal requirement that all men, upon reaching their eighteenth birthday, register with their local Selective Service or "draft" board, thus providing the nation with a continuing supply of future soldiers if needed. The individual we were looking for was long overdue for registering for the draft, and Ray and I hoped to find him. There was a federal warrant outstanding for his arrest. His parents resided at the last known address we had for the subject, and we headed that way to pursue his whereabouts.

We arrived at the address and saw a fairly large ranch-style home that was well cared for. Ray drove the FBI car up the long driveway, and we parked behind a well-used tan pickup truck. We exited from the car and walked to the front door and rang the bell. We didn't know what to expect and hoped the fugitive might be at home. A man opened the door wearing denim bib overalls, a worn green-flannel shirt, and a Ford tractor cap. We identified ourselves to him, and he invited us in. He offered us a seat, but we remained standing as it was possible we might need to make a quick arrest should the subject appear.

Ray initiated the interview as it was his case. He explained to the man that there was a federal arrest warrant existing for the subject, charging him with a violation of the Selective Service Act. Ray asked if the boy was present in the home, or if the man had any idea where he was at the moment. "I haven't seen my son in a long while, and I have no idea where he is. Besides, I wouldn't tell you even if I knew his whereabouts," the man replied, revealing he was the subject's father. Again, Ray calmly asked him for his cooperation, noting that his son would be better off turning himself in than staying on the run from the authorities. This caused his father to launch into a diatribe about the unjustness of the Vietnam conflict as well as the evils of the draft law. Ray let him rant and rave for a few minutes, again attempting to secure his cooperation, all to no avail.

All the commotion in the living room brought the subject's mother and sister into the living room to see what was going on. The husband shouted, "These two FBI agents have an arrest warrant for our son and want to know where he is. I told 'em I have no idea and wouldn't tell them if I knew." Ray gently asked the subject's mom if she would help us out for her son's sake, pointing out the simple truth that it would be better for him to surrender himself and handle the matter with an attorney than to remain on the run, always wondering when some police officer would eventually arrest him. Common sense and compassion seemed to do no good. His parents simply refused to cooperate and give up his location. They denied that he was at the house and refused to cooperate further. Our interview was going nowhere.

By this time, I'd had enough of their crap. It was pretty clear to both Ray and me that they knew full well where their son was residing. I put on my best tough-guy face and told mom, dad, and sis that if they were deliberately concealing the whereabouts of their son, a federal fugitive, they were all in violation of the harboring-a-federal-fugitive statute, and charges against all three of them could be forthcoming. "If I can prove that you folks are concealing the whereabouts of your son, we will be back with arrest warrants for all three of you. Then it will be too late for your cooperation," I stated, as authoritatively as I could sound. There was silence for a brief time, followed by more denials. With nothing more to be gained, it was time for Ray and me to depart. I warned them one more time that we'd be back, and we left the house. We walked to our car in the driveway and began backing down the driveway to the road.

About halfway down the long driveway, Ray somehow managed to get the rear right wheel of the FBI car off the driveway and hung up with no traction under it. Like most roads and driveways in the Delta, this one was raised three or four feet above level ground to preclude flooding problems.

We were stuck! We could not move the car forward or backward. We sat there for a moment before getting out of the car to look at the ridiculous situation we had just created. It was hopeless as we could not push the car back up onto the driveway and could not drive over the edge of the driveway without destroying the car. We stood there trying to think of our next plan and decided all we could do was to call for some kind of roadside assistance to tow us out of our predicament. However, it wasn't like service stations were plentiful in the rural area.

Just as we were considering our only option, the man who I had just threatened to put in jail for harboring a federal fugitive came walking slowly down the driveway from his house. "Need any help?" he politely inquired. Talk about feeling like a complete jerk.

"Yeah, looks like we missed the edge of the driveway," Ray responded.

The man came over to the car, took a look at the rear wheel, and slowly walked back to his pickup. About now I was wishing I could be anywhere but here. He returned to our car, backing up in his truck. He got out of the truck and took a length of heavy chain from the cab. He crawled under the FBI car and attached the chain to the axle. He crawled back out and told Ray to put the transmission in neutral. He got into his truck and towed the FBI car back up onto his driveway. Exiting his truck, he crawled once again under the FBI car to remove his tow chain. At last, we were able to move the car on its own. We said a simple "Thanks for your help" and sheepishly drove away. It was one of those moments you had to experience to fully understand the insanity of it all. I can't imagine what the man was thinking. Probably something like, "I guess I've got to go help those pathetic assholes just to clear my driveway." I suppose he was right.

Early on the morning of September 6, 1973, Donna woke me from a sound sleep, saying she thought it was time to go to the hospital for the birth of our first child. We did not know the sex of the child, and I'm not sure if technology was advanced to that stage yet. I had spent some time painting one of our bedrooms for the baby and assembling the new crib and bassinette Donna had purchased. Somewhat more complicated was the assembly of a bentwood rocking chair, another baby necessity at the time. We had wall-to-wall carpeting installed to add warmth to the room and hung curtains on both windows. It was nice to complete another room of our house, especially since it meant we'd soon be welcoming a new family member. There were two hospitals in Greenville at the time, which was certainly convenient for us. Donna's doctors worked out of King's Daughters Hospital in downtown Greenville, the more stately and older of the two hospitals.

As she got ready for the trip to the hospital, I packed her bag in the car and steeled myself for the upcoming adventure. Donna seemed very calm, which I found a bit disconcerting as this was her first time at childbirth. I was calm on the outside but a bit worried, hoping that all would work out fine. We got in the car and made the ten-minute drive to the hospital, where we went to the maternity ward and were met by a kind, experienced nurse. She told me she was taking Donna into the back and that she would return shortly. I kissed Donna and wished her luck as she went off with the nurse. Now I was alone in the waiting room. I wondered if this was the time I was to start pacing as I awaited news about the baby. I sat down and pretended to look through a magazine, knowing full well I couldn't concentrate on anything but what I imagined was going on in the back room. I didn't like having no control whatsoever in the situation. So I sat, fretted, worried, and waited.

A half hour later, the nurse returned to the waiting room. It was about 6:15 a.m. "Mr. Whiteside, your wife is resting comfortably outside the delivery room, and it's going to be a while yet before she is ready to have the baby." I'm sure she had taken a good look at me and decided I shouldn't wait for some indeterminate time. She said, "Why don't you go back home, shave and take a nice shower, then go out and have yourself a nice breakfast. Once you finish breakfast, come back to the hospital. Your wife will be fine here."

I didn't know what to do. I'd never heard of a prospective father-to-be who left the hospital before his wife gave birth, while she was still in labor. Was this some sort of a southern thing? I wondered. I must have looked very indecisive to the nurse as she said again, "She'll be fine. Come back in a couple of hours after freshening up and having breakfast. Go on now, and we'll see you soon."

    I decided it was best to do as I was directed, so I returned home and did exactly what the nurse told me to do. After showering and shaving, I dressed for work. I drove to Jim's Café and ordered a delicious southern-style breakfast. I even enjoyed my cup of chicory coffee, although my thoughts were of my wife and her current predicament. I finished breakfast, and it was almost nine o'clock. I returned to the hospital and sat in the waiting room. I was still alone, so it looked like we were going to have the only new baby born in Greenville that morning. After a few minutes, the nurse came into the waiting room and complimented me on my improved looks. She said the baby would be here soon, to just sit down and wait. Again, I did what I was told to do, making another feeble effort to read through a magazine or two.

    At 10:47 a.m., the nurse came into the waiting room and announced, "It's a boy! Eight pounds and six ounces, twenty inches long. Your wife said his name is Jason William. Mom and the baby are doing fine. I'll bring him out to the window so you can see him in a few minutes." With that, she returned into the hospital area.

    I was thankful everyone was well and thrilled I had a son. I was not asked to be with my wife during the birth process. I guess that just wasn't done back then, or at least not there. In a few minutes, the nurse appeared at the nursery window, holding up my new son. I quickly checked that all fingers and toes were present, and with that he was taken away and put back in the nursery. The nurse appeared a few minutes later. She told me that Donna was resting and that there was nothing more for me to do there. She suggested I go back to work and come back to the hospital at the end of the day to see my wife and new son.

    That was it! I played no role at all in the birth of my son. I couldn't even see my wife after it was all over. Not knowing any better, and with no one to consult, I again complied with the nurse and went to work, after stopping at a local tobacconist and buying a box of "It's a Boy" cigars to hand out. It was difficult to concentrate at work, so I ended up helping other guys work cases where they needed an extra body. Ray invited me to his home for dinner that evening after I stopped by the hospital to see Donna and Jason.

In a couple of days, Donna and the baby were discharged from the hospital. I went and picked them up and drove them home. Home...it was getting to sound more and more like it truly was our real home, and those past residences were just that, past. We began our lives together in Greenville, and now we were starting our family together in Greenville. It was not difficult to say that Greenville was home at this point in our lives and for the foreseeable future.

In the days that followed, work continued to have some lighter moments. One day, I was again working with Ray. It was a brilliant, sunny October day with just a touch of fall crispness in the air. Ray had some information that a man wanted for unlawful flight to avoid prosecution for murder may have been frequenting a local juke joint or honky-tonk in town. We decided to check out the place just before lunchtime. Even if the killer wasn't there, we might locate a cooperative employee or bartender who would be willing to help us on the case.

The sun was fairly high in the sky, reflecting brightly off the sun-bleached sidewalk as we entered the rather seedy bar and pool room. Closing the door behind us, we found that we were completely blinded from the sunlight as we walked into the dimly lit lounge. For close to fifteen seconds, a long time if a fugitive wanted for murder is looking at you, neither one of us could see a thing. Gradually our eyesight adjusted to the dim light, and we were able to make our way to the bar. Ray identified himself to the bartender and stated that we were looking for the subject who had been seen in the place. She denied seeing the fugitive after looking at a photograph Ray displayed to her. There were several other patrons in the joint who also looked at the photograph and could not provide any help.

The bartender told Ray that she was the daytime-only bartender, and that the evening bartender would be in at one o'clock and might have more information to share about the fugitive. Ray told her we'd come back later in the day.

We left the juke joint and decided to walk a couple of blocks to our favorite lunch spot, the One Block East, aptly named as it was located one block east from the river levee. During lunch, we both agreed that we were certainly at risk walking into the juke joint blinded from the sun. We decided we would need a better plan upon returning to the place so as not to make ourselves such obvious targets. While enjoying our meal, a plan was cleverly conceived. It was quite simple in its execution. If it continued to be as bright outside as it was before lunch, we would close our eyes prior to entering the place and leave them closed for a quick count of five. We would then open our eyes, hoping our vision would not be impaired in any way. Based upon the layout of the place, as silly as it sounds, the plan seemed feasible, and we both quickly concurred it would work. We finished our lunch and headed back to the juke joint.

It was just as sunny and bright as it had been when we entered the first time. We were prepared to put our plan into full operation as we stood close to the front door and closed our eyes. We counted to ten, agreed we were ready, opened the door, and walked in. A slow count to five was made as we readied our eyes for the darkened parlor. "One, two, three, four, five and… eyes open," Ray whispered. Much to our shock and surprise, and likely to the few patrons of the place, all of the house lights had been turned up since we last were there, and the patrons stood gaping at two fools standing in the doorway of the bar with their eyes closed for a few seconds. It didn't take but a second to realize how simple we must have looked to everyone there. Once again, we made perfect targets for the fugitive had he been present in the bar, standing there in full light with our eyes closed for five seconds. Hell, we wouldn't have even seen the shooter.

The couple shooting pool returned to their game as Ray and I sheepishly approached the new evening bartender and conducted our interview. After looking at the photo of the subject, he also claimed he hadn't seen the fugitive in the place and could not provide any assistance. We hightailed it out of there and had a good laugh about our "clever plan" on the drive back to the office. We concluded that a good pair of sunglasses would have been a much better choice.

There were a lot of fun times after working hours shared between most of the agents in the office. Ray and Ron decided to take me golfing for the first time. I borrowed a set of golf clubs from a friend of Ray's, who was looking to sell them. There was a public golf course located adjacent to the grounds of Greenville Airport, on an old air force base. Early one Saturday morning, we arrived at the clubhouse and paid our greens fees. Ron asked if I had any golf balls, and I replied that I did not. He suggested I buy some before playing. I bought a sleeve of three golf balls, thinking I would have plenty. I did not realize that fourteen of the eighteen holes on the course had some sort of water hazard nearby. That knowledge wouldn't have made any difference to me at the time, since I had never played the game, and I would soon be returning to the pro shop for a dozen more golf balls to get me past the first tee. Golf was a real challenge to me in the Delta, vying against not only the water hazards and the red-winged blackbirds that nested close to the water but also the raging Mississippi heat and humidity.

During golf sessions, Ron was the guy who first introduced me to chewing tobacco. He asked me to try a mouthful of Red Man. Always game to try something different, I reached into the pouch, grabbed some tobacco, and stuffed it into my cheek. I remain amazed to this day by the intense strength and sickening sweet taste of this tobacco chew. I was able to keep it in my mouth for a hole or two, but by then I had had enough. Weeks later, with practice, I was able to finally play nine holes with a chew of Red Man, but it took a lot of patience. I finally decided it wasn't for me. On my birthday, Ron did buy me a plug of Lucky Strike leaf-chewing tobacco to try. Being from Nebraska, he always enjoyed some form of chewing tobacco. I did try one bite, one time, out of the plug. It was worse than the Red Man, coming apart in my mouth. I tossed it away after the remainder of it had dried out in my desk drawer.

We also played poker together once a month. Ray, Ron, Chuck and I, along with three other friends we met in town, would get together at each other's homes for a Friday night game of nickel-and-dime poker. Even on a terrible night, one could only lose about eight dollars. Tennis was another occasional pastime, although it was too hot to play until evening arrived. An occasional evening football game at Greenville High School was the closest thing to watching live college or professional sports in the Delta. While in Greenville, we did get to see Wilbert Montgomery play football as a high school running back. He was a student famous for his athletic prowess, setting many local high school records. We did not know it at the time we watched him play, but he would eventually become a professional running back with the Philadelphia Eagles, and he played for them in their first Super Bowl appearance in 1981.

Agent Whiteside clowning around with Washington County deputy sheriff George Martin, 1973

CHAPTER 11
RACISM AND SLURS

Racism is still with us. But it is up to us to prepare our children for what they have to meet, and, hopefully, we shall overcome.

—ROSA PARKS

Overt racial discrimination and the extensive use of racial slurs in the Delta area were not nearly as bad as I once thought they would be. However, it isn't as if I was not aware that some deep-seated hatred between the races still existed; it certainly did. Some of the more obvious clues still remained on deserted buildings and failed businesses, where signs above separate doorways provided entrance instructions for whites and colored. Yet, although that specific policy of segregation had seemingly ceased to exist a few years ago, the old rules still applied in many cases. I often wondered why I never saw a black person at the barbershop, in the doctor or dentist office, or eating at a nearby table in a nice restaurant. Since the population in Greenville was more than 75 percent black, odds were I'd run into a black person at one of these spots. But I never did, unless the black person seen was working in a service capacity. It would take a while before I learned the concept of defacto segregation. In some cases, like the barbershop, the blacks had establishments of their own in their sections of town, and while there were black employees in all of the restaurants, black patrons usually ate at small restaurants also found in the black areas of town.

But what about the doctors and dentists? I was not aware of any "black only" doctors and dentists serving the black community. Where did they go when they needed medical care? The answer was made clear when my wife was discussing that very issue with a friend at work. She told Donna that black patients were scheduled on certain days, while white patients were scheduled for different days. In that way, no one, black or white, would think that a person of a different race was being examined by the same doctor with the same set of instruments.

I thought I would hear the word "nigger" and other racial slurs used frequently in the Delta during the course of interviews during my investigations with the locals. To my pleasant surprise, it never happened. However, during one of my first contacts with a local sheriff and my partner Ray Mislock, I learned differently. The sheriff was teaching us a little something about the Delta, knowing us to be relatively new to the area. He said, "We have four types of people in the Delta. We have whites, we have blacks, we have white trash, and we have niggers. And the worst of the group is the white trash. They are law enforcement's biggest problem. They are the ones responsible for most of the racial troubles in Miss-sippi."

The use of the racial slur "nigger" was almost exclusively used by blacks themselves when talking about another black person. It seemed to me to be a more common familial term when used in that way. Most white folk in the Delta did not use that racial slur when referring to blacks, although it seemed to depend more on their socioeconomic status. The most common name of referral for African-Americans seemed to be "blacks" or "Negroes." Yet the usage of the word "Negro" was not without some possible slur intended. Many locals with a heavy Mississippi accent referred to the "Negra," which seemed to me like a lazy southern-drawl way of saying Negro. However, when "Negra" was spoken softly with the accent, it often sounded like "nigger." What exactly it was that they wanted to say but were careful not to is not mine to guess.

Another offensive term often used to describe a black person with a very light complexion was "high yellow." It was a way of describing a black person who had a lot of Caucasian blood mixed into his or her genetic code. It was heard often in police circles, where describing a person's complexion was important in providing a full description. Rather than using the more accurate term "light complexion," it was common to hear the spoken description as "high yellow."

I don't recall working even one Ku Klux Klan or white extremist / white hate case during my assignment in the Delta. While there had been violence against the blacks in the local area, it seemed the preponderance of racial hatred and violence occurred in areas outside of the Delta. Perhaps part of the reason for more racial tolerance in the Delta was that the black laborer was an integral part of the success of the economy in field crops. There was plenty of work for all at the time of racial unrest in the state, and despite unfair work practices at times, the blacks and whites seemed to be working together for the greater economic good of the region and each other. With very little contact with the white "redneck" type in my cases, I simply did not hear many racial slurs used in the Delta.

Perhaps another reason for the lack of racial slurs was the simple truth that the blacks themselves were directly responsible for raising and caring for many white families. Black wet nurses and nannies were employed by the hundreds, raising the more wealthy white children. In many cases, they assisted in the birthing process of the white babies as there was a lack of adequate medical facilities in the rural areas of the Delta. They prepared meals for the families and kept the plantations clean and looking beautiful. Why hate the very people responsible for the upbringing of their children and for the welfare of their homes? It was a difficult concept to understand then, as it still is today.

To be sure, there were still evidences of racial inequality on the job. I recall early in my assignment, stopping in to the Greenville Police Department to check on a few arrest records. It was always important to obtain full descriptive data of a wanted suspect. At the very least, that would include sex, race, date and place of birth, height, weight, hair and eye color, and complexion. Other descriptive data was also important when available, like scars, marks, and tattoos. Job occupation, marital status, social security number, past criminal record, and relatives' addresses were also important when sending out a lead to another FBI office or police department when seeking a fugitive.

On this particular day, I was copying down some descriptive data from a former arrest record on file in the records section. When I came to the description of the subject, a black man, I saw that his eye color was listed as "maroon." While I knew what the color maroon looked like, it was the first time I'd ever seen it used to describe an eye color. Thinking it must have been a mistake, or a very unusual eye color, I asked one of the records clerks if it was a mistake. He replied, "Haven't you ever looked at 'their' eyes? They're all maroon!" When he left the room, I decided to check out a few other arrest cards in order to see if he was kidding. He wasn't. Every black male or female arrest index card I checked showed their eye color described as maroon.

Racism and Slurs

I received a call one afternoon from a young black woman who complained that she and her husband were being evicted from their apartment for no reason. She inferred that the eviction was because they were black. I traveled to see the woman at her apartment to try to determine whether there was a violation of any of the civil rights laws or any discrimination in housing laws. I was met at the apartment by a twenty-five-year-old black girl who was almost in tears. She explained that her landlord had ordered her and her husband to vacate the apartment in two weeks. She said they had no place to go and didn't know what to do. She denied having been any problem at the apartment house and said that she had never been in any trouble. Up until this time, she had never had any contact with the landlord and simply could not understand her eviction notice, giving no cause whatsoever for the eviction decision. He husband was working, and she was looking for a job. My interview with her failed to identify even one minor reason why this couple should be told to vacate the apartment. All of their rent had been paid on time, as she showed me all her rental payment receipts. None of this made any sense to me. I kept trying to identify even one disagreement with the landlord, or some comment made by the couple that caused him to evict them. But there was simply nothing to be found.

I finally asked the young lady if she had a copy of her lease. She obtained it from her bedroom and handed it to me. It was only on one sheet of paper and was fairly simple in style. I read carefully through it until I reached a small sentence near the end of the lease. It stated something to the effect that "the landlord reserves the right to remove the tenants from the apartment lease for no cause." There it was, simply stated. They could be evicted for no cause or "just because"! I had to wonder how many other leases were written in this manner to give an unsavory landlord exclusive permission to oust anyone he didn't like from his apartment complex. It wasn't like the landlord didn't know the couple was black when he leased the apartment to them, despite the fact that they were the only black couple there. But it was still a legal way to evict someone for no reason, even if that reason was the color of their skin.

I tried to explain to the young lady that it seemed that the lease gave her landlord legal permission to evict her and her husband, like he said, "for no cause." I pointed out the line in the lease giving him that authority. She asked if an attorney would be helpful in keeping them in the apartment. I informed her that it was her choice to try that route, but it looked to me that the signed lease was pretty solid in favor of the landlord. I didn't want to see her get ripped off by an attorney looking for a quick score, knowing full well that the lease would likely still win out in the end. I offered to contact the landlord in an effort to try to find out why he was trying to evict them. My thought was, if he told me it was because they were black, I might be able to find him in violation of one of the laws on discrimination in housing or civil rights. She provided me with his name, address, and telephone number. I promised her I would try my best, but I also let her know that she would probably be evicted, even if he was charged with a crime and the case went on for some time. She understood what I was speaking about; sadly, she couldn't understand the eviction notice. I couldn't either.

The following day, I decided I'd try to locate the landlord at the address I was given by the young lady. I didn't want to call first and set up a time to meet as I thought he'd simply hang up on me. I took one of the agents with me, and we went to his home or to a rental property he was using as his home. It was a typical run-down place in a neighborhood full of seedy homes. We knocked on his door, but no one answered. I decided to leave him a note to have him call me at the office. I let him know I was from the FBI.

Later that day, the landlord contacted me by telephone at the office. He started with the usual tough-guy act, asking what this was all about, claiming he hadn't done anything wrong. I informed him that I needed to see him in person about an eviction proceeding that he had initiated involving a black couple in one of his apartments. He immediately claimed again that he hadn't done anything wrong, and that the lease allowed him to evict whomever he wanted. I suggested to him that there were laws against discrimination in housing and that I would pursue the issue if need be. The landlord said he had nothing more to say and told me to go speak to his lawyer. Without identifying one, he hung up the telephone. I knew there really wasn't much I could do other than to continue calling his bluff.

In a few days, I contacted the black couple to see if they had heard from the landlord. They had not heard from him and still had not made preparations to move out. Another rent payment was due, and they made it on time. They were hoping to stay there as long as possible, as they had no other options at the present time. I kept in touch with the couple and knew that the landlord did not follow up on his effort to evict them. I don't know if my contact with him made any difference, but it seemed that at least this one time a racial injustice might have been prevented.

One late-fall day, I was returning to Greenville with Ron, whom I had accompanied on a lead into the upper part of Sunflower County. He was driving as we neared a small town along Highway 49. While it was late in the afternoon, it was still light out, and there was no reason to turn on the car headlamps. As we approached a crossroad, we watched in horror as an oncoming vehicle hit a person who was crossing the road on foot. I recall seeing a body fly up into the air, twisting about and landing on the shoulder of the road. I yelled out to Ron to pull over. The vehicle that hit the pedestrian had stopped along the shoulder, and Ron maneuvered our car in front of that vehicle as we parked.

Suddenly, several things began happening at once. We both approached the victim, who was a young black boy, maybe twelve years old. He lay on the road's shoulder, moaning in some degree of pain. With a quick look at him, we ascertained he probably had a broken leg. He did not seem to be bleeding or in any immediate danger of losing his life. We tried to comfort him, telling him he'd be all right and that help was on the way. Ron returned to the FBI car and radioed for a highway patrol unit or an ambulance to get to the scene. While this was happening, a small crowd of black residents began to gather at the accident site. I noticed the driver of the car that hit the child was a white woman. She had remained seated in her car. I didn't want to leave the boy while I waited for Ron to get in contact with some emergency unit. However, I began to hear the crowd swearing and cursing. I heard someone say, "This is the second time that she's hit someone." The accident scene was suddenly turning into a situation that wasn't looking too good.

Ron returned to the boy as I stood up to tell him the crowd was getting involved and wasn't too happy with the driver of the car. He stayed with the boy as I walked over to the driver. I asked her for her name and identified myself as an FBI agent. She said she thought the crowd was going to hurt her. I assured her that wasn't going to happen and told her to stay in her car. I walked toward the back of her car and approached the group of blacks who were gathering. I again identified myself and told the group that the boy was okay and that help was on the way. Someone shouted out that she hit another black person with her car just a few months ago. He insinuated that she had done so on purpose. I explained to the group that we would look into the situation, but that our first priority was getting medical help for the boy. The entire time I was thinking that the group of angry people was going to pull the woman out of her car and beat her up. If what they said was true, I could understand the anger. I'd want to do the same, but I couldn't let it happen here. Fortunately, I heard sirens in the distance and knew that help was arriving. That seemed to mollify the crowd to some extent, and they kept their distance from the woman.

A Mississippi Highway Patrol officer arrived with siren screaming and blue lights flashing, adding to the eerie onset of dusk. Ron had already put his blue flashing light on top of the FBI car. Several minutes later, an ambulance arrived on the scene. Once the child was being taken care of and placed on a gurney, the officer took a statement from Ron and me. He asked us to hang around until he spoke with the driver about the accident. He was not aware of the fact that she had allegedly been involved in a similar accident several months ago. As he took a statement from the woman, the crowd began to leave the scene. I was thankful that nothing more serious developed out of the situation, but I could see how tense the racial problems were in the region. Ron and I eventually got under way and returned to Greenville. I never learned whether the woman had been involved in a previous accident involving another black citizen. I did find out that the young boy suffered a broken leg and had no further serious injuries. He had been released from the hospital and was back in school.

CHAPTER 12
Delta Ways

*Valor and Arms; Magnolia; Mockingbird;
Wood Duck and Largemouth Bass.*

— Mississippi State Motto, State Flower,
Bird, Waterfowl, and Fish

In the FBI, things constantly change. New laws get passed by Congress as new threats develop, always challenging the Constitution and the status quo in our country. The FBI is frequently called upon to be the first on the scene when disturbing events begin to occur with greater regularity, much like the civil rights crimes that had occurred in the early sixties. Change also happens frequently within the FBI family itself, and did so in the Greenville office.

Since Ray had spent a little more than a year or so in Greenville, policy at the time required him to be transferred to a second office. For his new assignment, Ray drew the Los Angeles office. Hailing originally from Texas, Ray seemed to think this was a good assignment and expected that a large office would have a lot more excitement than our small Greenville Resident Agency. In that thought, he was probably right. I would miss Ray as we had done a lot of work together and had some interesting, fun times. We were also friends, and so were our wives and young sons, a relationship we were all going to miss.

Prior to Ray's transfer, we had begun working on what we thought was an organized-crime matter in Greenville. During the fall seasons of both 1972 and 1973, we noticed that betting pools on college and professional football games were openly available to patrons who frequented a few local pool halls and restaurants. In discussing the situation with local friends, it seemed that gambling on football pools had gone on in the Delta for a long time, and no one thought anything of it. The Delta was not known to be a haven for organized crime, nor did it have any known members of La Cosa Nostra living in the area to the best of my knowledge. The closest that any known organized-crime group existed was in New Orleans. It was said to be controlled by mafia boss Carlos Marcello. There was no known connection with football gambling in Greenville or any other criminal connection with the Marcello organization. Nonetheless, Ray and I decided we would at least explore the extent of the local gambling operation to see if it fit into violations of any provisions of the new Illegal Gambling Business Act, enumerated in federal statute law, Title 18 U.S.C. Section 1955. In brief, the statute applied to anyone conducting, financing, managing, supervising, directing, or owning an illegal gambling business, and whose operation involved five or more persons, in violation of the law of the state or political subdivision in which it was conducted, and who operated for a period exceeding thirty days, or earned gross revenue of $2,000 in any single day. The statute seemed to be a perfect fit for the football gambling activity in Greenville. All we needed to do was to see that all elements of the statute were met before we could prosecute the offenders.

We identified at least five or more establishments where football-pool sheets sat out in the open on store counters. We knew at least five different men who were the store owners and who were taking the bet money. In fact, Ray and I bet on football games in each of the establishments for evidentiary purposes. We also knew that this type of gambling was a violation of both Mississippi state and local law. Our evidence showed that the gambling activity lasted more than thirty days as the football betting slips were out for all games from early September until the end of football season. All of the requirements of the statute seemed to be met.

Ray and I discussed our evidence with one of the assistant US attorneys in his Oxford, Mississippi, office. He agreed there might be a violation. He asked if we could obtain additional evidence to determine what amounts of money were involved in the operation. He did not want to prosecute a group of people if they were only taking in a few hundred dollars a week as there would be little jury appeal for such a case. We promised to do what we could to identify some figure of the weekly take from the bettors.

Using a few local sources, we were able to obtain discarded gambling slips on the Monday evenings after the weekend football games. A review of the torn-up slips quickly determined that the threshold of $2,000 of gambling activity per day was easily met. We saw betting slips as high as $500 per person. In 1973 dollars, that was a pretty substantial wager in what we first thought to be minor gambling activity.

We continued to acquire all the evidence possible before we were ready to again attempt to get search or arrest warrants for the gambling businesses. In doing so, we decided to discuss our results with our supervisor,

John Neelley. John was a reasonable and very cautious man. He was well respected in the community, and he in turn respected the members of the community. That went for the law enforcement community as well. John suggested that we would need to get the Greenville Police Department and the Washington County Sheriff's Office on board before going any further. We would likely need their resources and assistance if we planned to do simultaneous raids on the gambling establishments. Ray and I concurred with his decision, and he volunteered to set up a meeting with the chief and sheriff.

A day or so later, John came to us and told us we were scheduled to have a meeting with Tom Nance, the chief, and Harvey Tackett, the sheriff, that afternoon. Ray and I prepared our material to brief the law enforcement officials. Following lunch at the One Block East, John, Ray, and I went to the Greenville Police Department for our scheduled meeting. As promised, it was only the three of us FBI agents and the chief and sheriff. Ray and I discussed what we had discovered, and both law enforcement leaders expressed some surprise as to the extent and volume of the gambling activity. They agreed on the spot that something needed to be done and seemed to support our request for search warrants and simultaneous raids on the establishments.

Then suddenly, without much warning, the tide quickly turned. Sheriff Tackett explained that this type of activity had gone on for a long time in the Delta, and nothing was ever done about it. It seemed to him that football-pool gambling was accepted by the public as a recreational activity of sorts. It was just the way it was in the Delta, he explained. He then looked at Tom Nance, who hadn't said much, and said, "You know, Tom, you're up for reappointment at the end of the year, and you need to think about what a gambling raid might do in that regard. We haven't said anything about this to the community, and maybe we should consider another approach before going ahead with these raids. We can always hit these joints later if they don't stop the gambling." Tom reacted quietly, agreeing with Harvey that maybe we needed to put out a warning first to remind the citizens that betting on football games was illegal, and that it needed to stop or arrests would be made in the future.

Ray and I sat there shocked! A warning? Surely they didn't really mean it. John thought that the law enforcement leaders probably had a good idea. We continued the discussion a bit longer until it was clear that two young, aggressive FBI special agents weren't about to change the way things went on in the Delta. Both the chief and sheriff promised that if gambling did not stop, they would welcome future gambling raids and would be there to assist. However, they thought that a community warning would be only fair for the first step.

Ray and I were incensed as we returned to the office. John tried to explain that things operated differently in the Delta than in the northern part of the country. He felt sure that the law enforcement officers were doing the right thing at the moment and pleaded with us for patience. He reminded us that Harvey Tackett ran for sheriff on a pledge to enforce the local blue laws—laws enacted to restrict otherwise legal activities on Sunday—and to rid the county of illegal gambling and slot machines, as late as January 1972, shortly before Ray and I arrived. He was sure the sheriff would do the right thing. We had no option other than to give up on our big organized-crime bust and move on with other cases.

Imagine our surprise on December 14, 1973, when we read in the local newspaper, the *Delta Democrat-Times*, an article entitled "Gambling Warnings Are Issued." The article read as follows:

> Greenville police and the Washington County Sheriff's Office have warned seven businesses in and around Greenville to stop taking bets on sporting events, the *Delta Democrat-Times* has learned. Police Chief Tom Nance said six Greenville businesses—which he declined to name—were warned to stop taking bets Thursday afternoon during a series of visits by Assistant Chief Robert Skinner and Captain Emmett Sweeden.

Sheriff Harvey Tackett said one county establishment was told "this morning" to stop taking bets. "We are going to strictly enforce the football card law," Tackett said.

Nance said the warning resulted from a six-week investigation by members of the Greenville Police Department and agents from the Federal Bureau of Investigation.

The chief estimated that "approximately $50,000 to $60,000 worth of bets, primarily on football games, are being placed each week. This thing has gotten much bigger than any of us ever realized," Nance said, "and we intend to do everything we can to see that this activity is curtailed."

Nance said the FBI took part in the investigation "to look for the possibility of violation of federal laws," but the chief said he was "not in a position to say" if federal laws were violated.

"This (gambling) has been done fairly openly, and it hasn't been a question of our not caring," Nance said. "It's simply much bigger than any of us realized."

Nance said no moves "have been made to prosecute" anyone on the basis of information gathered during the investigation but said that evidence gathered may be used in future prosecutions "if this business doesn't stop."

Under Mississippi law, it is a misdemeanor to gamble or to take bets. One section of the Mississippi code provides for a fine of not more than $500, while the other code section dealing with gambling provides for a fine of not more than $2,000.

Wow, weekly football and other sports bets of between $50,000 and $60,000 here in a small Mississippi town, and law enforcement issues a warning. So be it. Our gambling case became a fast victim of the old ways of the Delta.

Once Ray left the office, another agent transfer followed on the heels of his leaving. Joe received an intraoffice transfer to the Oxford, Mississippi,

Resident Agency. That left us with only five agents to cover the six Delta counties. Since Ken was still working on a special assignment, only four of us were available to do most of the routine work. John decided he needed to realign the county assignments, even though we would all work wherever needed. John kept responsibility for Washington County, and he took Sharkey and Issaquena Counties away from me. He put Ron and Chuck together in Bolivar County and assigned me to Humphreys and Sunflower Counties. Joe had worked Sunflower County with Ron prior to the new change. I was happy with the new assignments, especially to be rid of the extremely rural counties and to pick up the more populated Sunflower County.

Before Joe left, he and I took a ride to Indianola, the county seat of Sunflower. He re-introduced me to the high sheriff, C. O. "Jack" Sessums, who was a high-energy-type guy who really seemed to know his way around the Delta. He, like the others, enjoyed mimicking my Yankee accent. As he introduced me to his deputies, who were in the office at the time, I noticed they all carried the "Dirty Harry" model .44-caliber Magnum, six-inch-barrel revolvers. These were law enforcement people one didn't mess with. It was good to know they were on my side. At least I hoped they were! Sheriff Sessums discussed the various small towns in Sunflower County and identified the chiefs of police in each area. Some of the police departments were so small they only had one chief or police officer. Some towns actually hired a night watchman. I felt like I was living back in colonial days and wondered to myself if the night watchman called out "all is well" on his rounds. This was just another peculiarity in the Delta that I hadn't expected or even thought about.

Bank counter checks were another item peculiar to the Delta. At least I had never seen them prior to my assignment in Greenville. Perhaps they were common in other small towns in the South, but it was a new experience for me. Every bank in Greenville printed a packet of blank counter checks, bearing the bank's logo on the check and leaving an open space for an account number. These counter checks could be found at the front desk of every store, restaurant, and business where the cash register was located. They were often placed on a metal rack, displaying each bank available for use. The theory behind them was that a patron forgetting his or her checkbook could simply select a blank counter check from his or her own banking institution, fill out the proper account number, and make out a check that would be honored by the bank for the amount owed to the store or restaurant. It was an honor system that I had never seen, before or since, and that seemed to work very well. The counter checks were in such abundance that many people used them at home as telephone message pads. They could be picked up for free at any local bank.

Even more amazingly, a patron could cross out the name of a bank on a blank counter check and pen in his own bank's name if the business was out of a particular bank's checks. Such a check was still easily accepted. And most amazing of all to me was that many businesses would accept a plain piece of paper, paper napkin, or any other scrap of paper as a check as long as the bank name and personal checking account number were printed legibly on its face. I would not have believed it if I hadn't tried it myself. There was great trust among the citizens in town and the banking community to continue using such a system.

I do not think the black community shared the same sense of trust in using counter checks at various establishments. At the time, it was rare to see blacks patronizing businesses outside of their own black-owned shops and neighborhoods. Things were simply different for the black population in Greenville. I suspect few of the black citizens even had bank or checking accounts, and those who did probably wouldn't be trusted to use a counter check at the time. I hadn't heard of any illegal check cases or fraudulent-check schemes in connection with the use of counter checks either. Little did I know I'd be in for a rude awakening in that regard.

One day I traveled to a more rural part of Sunflower County in order to interview yet another victim of an impersonation fraud. It seemed this was a recurring type of scam in the Delta, an easy way for a low-life criminal or two to take advantage of an unsuspecting older citizen. Usually perpetrated by a couple of white males on an elderly black family, the scam lured the family away from the house while one of the impersonators went through their belongings, stealing whatever amount of cash they could find. This case was no exception.

As I drove up a dirt driveway to an isolated sharecropper home, I was greeted by a large German shepherd, snarling ferociously. I waited in the car until an elderly black woman approached me and asked my business. I identified myself (careful to show my gold badge rather than my credentials this time) and told her I was there as a result of her complaint to the sheriff's office about an impersonation matter. She was quite excitable and asked me to come into her home. We got as far as her screened-in front porch when she began explaining how the man claiming to be from the US government went through her things while another man held her attention at the rear of the house. She was talking so fast it was difficult to ask her a question. I finally calmed her down enough to acquire somewhat of a description of the two middle-aged white males and their automobile.

She explained in a rapid voice that they had stolen "all [her] money out of the shifrow on the streamed in gallrey." I asked her to repeat where the money was taken from. Once again, I knew what I thought she had said, but I had no idea what she was talking about. After learning there were no witnesses to the incident, I finished up the interview and left, trying my best to assure her I would do my best to find the men who stole her money. I decided to stop back at the sheriff's office to give them the results of my investigation and to see if they had any suspects or if they could assist in any way. After parking the car, I headed into the courthouse where the sheriff's office was located and immediately ran into Sheriff Sessums.

"Well, howdy there, Mr. FBI. How's everything in the fed's world?" Sessums joked as he held out his hand.

"Fine as frogs' hair," I replied, using a familiar phrase I'd often heard in the Delta. "I just got back from my interview with the victim of an impersonation you told me about. I was wondering if you have any potential suspects in the case."

Sessums replied that he had no suspects and that these cases seemed to be common in the Delta. He was of the impression that the perpetrators were definitely from out of the area, perhaps from out of the state. It was then that I decided to ask him what the victim was actually telling me about the loss of her money.

"Jack, when I spoke with the victim, she spoke very fast. It was difficult for my Yankee ear to understand her. She told me the money was taken from what sounded to me like a 'shifrow on the streamed in gallrey.' I have absolutely no idea what she was talking about, and I was afraid to keep asking her to repeat herself as she kept saying the same thing."

Sheriff Sessums stood there quietly for a few seconds before bursting out laughing. He called over Herman Parker, one of his deputies and a fellow I worked with often in the county. He told me to tell Herman what I just told him. By this time I realized the joke was on me, but given to good relations with fellow law enforcement officers, I related the same story to Herman. When he began to laugh, I knew it was time to learn what was so funny.

Sessums laughed and said, "They send you damn Yankees down here, and you can't even understand us Delta people."

I looked over at Herman, and he said, "John, what she was saying to you was that her money was in a chifforobe located in her screened-in porch, or gallery."

Sadly, I had to ask, "What's a chifforobe?"

More laughter was forthcoming from both of them until they finally explained that it is a piece of furniture that has both drawers and a place to hang clothes, a combination of wardrobe and chest of drawers. I was completely unfamiliar with that item and was glad they got a good laugh at my expense. "That's just how some folks talk here in the Delta," Herman offered. Considering I was among a group of Delta folks who often used the term "usta culd" in the context of "he usta culd build homes by hisself" and so on, I wasn't too concerned about my lack of understanding the local pronunciation of words. And for a town that had a gasoline service station called "Hep-U-Sef," I knew there would still be more attacks on the King's English yet to come.

Delta Ways

There were other sights in the Delta that were totally unfamiliar to me coming from Pennsylvania. On occasion, I had to drive outside of the flatland area into other parts of rural Mississippi. There, the topography quickly changed into green, rolling hills as I traveled north or east. There were dense trees, which led to a valuable pulpwood business for those who owned the land. Pulpwood trucks, usually overloaded to the point of almost rolling over, clogged the local roads and highways. It was necessary to keep a good distance behind them for fear of them losing a load of logs. Passing an overloaded pulpwood truck was a great danger in itself, as it was impossible to see ahead of them without moving into an oncoming lane of traffic.

There was an eerie beauty to many of the hilly roads in the area around the Delta. A pesky vine known as kudzu covered huge sections of forest wilderness, smothering the flora underneath it while exhibiting a brilliant green hue to the surrounding area. The plant, native to Japan, was first introduced to the United States around 1876 as an edible plant for cattle grazing. However, it spread far faster than the available animal population could eat it. Mostly a destructive plant, it smothered all light from the plant life it covered. At night, the moonlight would cast an eerie shadow on the kudzu-covered flora of the area.

On a trip one day to cover a lead in the upper part of Sunflower County, I had the occasion to stop at the site of a working cotton gin. During the Civil War, just about every cotton gin in the Deep South was destroyed by Union forces in an effort to bring a halt to any southern economic progress. Every time I passed what I knew to be a working cotton gin, I was of the opinion that each one must have been built immediately after the Civil War. I never saw a new one, and those I saw looked as though they were about to collapse on the spot.

I stopped at this one cotton gin and located the individual I needed to interview. He was a middle-aged black man whose blue, cloudy eyes lent a bit of mystery to him. He eventually provided me with the information I was seeking. As we walked back toward my car, I noticed a peculiar odor, apparently coming from a steaming cauldron that was cut from half of a fifty-five-gallon steel drum and sat nearby over a wood fire. I innocently asked this fellow what was boiling in the kettle, and he walked me over to the steaming cauldron and simply replied, "chitlins." While I was looking puzzled and feeling a little nauseous at the smell, he explained to me that they were hog intestines and were being boiled to be eaten. One of my grandfathers was a butcher, and I couldn't recall ever hearing of such a meat product. Out of curiosity, I asked my guide what one does to prepare them. My question seemed to set up his whimsical response. He answered, "First, you have to clean them, and there are only two ways to do so. You can either stump clean them or window clean them. You have to empty those intestines of their waste before you can cook them."

By now, taken completely in by this kind fellow, I asked him what the difference was in the way they could be cleaned, unknowingly playing right into his hands. He replied, "To stump clean them, you just fling them against an old tree stump until the contents come flying out. But the best method is to window clean them. We just put the closed end of the intestine on the windowsill, close the window, and then pull the intestines through the tight closure, forcing all the contents out." With that, he gave a great belly laugh and began walking away. "You're welcome to stay and share some with us when they're finished," he added with yet another laugh.

"No, thanks. I'd better be getting along, but I appreciate your help and the kind offer."

I'd come a long way with my culinary tastes and southern food. Sow belly and biscuits, venison cooked all sorts of ways, catfish, crawfish, black-eyed peas, and greens of all kinds. I loved them all, and knowing that I always enjoyed a new southern treat, a small part of me wanted to try those chitlins. But it just wasn't a big enough part of me at the time to accept the mighty challenge. Perhaps another day, maybe—or perhaps not.

But the most important event, without any doubt, that occurred once a year in the Delta, was not to be found in the cotton fields or the catfish ponds. Nor was it Lee-Jackson Day, still celebrated in the Magnolia State some 110 years after the Civil War. Rather, it was an event given the somewhat unusual name of the Egg Bowl (so named in 1979). It seemed there was no single event in the Delta that captured as much attention every day of the year as the next outcome of the Egg Bowl. It was the annual college football game held between Mississippi rivals in either Starkville or Oxford.

The football game occurred on Thanksgiving Day or weekend and was held between the Ole Miss (University of Mississippi) Rebels and the Mississippi State Bulldogs. It was a game talked about in every restaurant, barbershop, church, juke joint, café, school, store, mall, and any other place where folks gathered, from the day one game ended until kickoff of the following year's game. It was nonstop excitement and argument as to which team would take home the coveted Egg Bowl victory. The locals knew all the players and followed the high school drafts of potential football stars. The planning for the next season consumed all of the locals, and likely included the black population as well, especially since the colleges were integrated in 1963. It was the singular event that took precedence over all political, social, and even racial concerns in the Delta on a daily basis. For those whose school won the coveted game, it did not matter whether the team had won another game all year. All that mattered was this one game, every single day. And most folks I met could tell me who won each game for many years past.

There were other football teams in Mississippi, like Southern Mississippi University, that were on par athletically with the likes of Ole Miss and State. And there were smaller black colleges that played football as well and were of keen interest to their respective following. But for some reason, it was this one athletic contest that seemed to possess the hearts and minds of most who lived in the Delta. Even before my arrival in Mississippi, I can remember watching Archie Manning playing football for Ole Miss and watching him perform incredible football skills. His hometown, Drew, Mississippi, right here in Sunflower County, had a billboard on the outskirts of town, welcoming visitors to the small town with the words "Welcome to Drew, Mississippi—Home of Archie Manning." And now he was starring in the National Football League with the New Orleans Saints, a home team to many of the folks who lived in the Delta.

CHAPTER 13
Race Riot

I feel sorry for anybody that could let hate wrap them up.
Ain't no such thing as I can hate anybody and hope to see God's face.

—Fannie Lou Hamer, civil rights activist

Fannie Hamer was born Fannie Lou Townsend in 1917 in Montgomery County, Mississippi, the youngest of twenty children. Her parents were sharecroppers in the Mississippi Delta, and by the age of six, she started working in the cotton fields. Once she married Perry Hamer in 1944, they began working on a cotton plantation near Ruleville, Mississippi. She started her civil rights activism after attending a protest meeting in 1962, encouraging other black Americans to register to vote. From that time on, she dedicated her life to fighting for civil rights. In 1964, she helped found the Mississippi Freedom Democratic Party and brought national attention to the civil rights struggle in Mississippi. She was threatened, arrested, beaten, and shot at during her struggle for civil rights. In 1976, although diagnosed with cancer, she continued her fight for civil rights until her eventual death from the disease in 1977.[7]

It was a rather warm Sunday morning on November 18, 1973, as my wife and I loaded our son into the car for a short trip to Greenville Presbyterian Church. We took him to the nursery in the church, where he would be cared for during the service by some kind black ladies. Following the end of the service, we picked up our son and returned home. After feeding the baby, who was nearing three months old, I grabbed a sandwich and headed into our little den to watch an eagerly anticipated football game. On this day, the Philadelphia Eagles were to play the always-hated Dallas Cowboys in Arlington, Texas, and the game was being televised. I had been a Philadelphia Eagles season ticket holder since 1965. When I realized I would be entering the FBI, I gave up my tickets after the close of the 1970–1971 football season. Since moving to Greenville in 1972, I hadn't seen the Eagles play football. This would be the first game I'd been able to watch in some time. I was very excited and looking forward to spending

---

7. "Fannie Lou Hamer" (2014), The Biography Channel Website, www.biography.com/people/fannie-lou-hamer-205625.

my afternoon glued to the television set, hoping my favorite team would upset the Cowboys.

The game was still early in the first quarter when the telephone rang. I thought it was probably a relative from home asking if I was watching the game, or a local friend giving me some razzing about the Eagles. But I wasn't so lucky.

"John, it's Sheriff Sessums. I'm calling you from Ruleville, and I need you to get up here right away. We're about to have a major race riot here. There's just been a murder, and all kind of hell is breaking loose. Get here as quick as you can."

I told the sheriff I'd arrive as soon as possible. I couldn't believe my luck. It was the first time in a couple of years that I could enjoy an Eagles game, and when it finally came, it was only to be interrupted by work. Even if I just drove to Ruleville and back, staying only a short time, the distance and time involved would not get me back home in time to see any of the game. But FBI agents were on call seven days a week, twenty-four hours a day. The sheriff needed me, so I got up, put on a suit, grabbed my Magnum, credentials, and gold badge, and headed out to Ruleville.

On the way, I pondered the sheriff's message that a race riot was about to occur. Race riots were not something the FBI worked as a rule, although agents were often interested observers. Civil-disobedience matters were handled by local or state law enforcement organizations. And I was sure that the Ruleville police and Sunflower County Sheriff's Office were better equipped than me to handle any such disturbance. The sheriff did not elaborate about the murder any more than he had about the race riot. Murder was not a matter handled by the FBI either, unless it involved a police killing, government official, or a presidential assassination. I simply had no idea as to what I was driving into upon my arrival in Ruleville.

I was told to meet the sheriff at a small hospital located in town. As I drove into the parking lot of the health facility, I did not observe anything out of the ordinary, with the exception of a Sunflower County patrol car or two. When I was driving into town, it seemed like everyone must have been home watching the football game. I'd steeled myself for a huge riot and burning buildings, rocks being thrown and looting everywhere, but there was nothing of the sort. As I parked the car and entered the hospital, I wondered where the race riot was occurring, and what I was going to do to prevent or resolve it.

The sheriff's deputy met me in the hallway of the hospital facility. The deputy told me that Sheriff Sessums was waiting for me and led me into a small operating room. The sheriff was standing by a metal operating table covered with a white sheet, along with another deputy and several other unknown individuals. He looked over at me and exclaimed, "Well, the FBI's here. We can get started." With that, he yanked the white sheet off of a completely naked black female, whose lips were parted in a death grimace, showing her pearly white teeth. She was dead and had been for some time. I'm not sure what the sheriff's reason was for his dramatic removal of the sheet covering this young victim, unless he thought I'd pass out from the sight of a dead body.

I wasn't a stranger to dead bodies, thanks in part to my job as a Stone Harbor police officer. On three different occasions, I was the first police officer on the scene of a call where a sick person was reported. In all three of those instances, the person was not sick but deceased. In each case, the dead victim was an elderly person who had previous health issues. There was much panic and sadness in the victim's family members at those death scenes, and quick action had to be taken to make every effort at resuscitation of the deceased, even though it would be unsuccessful. I always tried to calm the family members until the ambulance arrived, and I administered oxygen to the victim, making an effort to aid as best as possible. But this time it was different; it was my first murder victim. There wasn't any family present, only law enforcement personnel. And she had been taken from the crime scene and placed on this hospital operating table. My initial observation of the girl was that there was no blood and no immediate indication of any fatal wound. As I approached her body, still wondering what it was the sheriff wanted from me, he identified the victim.

"Her name is April Unger, and she is fourteen years old," Sessums stated. "Her body was found behind a local doctor's office in Ruleville at about noon today. The coroner says she has been dead for about twelve hours, and he believes the manner of her death was from strangulation."

I said nothing as I moved closer to the body to see if there was anything I could remotely do to help out in the investigation. No one said a thing, and I still wasn't sure why I was here. Surely the sheriff's office had worked homicide cases before. What was it they wanted me to do? I wondered. There was still no sight or sound of any race riot or civil disturbance outside.

I noticed some discoloration or bruising on the victim's neck, which probably indicated strangulation marks. More interestingly, I noticed bite marks on both of her breasts. The marks were made by someone's teeth, and they were so clear that I knew it was imperative to get photographs made of this physical evidence. I told the sheriff that I believed these teeth marks could be positively identified as coming from a suspect, once we had one. I pointed out the marks to him and his deputy and told him he needed a camera as well as a ruler or some other device to carefully measure the size of the marks and the gaps between them. He also needed to include the ruler in the photos of the bite marks to show their relative size in the developed pictures. While not a forensics expert, or even a novice, I knew that these bite marks would be a strong part of any future prosecution and that care needed to be taken to preserve the evidence.

With that examination completed, the sheriff escorted me into a large waiting room where another group of unknown officials had gathered around a large table in the center of the room. Everyone was talking loudly, at times even shouting. Sheriff's deputies were coming and going, and it appeared that they were trying to locate a suspect or two in town. I had to wonder if the girl's family had been notified, as I did not see any grieving black parents in the room or anywhere else in the area. It quickly became apparent that the authorities thought April Unger's murderer was a boyfriend or acquaintance of hers. The deputies had been working on the case prior to my arrival and had apparently come up with a few leads. They were out in the town looking to round up a few of April's beaus for questioning. The sheriff asked me to take a seat at the table as they were bringing in a suspect, and he wanted me to be in on the interview.

While I was waiting for a possible suspect to arrive at the hospital, I discussed the murder with the sheriff, reminding him that the coroner should check the victim for hair and fiber samples. I knew the FBI laboratory was well known for its forensic examinations, and I wanted the sheriff to be sure he found all possible physical evidence on the victim's body that might lead to the identity of her killer. I also reminded him of the necessity of the photographs of the bite marks on her breasts. I also suggested that the crime scene where her body was found should be checked for fingerprints and footprints, as well as any other evidence leading to the identity of her killer.

In a few minutes, a couple of deputies brought in a young black male who was considered to be a boyfriend of the victim and a possible suspect in her murder. The first thing the sheriff ordered the deputy to do was to take the suspect to a corner in the now-crowded room, have him drop his pants, and comb out his pubic hair to collect any loose hairs or fibers. I watched in stunned amazement at these proceedings. The suspect was not taken to a bathroom or other quiet facility where he could do this in private. I had no idea whether he was advised of his Miranda rights prior to this exercise. It was possible that the suspect had given his consent to come to the hospital for an interview and to provide the sheriff with evidence of his innocence or guilt. But it was simply the worst investigative situation I'd ever seen in my two and a half years as an FBI agent. Nothing like this would have ever happened in Stone Harbor, New Jersey, or Akron, Ohio. I was simply speechless.

Regaining what composure I had left, I suggested to Sheriff Sessums that any body searches of suspects be undertaken in a more private area. With that, he advised that he would like me to interview the suspect who was just brought into the hospital, and who had suffered the personal indignity of dropping his pants in the crowded room. Before I could speak, the deputy brought the suspect over to me and sat him down at the table across from me. At the moment, I did not realize that the man sitting next to me was the mayor of Ruleville, Mississippi. I identified myself to the murder suspect as a special agent of the FBI. I explained to him that the investigation concerned finding the person who murdered April Unger. I then advised the suspect of his rights, as I had no idea what had been said to him by any other law enforcement official who found him and brought him in.

As this interview was transpiring, I noticed that every word I was saying and every response from the suspect was being typed on a loud manual typewriter by the mayor who was sitting next to me. Not only was the noise of the typewriter an unbelievable distraction, but the activity in the rest of the room with deputies coming in and going out, as well as shouts and other conversation taking place, made the interview impossible.

I turned to the mayor next to me who was trying to type every word I said and asked him what he was doing. He replied that he was typing the statement from the interview. I politely informed the mayor that he was not entitled to sit in on the interview and asked the deputy to find us a small room where the three of us could conduct the interview. Besides that, it was impossible to concentrate on questioning the suspect with the constant click-clacking sound of the manual typewriter keys immediately to my left. Fortunately the deputy succeeded in locating a small room, and a proper interview was conducted. The subject subsequently admitted knowing April Unger and admitted dating her. But he denied being involved in her murder. In fact, the suspect had a solid alibi in that he was not with April at any time during the weekend. After the interview was completed, the suspect was allowed to return home.

As I returned to the large waiting room, I noticed yet another black male with his pants pulled down, standing in the corner of the room combing his pubic hair. This was simply unbelievable to me! I wasn't sure if the point was to shock me or to show that the sheriff's office was trying to collect scientific evidence. In either case, they were failing in just about everything. However, I was still waiting to be of assistance in any manner that I was able.

Just as I pondered what I should do next, or what other leads might need to be worked, the sheriff came over to me and asked me to assist on the interview of the new suspect. He was pretty sure they had found the right guy this time and wanted me to be present for the interview with his deputy. This time, we started immediately in the small room without any interruptions from others who had gathered and were simply lingering in the great room.

I sat down with the deputy, and we began the interview. This second suspect was advised of his rights and was provided with a written Advice of Rights and Waiver form, which he signed, stating he understood his rights. As I was not sure if the suspect could read, I asked him to read the form back to me, which he did successfully. I didn't want someone later in a courtroom to claim the suspect couldn't read what he was signing. Satisfied that the suspect could read and understand his rights, the interview began.

His name was George Ratliff Jr. He admitted he knew April Unger, and that they had dated. He denied any participation in or knowledge of her murder. However, his body language indicated he was being deceptive. He had difficulty looking at me or the deputy when answering questions. He began to fidget and looked quite uncomfortable. Further questioning of Ratliff determined he had no alibi as to his whereabouts at the time of Unger's murder and no witnesses who could place him some distance away from her. Eventually, and slowly, George Ratliff Jr. confessed to strangling April Unger during a date together the previous night. He provided a signed statement to that effect to the deputy and me. He was subsequently transported to the county jail in Indianola until his initial appearance in court scheduled for the next day.

The murder investigation was over as far as I was concerned. There were no witnesses to be interviewed unless the sheriff could locate family or friends who knew that April went out with Ratliff the previous evening. There were those sorts of loose ends to tie up, as well as to properly collect any forensic evidence like matching pubic hair and comparisons of the teeth-bite marks on the victim's breasts. But that was the job for the coroner and the sheriff. My job was to provide whatever guidance I could as another law enforcement professional and to ascertain the facts involved in any occurring race riot in town.

It was dark now, the football game long since over. I was hungry and tired, and somewhat gratified that my first homicide case had seemingly been resolved. Even more so, I was thrilled that there was not even a hint of a race riot in Ruleville that night. I never knew why the sheriff thought there was going to be a riot, unless his thought was that April Unger's killer was a white man, much like the event precipitating the riots that occurred when Joetha Collier was murdered in nearby Drew in May 1971. Sadly, there seemed to be a preponderance of black-on-black murders throughout the Delta. While certainly not a good thing, murder being murder, it was just a bit better than the white lynchings and murders of blacks for racial hatred alone.

As I drove home through the flat, desolate, and deserted two-lane roads of the Delta, I could only wonder what future there was for the poor black folks who inhabited the majority of this region. Few jobs, with what jobs there were paying a meager wage, and life in a sharecropper shack didn't seem to forebode a bright future. The public schools were some of the worst in the state, and the state itself usually ranked at or near the bottom of the list when it came to education standards throughout the United States. April Unger was a beautiful, fourteen-year-old girl with her whole life yet ahead of her. Now she lay dead on a coroner's slab. Just one more victim in a society that couldn't seem to get untracked and move forward in a positive and caring way. At least her killer was identified and arrested; I was thankful that I did not have to meet with her parents and deliver the sad news.

I returned home to a sleeping wife and son, thankful for the fact that I had a great job, nice home, and loving family. How different the night must have been for the Unger family. I poured myself a strong bourbon and branch as I wasn't able to sleep just yet. I turned on the late news to try to unwind from the sad, tragic day. The fact that the Philadelphia Eagles were beaten by the Dallas Cowboys 31–10 earlier that afternoon seemed awfully insignificant to me.

The trial for George Ratliff Jr., who was nineteen years old at the time of April Unger's murder, was not scheduled to get underway in Sunflower County Circuit Court until June 18, 1974. Unbeknownst to me at the time of the initial homicide investigation, George Ratliff Jr. was a nephew of veteran Mississippi civil rights leader Fannie Lou Hamer and was identified as such in a *Delta Democrat-Times* newspaper article on August 11, 1975.

During my assignment in Greenville, I knew that a civil rights activist resided in the Ruleville area. Even though I was working there closer to the end of Fannie Lou Hamer's life, I was not aware of her presence or of any problematic civil rights issues involving her. And while she was still active in civil rights issues, she had slowed down considerably due to failing health. I can only wonder what she thought about the arrest of her nephew, and whether she was the one who pushed for an appeal for him to the state supreme court.

I testified at the trial in connection with taking a statement of guilt from the defendant. The trial lasted for a couple of days and finally went to the jury on June 21, 1974. The jury subsequently found George Ratliff Jr. guilty of manslaughter in the death of April Unger, throwing out the more serious charge of murder. He received a fifteen-year sentence, to be served at the state penitentiary at Parchman, Mississippi. But that was not the end of the matter.

George Ratliff Jr., like many other prison inmates with nothing to lose and nothing better to do with their time, filed an appeal to vacate his sentence. His attorneys argued that the trial court erred by not suppressing a written statement given by the defendant on the night of the slaying. They maintained that Ratliff had been told the charges against him would be reduced if he made his statement. His appeal went all the way to the Mississippi Supreme Court. On August 11, 1975, the *Delta Democrat-Times* reported that the court upheld the manslaughter conviction of Ratliff, rejecting defense arguments that the manslaughter verdict was "'contrary' to the overwhelming weight of the evidence." The Mississippi Supreme

Court noted that a lengthy hearing had been conducted on the defense motion to suppress the statement, and authorities denied that such promises were made. The trial judge found the statement was given "freely and voluntarily."

George Ratliff Jr. was given every legal opportunity to have his case reviewed and appealed. He has probably been out of jail for at least twenty-five years, if he is still alive today. I hope he became a productive member of the community and has a family of his own. I hope his crime was one of passion and accidental, that he is not a recidivist and back in prison. But I still cannot forget young April Unger. Fourteen years old, a beautiful girl with her whole world waiting...and in an instant her life, hopes, and dreams were snuffed out. How many legal opportunities did she get to keep her life? Where were all those caring people who helped George Ratliff Jr.? Where are they? April Unger must still wonder...May she rest in peace.

CHAPTER 14
TRAINING

*Through rigid training and firm discipline we endeavor
to discharge our responsibilities to our country.*

—J. Edgar Hoover - Director, FBI

Training was omnipresent at the FBI. Whether it was new-agent training, on-the-job training, specialized training, language training, police training—how to teach skills to local police personnel—or any other kind, special agents in the FBI never stopped training. It was important to stay current on all the latest laws, investigative techniques, and technical improvements relating to equipment and computer systems, weapons, and fingerprinting. The field offices kept detailed files on all training periods and the topics afforded to each special agent in their respective divisions. However, for those of us assigned to distant resident agencies, we would have to make a trip into Jackson Division headquarters for training purposes. There was simply no way to receive the training required at our "charming" rural Delta outpost.

Training sessions were usually enjoyable as we got to reunite with our friends and colleagues in the field office and to meet with other colleagues from other resident agencies as well. Generally, there was a one- or two-night stay at the local Ramada Inn, in order to maximize the value of travel to headquarters. In addition to whatever training was offered, we would usually spend another day having file reviews with the various supervisors who were responsible for our respective cases. Most of us in the resident agencies had cases falling under the purview of all five office leaders.

During the time I was assigned to the Jackson Division, the office was led by Special Agent in Charge (SAC) Roy K. Moore. He had an assistant special agent in charge (ASAC) under him and three squad supervisors who reported to him directly. These five men composed the field office management team as it pertained to the special agents. The clerical support staff, secretaries, and stenographers were supervised by a chief clerk and chief stenographer, who also answered to SAC Moore.

When scheduled for a file review, agents' files would be pulled from the individual rotors—revolving file cabinets—by the rotor clerk for each squad supervisor. A stack of all pending cases would await the agent who arrived for his file review. The agent would sit down with his case files and review what work needed to be completed, in both the short term and the long term, if necessary. Once he checked through all his files and made appropriate written comments, he would visit with each supervisor who would review each case and the agent's plans for future investigation. File reviews of this nature were generally held every sixty days. This was a management effort to ensure that all assigned cases were being given appropriate attention and investigation. It was also a way to ensure that case assignments were distributed fairly equitably between the agents on a squad in Jackson or assigned to a resident agency territory. File reviews were not a fun activity, but they were necessary and a great way to help manage individual investigative assignments. They also served as a reminder to the agent if a case had not been worked on in some time.

Usually the day before or day after an agent scheduled his file reviews, he would attend a training session. This often included some sort of legal lecture to both refresh and update changes in policies like search and seizure, arrest warrants, and Miranda warnings. At times, moot court sessions were held to allow agents some practice at testifying. But most of the training occurred on the firearms range, where agents were required to attend four outside shoots per year and four additional indoor shoots or shoots at facilities near their own offices. FBI special agents went to the firing range eight out of twelve months of the year, to make sure they were well qualified to use their revolver if the need arose. During firearms sessions, we also trained using the pump-action shotgun and whatever rifle the bureau preferred at the time. While assigned to Greenville, we were using a pump-action Remington rifle. Additional training in defensive tactics was also held at the firearms range and usually included handcuffing techniques, disarming methods, and a variety of holds used to subdue a criminal subject if necessary.

Once a year, the Jackson SAC would permit the secretaries, clerical support personnel, and stenographers to attend a firearms shoot, supervised by the firearms instructors. They always enjoyed the day out of the office, and it helped them to feel appreciated and a part of the FBI team. It would be embarrassing to be outshot by a stenographer, but it would happen on occasion. Those southern country girls all knew how to use a gun.

Serving in a resident agency required us to maintain liaison with all the law enforcement agencies located in the counties where we worked. I tried my best to maintain contact with every agency in my assigned counties. It was difficult at times as I was not always trusted by some of the old-school good ol' boys who did not want anything to do with the FBI. I recall one liaison experience I had with the chief of police from the town of Sunflower. I met the chief as a result of having worked a bank burglary in his town. He was about twenty-two years old and was a one-man department who relied heavily on the sheriff's office if he needed help.

Ray and I traveled on a Sunday afternoon to the bank in Sunflower. At the time, the town had no paved roads; they were all plain dirt. This was really small-town Mississippi. I had not met the chief yet, so this trip provided me with a good opportunity to get to know him. Upon our arrival at the bank, he told us that someone had broken into the bank and had attempted, without success, to open the bank-vault door. As he showed Ray and me the crime scene, it was apparent that the burglar tried to enter the vault by unscrewing the nine-inch-wide stainless-steel molding that surrounded the vault door. The subject was only partially successful in his efforts. After loosening the top three or four metal screws, he grew impatient and began pulling the top of the metal molding away from the vault door. The metal was considerably stronger than the burglar, and he only succeeded in pulling a small piece of the molding about a foot away from the wall. It was then that he probably noticed that the molding was decorative in nature, as there was still no way for him to enter the vault, even if he had removed the entire panel. The paneling did nothing more than hide the brick and concrete edges of the vault. He must have given up on his efforts at breaching the vault and looked around the bank for something else of value. All he managed to find and take was a small, clear Lucite paperweight disk filled with a set of current US coins, probably not valued at more than the actual face value of the coins, ninety-one cents.

However, breaking into a federally insured bank was still a federal offense under the bank-burglary statute. It was our job to collect whatever evidence we could in an effort to identify the perpetrator. Since the loss to the bank was negligible, it was likely that the US attorney assigned to the case would defer federal prosecution in favor of local or county prosecution, if the subject was identified and a prosecutable case was made.

Ray and I immediately got started processing the bank-vault area and teller-window counters for fingerprint evidence. We used our FBI-issued fingerprint-dusting kits to dust every potential spot the burglar may have touched. Our efforts resulted in acquiring quite a number of good latent-fingerprint lifts. Of course, many of the prints belonged to employees who worked at the bank. But we were hopeful that the fingerprints found around the metal molding were those of the burglar exclusively. While we worked, I explained to the chief what we were doing, showing him how to examine the crime scene. He was keenly interested in the process we used to lift the latent fingerprints after dusting them so they could be preserved for examination by the FBI Identification Division.

We had just about finished processing the bank for evidence when we looked at the back side of the metal molding that had covered the edge of the bank vault. The back of the metal was coated with grease and grime from years of remaining in place. And there, embedded in the grease and grime, were clear fingerprints the burglar had left as he tried to pull the molding away from the wall. Unfortunately, we did not have a fingerprint camera with us at the time. They were rather unwieldy items—box-shaped, eighteen-inch-long rectangles with a lens at one end and four small flashlight-type bulbs to provide illumination for the camera as a long shutter release was engaged. Sadly, we had no way to photograph these greasy prints, knowing full well they were left by the burglar.

Ray made an attempt at trying to lift one of the prints using a piece of fingerprint-lifting tape, but the image simply mashed together into an unreadable mess. Since we believed we had sufficient latent prints taken from the outside of the molding, I suggested we make another attempt at lifting a greasy print using some fingerprint powder. We weren't expecting any great outcome at the effort, but we gave it a try. And not surprisingly, the powder mixed with the grease and left a complete mess. While we worked, we remained under the watchful eye of the chief. We explained our predicament to him and let him know that we had plenty of prints already and that our experiment was just that. Had this been a major crime scene, the entire panel would have been removed from the vault and shipped to the FBI Identification Division for processing. But there had barely been a crime, and we had obtained enough evidence for prosecutive use.

As Ray and I finished up, I told the chief that I would stop by early next week and see whether any progress had been made by him or the sheriff's office in this case. Ray and I returned home after yet another weekend on the job. Since we had dusted spaces well above our heads at the bank, the extremely fine fingerprint powder was all over our clothes. And that wasn't all: I was blowing fingerprint powder out of my nose for a full week.

Later that week, I returned to Sunflower to visit with the chief. While there, he said to me, "John, I want to show you some fingerprints I just took of a guy I arrested. It was my first time since you showed me how to use a fingerprint card." With that, he opened a desk drawer and pulled out a fingerprint card for me to see his work. He was as proud as a peacock, and I didn't have the guts to tell him the fingerprints he had taken were worthless. He had simply inked the very tips of the subject's fingers and made what looked like tiny dots on the fingerprint card.

"Great job, chief," I replied as I looked in amusement at the card. "I'll tell you what to do next time to make these even better. Try to ink the entire end digit of each finger and then roll the finger on the card, almost making a large square imprint. It will be a lot easier for the Identification Division to make a good comparison with more detail on each finger."

I took his ink roller and showed him how to take a fuller image of the finger. This was just one of those moments as an FBI agent when helping other law enforcement officers was every bit as important as chasing after dangerous criminals.

Regarding the bank burglary, working with the Sunflower chief and the Sunflower County Sheriff's Office, we were able to come up with a suspect. During an interview at the subject's house, we saw in plain view the Lucite paperweight that had been stolen off of a desk at the bank during the burglary. The subject confessed to the burglary and was arrested and charged by the county sheriff. His fingerprints were subsequently positively identified by the FBI Identification Division, putting him in the bank and touching the metal molding around the vault. To my recollection, he received a short sentence for his crime.

Sadly, my training sessions did not end with the chief and his fingerprint cards. I vividly recall another incident that involved a police killing in Doddsville, Mississippi, another tiny hamlet located in Sunflower County. On April 2, 1975, John Neelley and I were contacted by Sheriff Jack Sessums and advised that shortly before seven that morning, the body of Carter Lee Curry, town marshal of Doddsville, had been found murdered at the Lion Oil gas station. It appeared to the sheriff that Curry had been surprised by his attackers and was shot in the head. Sessums asked for assistance, and John and I traveled to Doddsville in separate cars, in case the investigation would require us to work in different areas. Upon our arrival at the scene, Curry's body had already been taken to the undertaker, Doug Card, who served as county coroner.

Carter Lee Curry was a black man. Being a town marshal, he was usually assigned the night watch as the members of the Doddsville Police Department slept. The positions of town marshal and night watchman were somewhat synonymous with each other in southern law enforcement circles. These positions were not familiar to me in the North. There did not seem to be any immediate concern of a race riot in connection with this murder. Here I was, investigating a second homicide in less than five months, and a police killing at that. I knew John would be the case agent on this matter based upon his seniority in the FBI, which was fine with me. I would certainly be involved inasmuch as it had occurred in Sunflower County, assigned to me. I had not met Carter Lee Curry prior to his murder. I simply had never needed to work any criminal matters in Doddsville until this unfortunate incident.

As John went inside the gas station to speak with Sheriff Sessums, I wandered out to the side of the building where my buddy Deputy Herman

Parker stood looking at a window that appeared to be broken. "What have you got there, Herman?" I asked, hoping I could be of some help to him.

"Howdy, John. Looks like the killers got into the gas station through this window. Probably broke it in order to get in the place. I suspect Carter Lee Curry may have seen the broken glass and went inside to check it out. There wasn't any alarm system involved. Whoever did this probably hid inside and then surprised Carter when he came in. They just shot him in the head. He was shot a total of three times, twice in the head."

I took a look at the window and the windowsill where the deputy was standing. The old white paint was peeled, much like the downtrodden condition of the entire building. "Herman, have you taken fingerprints of the windowsill? It's possible whoever entered here left some," I suggested.

"No, John, I did not take any prints because the paint is all peeled, and you can't get prints off of that type of surface."

Once again, and in my kindest, most sensitive way, I informed Herman that it is possible to take and lift latent fingerprints off of peeled-paint surfaces. "Herman, you may not believe this, but I can distinctly remember during a training session at the FBI during our week of fingerprint work, the instructor specifically stating that it is possible to take latent prints off peeled paint. I'll give it a try, if you don't mind."

He said, "Go ahead, John. I'll stand here and watch you!" Once again, another training session opportunity for a good friend presented itself.

I prayed as I walked to my car to retrieve my fingerprint kit that I'd be able to identify some latent fingerprint on the windowsill. I returned to the window, stood up on a bench, and began a careful dusting of black powder on the peeled paint, once white in color but now graying with age. To my own astonishment, as well as that of Herman Parker, some traces of fingerprint ridge lines became evident on the ledge. "By God, John, that's amazing," Herman exclaimed. I thought so too but didn't say anything. I got out the lift tape and placed it carefully on the latent fingerprint. As I peeled it up, several pieces of chipped paint came along with the tape. I left the chips on the tape as I transferred it to a white index card for later examination by the FBI Identification Division. I didn't know if the lifted fingerprints would be of any value in the investigation into the death of Carter Lee Curry, but I was thrilled to know the technique worked. I also had a new believer in fingerprint lifting and evidence collection, and I had again helped in a small way to make a better law enforcement deputy out of an already great one.

The murder investigation grew considerably more complicated as the morning wore on. There was little else for me to do at the scene, so I returned to the office ahead of John Neelley. Following my departure, and much later in the day, a Ruleville resident named J. B. Winter contacted a Ruleville constable named Bill Whiting. He related a story to Whiting of what had occurred to him earlier that morning.

According to Winter, he had driven past the Lion Oil service station in the morning without noticing any police activity at the time. He was en route to pick up his daughter from school. As he drove on Mississippi Highway 442, he observed a black male standing by the side of the rural road with what appeared to be blood on his shirt. Thinking the man was injured and needed assistance, Winter pulled off the road to help him. The unknown male approached the car, a light green 1968 Plymouth Valiant, and pointed a short, black revolver at Winter's head. He told Winter to look straight ahead as he would kill him if he turned his head. As this happened, another black male appeared from the side of the road, and both men entered the backseat of Winter's car, still holding the gun at his head. Winter described how he was directed to drive along several rural roads, through the small towns of Linn, Boyle, and Skene. Winter was then directed to stop the car after leaving Skene and assumed he was about to be killed by the two men. During the ride, he was unable to look at the faces of the men in the backseat as his rearview mirror had been knocked crooked, and he was afraid to fix it for fear of being shot. One of the men then exited the vehicle and urinated on the side of the road, eventually reentering the car.

They continued on the trip for another few miles before one of the men asked Winter to hand his wallet to them, without turning around. Winter did as he was told. The men took $178 from his wallet before throwing it back on the front seat. After driving a short time, near the intersection of Mississippi Highway 1 and State Route 446, Winter was ordered to stop the car. Both black passengers got out of the car. The taller of the two then told Winter to drive back the way he came and to drive slowly, without looking back. He said, "If you tell the law, we will find you and kill you and your family, too."

Winter did as instructed and drove off without looking back. He returned to Ruleville to pick up his daughter and returned home. He was too frightened to go to the police but, after some time passed, decided he had to tell someone about the incident that morning. He drove to the police department in Ruleville to speak to the chief of police, Jerry McCool, but lost his nerve out of fear of the two black captors and left the police department without speaking of the incident. After getting back to his car to return home, he saw Constable Whiting and knew he had to tell his story.

Winter's recollection of the event was published in the *Delta Democrat-Times* two days later, on April 4, 1975. The two black males immediately became prime suspects in the murder of Carter Lee Curry. There was a reward posted of $500 for any information leading to the arrest and conviction of the person or persons who killed Carter Lee Curry. I'm not sure who posted the reward, whether it was the county, Curry's family, or some other organization. Looking back at that reward- even when considering the dollar's value in 1975- it doesn't seem like much for the death of a law enforcement officer.

As a result of my other cases, I was not assigned any follow-up leads to work on the Curry homicide investigation. I can only assume the murder investigation was continued by the Sunflower County Sheriff's Office with any requested assistance from the FBI. I never learned the outcome of this matter until doing research for this book. I attempted contact with the Doddsville Police Department and forwarded them an e-mail request for any updates on the Curry case. I never received any response to my inquiry. On the Officer Down Memorial Page site on the Internet, the biography and incident details of this homicide are shown in brief.

Curry was listed as being forty-nine years old at the time of his death, and he had been in law enforcement for six years. The cause of his death was confirmed to be by a gun. Sadly, the case was shown as never solved. (www.odmp.org/officer/3722-night-marshal)

During my assignment in Greenville, I was offered and attended two specialized training sessions back at the training academy in Quantico, Virginia. Those training sessions were better known within the FBI as "in-service" training. I was scheduled for organized-crime in-service training April 13–19, 1975. It was a one-week training course that specialized in organized-crime matters and the relatively new laws passed by Congress to combat organized crime in the United States. I guess I was selected because I continued to work the gambling cases in the Greenville area, never knowing whether I would ever be successful in obtaining search warrants for the local sports parlors. The course was very beneficial, and I got to meet a number of agents who worked organized-crime cases in New York, Chicago, Cleveland, Boston, and Los Angeles. Some of those agents may have wondered why some agent from the rural Mississippi Delta would be in the class, but they did not know I had a pretty significant case ongoing at the time. And, little did I know, I'd be working with some of those same agents in the not-too-distant future.

The other in-service training I attended while assigned to the Greenville RA was of a volunteer nature. It was a SWAT (special weapons and tactics) team in-service that took place June 3–14, 1974, fourteen months earlier than my organized-crime in-service class.

CHAPTER 15
SWAT

*A special mission, a dangerous takedown, a dignitary that needs protection—
That's when SWAT gets the call.*

—FBI WEBSITE - WWW.FBI.GOV

To the best of my recollection, there were no SWAT teams being utilized by the FBI when I entered on duty in 1971. For those unfamiliar with the term, SWAT is the acronym for special weapons and tactics. Some recent research into the origin of SWAT teams in the United States indicates that the first SWAT-team concept was developed by the Los Angeles Police Department around 1966 or 1967. The concept came about after the horrific shooting on the University of Texas campus when a man named Charles Whitman secluded himself atop a twenty-eight-story tower and began random shooting with a high-powered rifle. Fifteen people were killed, and twice as many were wounded. Case studies following the shooting determined that police departments were not suitably trained for acts of terror such as that committed by Whitman. This incident was not the only issue that resulted in the forming of the SWAT-team idea. Police were coming under increased attacks by rioters and protestors of all types. The standard beat cop on patrol was simply not equipped or trained to deal with these increasingly dangerous situations. Thus, the SWAT team was born.

Sometime around 1971, the FBI concluded that it, too, should form SWAT teams in its different field offices to address high-risk arrest and hostage situations. Sniper operations like the Texas tower massacre and a rash of airliner hijackings demanded a better-trained and more effective arrest team. So, the FBI got in on the creation of its own SWAT teams. I do not recall hearing anything about SWAT teams in the FBI while serving in Cleveland and Akron, Ohio. However, once established in Greenville, I started hearing that the FBI was running SWAT-team training at Quantico, Virginia. The larger offices were getting the training first, ahead of the smaller offices for obvious reasons. At some point I learned that the Jackson Division did send its first five-man SWAT team to be trained. I never heard of any way in which to volunteer for that first team. Once they returned from training, I got to talk with the agents, and they really enjoyed the two-week course at Quantico. I was still in pretty good physical condition from my days of teaching physical education and knew that this was something I'd like to try. I was told that Jackson would be sending another SWAT team to Quantico in a year or so. I prepared a memorandum expressing my interest to be considered for a spot on the next Jackson SWAT team scheduled for training.

Sometime in late March 1974, I was notified that the Jackson Division would be sending another team to SWAT training in June. I was one of the five agents selected for this second team. I was thrilled beyond belief to become a part of this elite group. However, there was a notice attached to the invitation to attend SWAT training, advising that the course was very physically demanding, and all who planned to attend must show up in excellent physical condition. The packet of information from the training unit mentioned that the marine corps obstacle course and the confidence course would all be part of the training experience. Additionally, all candidates would be expected to be able to run at least five miles in boots while carrying heavy gear. I knew, despite my reasonably good physical condition at the time, that I'd need to start getting into top physical condition.

I immediately started a running program, trying to go out early in the morning before work as it was much cooler than at any other time in the day. I found I was not enjoying the early-morning runs and decided to change my routine to start after work, when the blazing sun was at least lower in the western sky. I used the track at the Greenville High School and ran laps—a mile at first, then I pushed to two and three miles. I'd begin to lose count as to how many laps I'd run, so I would switch my car keys into a different hand following each completed mile. I had worked myself up to almost four miles when I developed a serious case of shin splints, some of the worst pain I'd ever experienced. I knew it was an overuse injury as I was pushing myself to get past the five-mile goal. But I needed to rest my legs in order to help ease the pain and heal the shin splints. The problem was that time was running out, and June was fast approaching.

The oppressive Delta humidity made the running experience even more debilitating. I was getting into great shape for sure, but at what cost? I was simply exhausted and in great pain every night. With ice bags on my shins and complaining to my wife, I didn't see how the pain would leave my legs before I actually started training. Yet I had to press on, as I didn't want to be left behind during SWAT training and disappoint my teammates. By end of May, I was in the best physical condition of my life, excepting the still-painful shin splints.

Naturally, I took a bit of good-natured razzing from my colleagues at work. Just before I was to depart for Quantico for the SWAT in-service training, my buddy Ken presented me with a poem he wrote specifically for me and dedicated to my upcoming experience. He was no Robert Frost, but here is his clever prose at work:

A Game of SWAT

This is a poem about a man
a hero to some, to others a sham.
One day he decided that he ought
to try out for that team, known as SWAT.
He dreamed of his name, wreathed in glory
but alas, we are getting ahead of our story.
Whiteside, John is the name
that we herewith nominate for the "hall of fame."

So Johnnie went to Quantico
to see if he could make it go.

But before he went, he worked out hard
he didn't drink or deal a card.

And so one bright and sunny day
he arrived at Quantico to have his play.

The obstacle course was his first test
our John passed it—among the best.

But here is where our Johnnie erred
at end of day he didn't go to bed.

Swat

That night to the beer hall he did go
so to celebrate that first day's show.

But the very next morning when he awoke
his head felt like hell, his back felt broke.

And this was the day of his final test
the Confidence Course would challenge the best.

Thoughts raced, on high, sublime
high ropes, big logs, were his to climb.

So to the site our John did travel
the Confidence Course to unravel.

The "Reverse Climb" and "Dirty Name"
were nothing more than small folks' game.

But as John rose up from the sand standing tall
the next problem on the course rose up like a wall.

"Skyscraper" was its proud name
and our Johnnie prepared to scale its frame.

Thirty feet is no small height
John gulped back a feeling of fright.

Don't look down, he said to himself
as he threw his belly on the lowest shelf.

His mind raced "first position"
place palms down, that's no imposition.

Cypress Shade

His biceps quivered, and with a strain
he hoisted himself to the second plane.

A pant for breath, a gasp for air
how Johnnie wished for an easy chair.

With a grunt, a tug, and some divine help
our John found himself on the next higher shelf.

One more to go to reach the top
God, what it takes to be a cop.

Thoughts of success were not slight
as he rose to conquer that one last height.

And so, there was Johnnie, up on top
soaked with sweat, wrung like a mop.

The easiest part now lay ahead
only to climb down—then on ahead.

The next instruction raced in his head

"lay flat on the platform, then hang your head—

"Over the ledge, then grasp the top—"
with those sweaty palms, wet like a mop.

"Rotate your body forward and down—"
three cheers, I can make it to the ground.

Keeping together his ankles and knees
Johnnie launched himself into the breeze.

Head over heels he tumbled down
until his ass caressed the ground.

You see, our John had made a mistake
too much in a hurry, no care did he take.

"Maintain a firm grip on the platform"
forgotten, this phrase had bruised John's form.

And so, as our hero, rear now in a sling
gazed over the airplane's homebound wing.

A hostess offered, "Martinis by the glass"
but, said good ol' John, "Hell, give me the flask."

I've made up my mind now, no more shall I wander
I'll stay home in Greenville, no future to ponder...

Bottoms up...by Dash

Little did Ken (or Dash) know how oddly prophetic his poem would be. Neither did I until I arrived for training. June in Virginia wasn't much cooler or much less humid than the Mississippi Delta. At least one thing I had going for me and my team at the onset of SWAT training was that we had trained in Mississippi and wouldn't be as affected by the heat or humidity. That was about the only edge we had over the other six teams who trained with us.

Our two-week class comprised SWAT teams from FBI offices in Little Rock, Louisville, Memphis, Mobile, Savannah, and St. Louis. Our Jackson team included Norm Stutte, Bob Agnew, Charlie Sheppard, Jerry Marsh, and me. We were all in great physical condition and ready for whatever the trainers were prepared to give to us. Or so we thought.

On arrival day, just when we thought we could chill out and relax before starting on Monday, we were told to report to the gun-cleaning room, where we were instructed in the proper way to devise a Swiss seat out of rope and a metal carabiner. This seat, wrapped around the crotch area and secured with a metal carabiner, would be used to rappel down the side of a building. Fear immediately gripped me, as I was not aware of this part of the course. Before I had time to untie my Swiss seat and head for an escape route, we were taken outside of the building and introduced to a wall where we began our first experience dangling from a rope tied to a railing. It was basic rappelling on a short, slanted ten-foot wall. I had yet to realize we would be rappelling out of a five-story building in the not-too-distant future.

During new-agent training, there was no place in the old academy building to share a beer with fellow students. We would have to travel to the Globe and Laurel restaurant if we wanted to have a beer while assigned in Quantico. Of course, we needed to be back at the academy by eleven, or the doors would be locked, and there'd be hell to pay for getting in late. When the new academy was constructed, there was a snack bar / beer hall built just outside of the mammoth cafeteria. One could buy a sandwich or hamburger and a soda or beer in lieu of a big meal. The snack bar / beer hall became a place for classmates to gather for a relaxing beer after a grueling day of study. It also became a place of trouble if one wasn't careful—not so much that evening, but more likely the next morning.

One case in point, a few of us had a few beers after our traumatic first experience with rappelling. The hall closed promptly at eleven o'clock to ensure all students were bright eyed and alert for class the following day. But most students simply attended class in modern, comfortable classroom settings. Not so for the SWAT teams. Out at seven in the morning, we started our day with a five-mile run in boots, singing along in cadence, "We are the SWAT team, mighty, mighty SWAT team, everywhere we go, people wanna know, who we are, and so we tell them, SWAT team, SWAT team…" and so on. While the cadence was designed to make the run seem to go faster, the beer in our bellies and the pounding headaches counteracted the "joy" of the run. Most of us made a silent vow to avoid the beer hall in the future.

Swat

After some serious workouts, we had a lot of classroom instruction at the firing range, and then we fired a variety of different weapons that would be included as a part of each SWAT team. Besides our own .357 Magnum revolvers, teams would carry two M16 rifles, a bolt-action sniper rifle, a shotgun, and an M79 grenade launcher capable of firing tear gas, shotgun pellets, flares, and a high-explosive round if needed. We trained in sniper-rifle fire, shooting at targets hundreds of yards away with a scoped rifle. Most of us became so proficient with the sniper rifle that we could shoot a hole in the tiny fluorescent marker that our spotters would use to mark the spot we hit on the target. I think everyone knew without any doubt that, if need be, we could shoot a hijacker holding a hostage without hurting the hostage. That was what this course was all about, training each team to build both team confidence and personal confidence in order to perform under extreme and difficult situations.

It wasn't too long, perhaps a day or two, before we moved to Combat Village for our first experience with real rappelling. Our rappelling instructor, Dave, was a true daredevil. After explaining how perfectly safe rappelling was, as long as the ropes were sound, he explained the belay system. A man on belay stood on the ground, holding the other end of the rope that the person rappelling was coming down. Should the person rappelling lose consciousness or in some way become disabled, the person on belay could gently bring him back to the ground in a safe manner. It was a system well known to mountain and rock climbers but totally new to most of us at the time. When the belay man pulled on the rope with slight pressure, the rope would tighten against the rappeller's carabiner and slow or completely stop the man on rappel.

To demonstrate the true safety of the belay position, Dave climbed to the top of a five-story building, stood on the roof, and checked his line. He called down to his belay team, now composed of two burly instructors rather than the usual one on belay. He shouted the rappelling command "On rappel" and received the reply "On belay" from his team below. With that, and to the surprise and shock of us all, Dave leaped headfirst off the roof and plunged toward the ground. Before fear could even enter our brains, the sound of loose gravel grating under the heavy boots of the belay team was all that could be heard as they strained to pull on the rope, tightening it against Dave's carabiner in order to keep him from a sudden meeting with mother earth. The belay team stopped Dave's fall about five feet above the ground. He was grinning like a Cheshire cat the whole way down.

That demonstration proved several things: It showed that the belay team or person was able to save the person on rappel in any circumstance. It also showed that Dave must have had some sort of death wish. And worse, it showed me that there was no way in hell I would be demonstrating that same feat, unless I was pushed off the roof. After a few moments of recovery for all of us, as well as a lecture about the safety of rappelling, Dave again went up to the top of the building. This time, he rappelled down in a more traditional manner, except he was holding his five-year-old son in his arms, demonstrating both a rescue-type use of the rappel as well as again proving his trust of and the safety of his rope and his belay man below. His son seemed to really enjoy it.

By this time, we all knew we'd have to man up and rappel out of the building. We started our experience working out of a lower floor, eventually working up to the top floor. Despite all Dave's earlier demonstrations, most of us felt a bit queasy during our first few attempts. For those who have never tried it, standing on the sill edge of an open five-story window, attached by a thin piece of rope, and preparing to take a large step backward and out of the window was no easy task. Not for me, anyway. It also didn't help to learn that if the twist of rope placed in the carabiner was applied in the wrong direction, the twist was called the "suicide loop" and would come out of the carabiner as the rappeller was on his way down. Something else to remember and always worry about. But by the end of the two weeks, most of us had mastered rappelling and actually started to enjoy it.

As the week progressed, we continued physical training on the marine corps obstacle course and the dreaded confidence course. It was interesting to see how simple fear would reduce one's physical strength and mental acuity, another purpose of the training program. Yet all the training built up a strong camaraderie between team members. We practiced swimming in the pool wearing full clothing while carrying an M16 rifle. No easy task there either.

During the one weekend that occurred during the middle of our two-week training period, we did not have the time off. Rather, that Saturday, each team was given a series of map coordinates that we were to use to locate numbered ammunition cans placed strategically in the deep woods of the marine corps base. It was a lesson in orienteering that I thought would be easy, especially based on my knowledge of map-and-compass work in Boy Scouts. Oh, how wrong I would be.

For starters, we failed to properly orient the map, thinking the correct lines were present from the last group who used the map. Taking what we thought was a clever shortcut resulted in us getting totally lost in the woods. Once we figured out our mistake, reoriented the map, and located our position, we were able to eventually complete the course. However, that was not before I suffered a painful injury to my shin, one of the still very sore ones from training for the SWAT team. I was running full out with all my gear when my shin struck a partially buried root or stick that protruded from the earth at an angle so as to ram into the front of my leg. I fell to the ground in a heap, worried that I might have broken my leg. But upon examination, all seemed okay other than a nasty bruise seeping blood. I got myself together and completed the exercise with my team. When we finally reached the finish of the exercise, at a staging area where the other teams were to meet, we were surprised to find no teams present but ours. Had we finished ahead of all the rest?

"Where have you guys been?" asked the counselor. "All the teams have finished, enjoyed the refreshments we had for all of you, eaten your share, and returned to the academy. We were about to send a search party after you." Embarrassed, we had to confess our misread of the map and admit to getting lost in the woods. But hey, at least we found our way home again. This misadventure resulted in a good-natured, occasional classroom chant of "Where's Jackson" for the remainder of the in-service.

With a final day of training remaining, we had all accomplished an incredible amount of physical training, firearms training and proficiency, and bonding with each other as a team. We had rappelled out of a window down the length of the five-story building. We had practiced a spider crawl off of a roof, learning to complete a controlled fall to the ground without being knocked out of action. We had overcome some personal fears, or at least learned how to deal with them. Our confidence in each other was complete, and we had worked together to overcome many difficult odds. We practiced assaulting a building or two in Combat Village, a set of cinder-block buildings used to simulate a small town. Unfortunately for the Jackson team, we got lost in the woods yet again, although we recovered more quickly this second time. That certainly didn't let up on the razzing from the other teams, however. We all stood a lot taller that Thursday evening, knowing we only had one more day of training before we'd be on the airplane home, trained and ready for action.

Not having learned a thing about our first night in the snack bar / beer hall, we all decided to have one last bash together as a group, saying our good-byes and saluting our respective FBI offices. Rumor had it that the last day of training was a half day, so we could be bused to Washington, DC, in order to catch our flights home. How bad could the half day be? We were the FBI SWAT team, the mighty, mighty SWAT team...invincible, ready for whatever challenge came our way. We thought it would be nothing more than some review, a few handshakes, awards given out for team records accomplished during training, and of course, one last chant of "Where's Jackson"! So drink up, my fearless boys, for a job well done.

We started the final day at seven with a short run in full gear. No one was feeling too chipper by this time, but we all assumed the worst was finished. All except the class counselors. We were bused to a place on the base that had some sort of endurance course involving sand dunes and rope climbing. It was without a doubt the worst challenge of the two-week period and was cleverly designed and planned to show the brave new little SWAT-team braggarts that they'd best stay in top condition to be ready whenever called upon. Clearly, we weren't ready, not after the previous night of frolicking. We had to run a timed course in full gear with combat boots and rifle through sandpits, up and down sand dunes, and occasionally needing to climb to the top of a rope at just that moment when we were totally out of air. It was a bear, for sure. I remember as I was finally climbing my last rope, I simply had nothing left in my body, not one more ounce of strength or energy. But I had to get to the top of the rope. It seemed impossible. There was no way I could do it. But just at that moment of deep despair, not divine power, my teammate Bob Agnew appeared below me on the rope and told me to step onto his shoulders. I did so and was able, with his support, to get to the top of the rope. That's how it had been all week. Whenever a teammate faltered, the others were there to lend a hand. I did it; we all did it. That's what the program was really all about.

Mercifully, the course was finally over. I was in the best shape of my life and had pure confidence in my skills as a SWAT-team member. I knew without any doubt that, if necessary, I could take the shot and kill a hijacker or any other criminal holding a hostage and threatening death. I was ready to go, and so were my team members.

So off to the airport we went, saying good-bye for the moment as I would fly alone to Greenville while the others had a different flight to Jackson. We knew we'd be training together with the other Jackson SWAT team following our return home. I boarded my flight and got seated and belted in. I couldn't wait for that pitcher of martinis that Ken spoke of in his poem. Every muscle in my body ached, and I was completely exhausted. How wonderful would that ice-cold gin feel coursing through my weary veins. I couldn't wait for the flight attendants to begin serving drinks.

I awoke as the plane began its descent into Memphis. I had never even heard the announcement to ensure seat belts were fastened, let alone the original call for cocktails. I was simply totally spent, having left everything in the woods at Quantico. After landing, I reboarded a Southern Airways flight to Greenville. I was finally home again, proud as could be, and looking forward to a long night's sleep.

Monday morning as I walked, or perhaps limped, into my Greenville office, I was standing quite a bit taller. The SWAT course had brought out the best in me, reducing some old fears, teaching me my physical and mental limitations during a time of stress, and producing a confidence in my own abilities that I never knew I had. What a marvelous experience, and one that stays with me to this day. My thought was that every FBI agent should be given the opportunity to go through this course, impossible as that may be.

When Ken arrived, he smiled when he saw me. "How was it, John? Anything like my poem?"

I nodded. "It was exactly as you prophesized," I responded. "We all made the critical mistake of enjoying a fond farewell the night before the last day, and we ended up paying a heavy price for our good time." Ken laughed. In some way we've all experienced that type of situation somewhere along the road we travel. "And I passed out in the airplane seat before the flight attendant came around offering martinis. I was so totally exhausted."

As the weeks passed, the two existing SWAT teams in the Jackson Division would meet together on a periodic basis to train together. At times, we would meet at the Jackson Fire Department tower to practice our rappelling skills. We also had an arrangement with Delta Airlines to learn about all the procedures that take place to get an aircraft ready to fly, or what happens when one lands. We learned about methods of entrance and exit other than the main cabin doors. We also learned about all the different land-support vehicles and how they were used to service the airplane, including refueling, baggage handling, and providing food and drinks to the galley. The true purpose of this experience was to better prepare us in the event we were summoned to an aircraft-hijacking situation, something that was occurring in the mid-1970s with alarming frequency. Training with the SWAT teams was a wonderful experience, and we all tried our best to be prepared whenever we were needed. That wait wouldn't take too long.

When I first arrived in Greenville in 1972, the special agent in charge (SAC) of the Jackson Division was Elmer F. Linberg. The SAC is the one person in charge of all field office and resident agency operations. Since I reported directly to the Greenville Resident Agency upon my arrival, I did not have the opportunity to meet SAC Linberg until my first trip to the Jackson office for firearms training. I only met him on that one occasion, as he either retired or transferred to another location at some subsequent date. The new incoming SAC was a man named Roy K. Moore, an iconic man with a huge reputation in the FBI. SAC Moore was the first man J. Edgar Hoover sent to reopen the Jackson Division office on July 10, 1964, after the rash of lynchings in Mississippi. Director Hoover traveled to Mississippi to attend the opening ceremony and to show his support to the agents who were about to face very difficult, dangerous, and demanding investigations.

Roy K. Moore first developed his reputation as a no-nonsense investigator while conducting the investigation of the midair explosion of an airliner over Colorado. Some forty-four people were killed in the blast. His investigation and that of his colleagues ultimately identified the suspect in the bombing as Jack Gilbert Graham. Graham had placed the bomb in his mother's suitcase prior to her departing on the airplane, in order to collect the life insurance following her death.

As his reputation grew, Moore was asked to lead the investigation of the Birmingham, Alabama, church bombing that killed four young girls in 1963. That effort, plus his past experiences, led the director of the FBI to appoint him as SAC in Jackson. He was transferred to the Chicago Division in 1971 and served there two years as SAC before requesting a transfer back to the Jackson Division in 1973. He was a disciplined leader and a former marine. But he had a whimsical side to him as well, and he was extremely popular with all of his employees. Everyone was well aware of his reputation in the FBI as the "go to" guy. Besides cleaning up the mess in Mississippi, he was involved in investigating a series of murders on St. Croix, the kidnapping of the editor of the *Atlanta Journal-Constitution*, the American Indian siege at Wounded Knee, South Dakota, and the kidnapping of Patty Hearst by the Symbionese Liberation Army in San Francisco—all high-profile cases.[8]

Sometime in late August 1974, the FBI was advised of an extortion case by a major communications corporation. Corporate security officers contacted the FBI to report that some unknown individual had damaged a bit of property just to show that he knew how to do more damage and his request wasn't superfluous; he meant what he said. He asked for a ransom of $1 million, or else he would destroy communications systems valued at far more money. The minor amount of destruction he had already caused convinced corporate security personnel that he indeed meant what he said and had the ability to create massive destruction to their equipment. They came to the FBI seeking help on the case.

But there was much more to the ransom request. The unknown extortionist set forth a very detailed description as to when, where, and how the company was to deliver the million dollars. He provided a date a week or so in advance to allow the company to secure the needed equipment to make his ransom payment. He asked that a small boat, a certain desired length, was to be equipped with two white lights set atop poles located ten feet apart and extending ten feet into the air, to be visible from shore or aircraft. This would make the boat stand out from any others that happened to be on the river at the time. The ransom money was to be loaded on the boat with the signal lights and brought to Memphis on a particular evening, and then it was to depart from the port at dusk. No more than two people could be in the boat along with the ransom money. The boat was to then travel south down the Mississippi River until a flashing red light was observed on either shore, Mississippi or Arkansas. At the sight of the flashing red light, the boat was to proceed to shore, and the money was to be dropped off at the shoreline. The boat was then instructed to

---

8. *Washington Post* obituary, October 20, 2008.

depart from the area. If no red flashing signal was observed, the boat was requested to stop at Helena, Arkansas, for the night and resume the journey down the Mississippi River the following night, starting at dusk, with the same set of instructions.

Initially, I knew nothing about the case until my supervisor, John Neelley, told me we needed to go to see Jesse Brent. Jesse Brent was one of the largest, if not the largest, towboat operators on the Mississippi River, and certainly the largest in the Greenville area. John said he needed to rent a boat from Jesse for an FBI operation in the near future. We arrived at Brent Towing located on Lake Ferguson, and John introduced me to Jesse Brent. He told Brent that the FBI needed to borrow a boat of a certain size for a week or two. He also cautioned Jesse that there would be some alterations made to the boat, hopefully not causing too much damage. Jesse Brent was the tough type of towboat operator who possessed a big heart. He told John he'd get him the boat, and he only asked that any damage be repaired before returning it to him. That's just the way things seemed to work in the Delta most times. Another rather simple and easy solution.

I do not recall where the ransom note was delivered by the communications company to the FBI, whether it was taken to the Memphis, Little Rock, or Jackson office. Since Tennessee, Mississippi, and Arkansas were all potential sites involved in the extortion, all three offices became involved in the investigation, and all three SACs participated in the scenario that would accompany the delivery of the ransom. However, the hand of Roy K. Moore and his grandiose operations seemed to be at the forefront.

He and others devised a very involved scenario to deliver the money as requested and be able to arrest the extortionist at the same time. The boat would be fitted with the lights requested by the extortionist before being taken to the Memphis port. FBI radio systems would also be added to the boat. Since none of the FBI agents were found to be qualified to operate a boat in the dark on the Mississippi River, John Neelley was able to find a Mississippi state game and fish officer who stated that "he knew the river like the back of his hand" to pilot the boat. FBI Agent Drew Clark, the largest FBI agent in the Jackson office and a member of the first SWAT team, was chosen to accompany the game officer as he was the only one strong enough to lift the bag full of money. Thus, the crew was chosen for the operation. The money would be loaded into the boat in Memphis by these two men in the event that the extortionist was watching from somewhere in the port. But that wasn't the end of the complicated scenario.

Roy K. Moore wanted to know if there were any qualified scuba divers in the three FBI offices. I, along with Chuck Wilmore and another agent from Memphis, Mike, volunteered my services in that regard. Moore advised that we would ride unobserved in the bottom rear of the boat. When the red flashing signal was observed, we would deploy into the river, using the boat as a shield, and swim to the shoreline to await the drop-off of the ransom money and subsequently arrest the extortionist. It sounded pretty simple, my first true FBI SWAT operation. We were all really excited after receiving the briefing about the case. Moore also told us that there would be plenty of other personnel and firepower out there with us. He would have two boats loaded with SWAT teams from Memphis, Jackson, and Little Rock moving parallel with our boat, keeping a distance behind and operating without lights so as not to be observed. Further back on the river, a party-type barge would follow the SWAT crafts, containing law enforcement officials, SACs and others, making a bit of noise to divert attention from the boats ahead and to serve as lookouts as well. And that still wasn't all to the grand plan.

Moore directed that a box truck containing agents on motorcycles travel along each side of the levees, in Arkansas and Mississippi, paralleling the ransom boat at all times. Should a chase ensue after the money drop, there would be immediate support. In addition, FBI automobiles were spaced about a mile apart for five miles, both ahead and behind the ransom-carrying boat. This would provide additional surveillance and any support needed in the event of a chase. Lastly, a small airplane was procured to fly above the river with full night-vision and radio capability.

It certainly didn't seem that there would be any escape for the extortionist, no matter what he tried to do.

At a final briefing in Memphis the morning of the operation, Moore and the other SACs went over the entire scenario until everyone was familiar with their roles. Excitement rose through the group of experienced special agents and SWAT-team members. All knew exactly what was expected of them that evening.

Just prior to adjournment, one last detail was given to the members of the scuba team. The management team did not want to put the divers on board the ransom boat at the port in Memphis, for the simple reason that the extortionist may be observing the launch of the boat at dusk. In order to prevent any accidental observation of additional men aboard the boat, the SAC had made contact with a towboat captain in Memphis. After Moore solicited the captain's cooperation without divulging the true purpose of the matter at hand, the captain agreed to take the three scuba divers aboard his towboat and travel down the river with them. As darkness fell that evening, the ransom boat would quickly approach the towboat, and all three FBI divers would leave the towboat, getting into the ransom boat. It was thought this was the safest way to get the divers on the ransom boat without being detected by the extortionist. As to a light cover story, the captain said he would tell his crew that the three of us were new deckhands, just joining his towboat staff. With the plans finally completed, the meeting broke up and all returned to their respective workstations to prepare for the evening's activity.

As we divers prepared to load our gear into large parachute bags to be taken aboard the towboat, Moore stopped us. Looking me straight in the eye, as was his way, he said, "You understand that this guy is not to get away." I could only offer up a meek "Yes, sir," and thereafter proceeded with my packing. I knew he meant business, and neither Chuck, Mike nor I had any intention of losing the extortionist on the banks of the Mississippi. I did have several vague thoughts about trying to run after the extortionist in my swim fins with a scuba tank strapped to my back. That seemed like a disaster waiting to happen. We would have to ditch the equipment as quickly as possible in order to have more flexibility to run after the subject if necessary. There was one comforting thought, however: he himself would be wrestling with a huge bag of money and wouldn't be able to move very quickly. The biggest fear was that he might be armed and hold his weapon on Drew and the fish and game officer, getting them to carry the money for him. Lots of crazy scenarios began running through my mind, and none of them were particularly good ones. And of course, we did not know if he would be acting alone. As in all arrest scenarios, even the most careful plan could quickly fall apart due to unknown factors and sudden changes that simply could not be planned for or expected.

After loading our scuba gear in the parachute bags, along with our .357 Magnum revolvers, we disassembled the shotgun barrels from their frames to better conceal them in the parachute bags. We carried plastic trash bags to protect the weapons while swimming to shore, as we would be swimming with one hand holding a shotgun. We were dressed in blue jeans and tee shirts, trying our best to look like riverboat deckhands. One look at our soft, manicured fingernails and hands would certainly belie the fact that we had never so much as set foot on a towboat, let alone served as deckhands. But all we really needed to do was get out of the port at Memphis, then under cover of darkness transfer to the ransom boat as it caught up to us. The captain knew who we were and never asked a question about the operation. The word of Roy K. Moore was all one needed in these parts to cooperate with the FBI.

We climbed into an old pickup truck, having stowed our gear in the bed of the truck. We were taken to the port where we arrived at the towboat. I'd never seen a towboat up that close, having only observed them moving barges slowly in the middle of the Mississippi River. This towboat appeared much larger and more powerful than I had ever imagined. We left the truck, grabbed our gear, and stepped aboard the towboat to the welcome of the captain. We were nowhere near the ransom boat, and any surveillance of us would appear to simply be three deckhands arriving for work on their towboat. The captain led us up to a lounge for the deckhands and told us to leave our gear there. He said we would be getting underway shortly, and once out on the river, they would be serving supper to the deckhands. He encouraged us to join the crew for supper.

None of the three of us had eaten anything since breakfast, and we were hungrier than we thought. We sat around a large table with the captain and the rest of the deckhands as supper was served by another member of the crew. I don't remember what was served, only that the food was surprisingly tasty and plentiful. We engaged in a bit of small talk with the deckhands and let the captain speak for us whenever we'd be asked a question about where we served on boats in the past. I don't think we were fooling any of the deckhands about being deckhands ourselves. But we were only along for a short ride, and they'd all have plenty of time to figure out who we were once we disembarked from the towboat.

After supper, the captain told us we could return to the lounge. He would give us about a twenty-minute warning when he heard from the ransom boat that they were nearing him for our pickup. We left the hospitality of the table and, along with the deckhands, returned to the lounge and began watching a television program. There was little conversation as I suspect all the deckhands knew something wasn't normal and all were being very cautious. Little did they know that things would only get crazier in a few short minutes.

The time had finally arrived. The captain poked his head into the lounge and told us that it was time to get ready. He left the lounge and was not seen again. It was then that the fun started. Chuck, Mike, and I began to disrobe down to the swim shorts we were wearing under our blue jeans. We began to get some strange looks from the deckhands, who were understandably confused. We opened our large parachute bags, retrieving our wetsuits, and put them on. Thankfully the air conditioning was working well on the boat, as the suits are very hot if not cooled by the water. Once we were dressed, strapping diver knives to our legs and depth gauges to our wrists didn't seem to overexcite the crew, who were watching intently. Having been around towboats and the river most of their lives, they saw nothing special or unique about divers. In fact, they may have guessed we were there to do some underwater repair to the boat. It wasn't until we added the last component to our outfits that we truly got their attention.

We took the dismantled shotguns from the bags and began to reassemble them. Noting we now had a captive audience, a few movements of the shotgun action, or "racking the action" added to the growing drama. We loaded the twelve-gauge shotguns with double-0 buckshot and then wrapped a plastic trash bag around each one to protect it from the water. It was so quiet in the lounge you could hear a pin drop. This was well before hijackings at sea were fashionable, but I could only wonder what these deckhands were now processing in their minds.

One final task remained to complete our readiness for the night's activity. We reached into our bags and retrieved our Magnum revolvers, checking the cylinders to see that they were loaded and spinning the cylinders a few times, again simply for effect and amusement. We then placed the revolvers inside small plastic bags and placed them inside our wetsuits. We packed our clothes back into the parachute bags, zipped them up, and walked to the portal that led to the walkway alongside the towboat.

As we stepped outside, it was dark, the mosquitoes were humming, and the humidity was as thick and oppressive as ever. We observed the ransom boat with its telltale white marker lights fast approaching. It was time to go.

As the ransom boat pulled along the starboard side of the towboat, we tossed our nearly empty parachute bags aboard and climbed down into the boat, quickly moving to the stern area and getting settled out of view of the riverbanks. As the boat quickly pulled away from the towboat, I glanced back at the side of the towboat. There, standing along the rail, were all the deckhands who just witnessed what to them must have been something out of a movie scene. Mouths agape and eyes as wide as MoonPies, the sailors watched in amazed silence as the ransom boat departed from view. The captain had agreed to let some time pass before he would continue his run down the river so as not to interfere in whatever it was the FBI had asked him to avoid. The covert operation was now fully underway.

Mike, Chuck, and I tried to get into as comfortable a position as three grown men could in the back of a small boat, keeping below the view of either riverbank. We had a pair of night-vision binoculars and took turns scanning both sides of the riverbank in an effort to observe any suspicious activity. Despite the stickiness of the Delta humidity, the sky was clear, and visibility was perfect. That was not always the case for the pilot of our boat, however. Without a spotlight to aid in navigation, passage down the river at night was a dangerous assignment. Sandbars and shallows, as well as drifting flotsam and tree limbs, made a much more difficult task for our pilot. I wasn't so sure he knew the back of his hand or the river as well as he said he did. While he and Drew struggled to keep the boat heading downriver, the three of us continued to search for something along the riverbanks that would alert us to the presence of the extortionist.

Time and time again, we would end up running aground at some sandbar that came out of nowhere. The divers would have to get out of the boat and into the river to push the boat off the sandbar and get us moving again. This was welcome relief in several ways. We would be able to stretch our legs and get some feeling back into them before reassuming our cramped position on the flat deck of the boat. In addition, and more importantly, it allowed us to get a bit of fresh Mississippi River water moving through our wet suits to help cool us off. Wearing those neoprene suits in that humidity was akin to sitting in a private sauna all night. The suits were a great help in repelling attacks from hungry mosquitoes though.

There were several drawbacks to entering the water in the pitch-dark blackness of the Delta night that did make us think before leaving the boat. There was the possibility of stepping on something on the river bottom that might seriously cut or tear our feet. We might also get hit by passing debris floating unseen down the river, or step off into a hole so deep we could be separated from the boat. In the dark with no lights other than those requested by the extortionist, it would be difficult to find someone lost overboard. And in spite of those unfavorable possibilities, there was one more drawback even worse than all of them combined.

That drawback was something called a cottonmouth, known equally as well as a water moccasin, the only poisonous water snake in North America. Scientifically known as *Agkistrodon piscivorus*, it is the famous snake that lives in the Mississippi River, streams, bayous, ponds, and creeks. It is one of the pit vipers and is famous for standing its ground rather than retreating from a potential adversary. While the experts say that the snake is not aggressive and won't attack unless provoked, I had to wonder how many of those experts had waded around in the Mississippi River during darkness, wondering about the aggressiveness of those snakes that were also swimming around looking for a meal. Had there been any snakes around us at the time, we would never have seen them. The river was their element, not ours, and our place was best served aboard the boat, not in the water.

Down the river we traveled, rarely seeing any signs of life on either riverbank. On occasion, we would pass a small opening along one of the riverbanks, which appeared to have been cleared by the county where a few charcoal pits were placed for recreation purposes. We would see an occasional car or two parked along these open areas where campers would spend some time. But we didn't see any flashing red lights. There was no way that we would miss such a signal as it was simply so dark and foreboding along the river.

Then it happened! Just as we were being lulled into a bit of a trance from the rhythmic rocking of the boat, the hum of the engine, and the soft splashing sound of the wake from the propeller, a flashing red light shone forth from the Arkansas side of the river. Senses on full alert, we called out to Drew and the pilot that we saw what appeared to be the brake lights of a car on the Arkansas side of the river. It seemed the brakes were applied only once, and then they were released. The brakes were not applied again. It was a one-time application and not something that would be considered to be "flashing." Was this the signal, or was this simply another camper, fisherman, or lovers parking a car with no other motive?

Drew radioed back to the following SWAT teams and command aboard the party boat that we had a possible signal. Did they want us to take the boat into the site or wait for another signal? Word quickly was relayed to us to wait and see if the brake lights were applied again. If so, we were to move toward the bank and put the operation into effect. The ground units were advised of the status of the situation as it occurred. We all were of the opinion that if it was the extortionist, he would flash the brake lights a couple of times, especially if he saw his ransom money leaving down the river. But the lights never flashed again.

Most likely, it was not the person we were looking for. Somewhat disappointed, but now wide awake again with adrenaline pumping through our veins, we settled in to watch and wait for another flashing red light. Hours passed...and still no red flashing lights. We finally reached Helena, Arkansas, at about two o'clock in the morning. The journey was finished for the evening per the instructions of the extortionist. We secured lodging at the local Holiday Inn, walking into the quiet lobby in wet suits, heavily armed, and soaking wet. It had been a fascinating and thrilling day. Ordered to bed, we were told we would get instructions at a meeting before noon the following day. I was too excited to get any quality sleep that night.

The next morning, we were assembled together after a late breakfast and given an update by one of the case managers. The extortionist, using a prearranged system of communication, had notified the victim agency that he no longer wanted the ransom boat to continue on its river journey. He asked that a small airplane be used to continue the journey down the Mississippi River, again seeking a flashing red light. At the sight of the flashing light, the ransom was to be dropped from the airplane. Thus, our river journey was finished, and we made preparations to return to our respective FBI offices. It was a bit of a disappointing finish to such an exciting case, but this is often the way things go in investigations. What the operation did do, for me and many others involved who were in the young stages of our FBI careers, was to show the willingness of the FBI to go to any means necessary to solve crime and protect the rights of our citizens and their property. I was never more proud to be an FBI special agent than I was that sunny morning.

Once the boat was returned to Greenville, John Neelley saw that it had received a lot of superficial damage from items hit while traveling down the river. In addition, all of the holes drilled to install the necessary signal lights and radio equipment had to be filled and repaired before the boat could be returned to the owner, Jesse Brent. It cost the FBI a few thousand dollars to do the necessary repairs.

As far as the continuing saga went in an effort to identify the extortionist, no signal was ever seen from the air the following night in connection with a ransom drop. The extortionist seemed to drop off the radar, and I never heard anything more about future demands from him. Work returned to normal for Chuck and me in the Delta. I did learn a few years later that the extortionist was subsequently identified by the FBI. However, I do not know if he was arrested and charged with a crime. I have not been able to confirm any additional details in this case despite my efforts to interview past agents who worked on the extortion matter.

The Jackson Division would eventually send a third SWAT team to Quantico for training, and upon their return, all three teams would practice together periodically at the fire tower and on the firearms range in Jackson. But there would never be another SWAT operation that was anything like the one on the Mississippi River, at least not as long as I was there.

SWAT team rappelling work with teammates
Sheppard and Marsh, 1974

CHAPTER 16
Parchman

*The housing units are unfit for human habitation
under any modern concepts of decency.*

—Collier v. Gates, US Court of Appeals, Fifth Circuit
September 20, 1974

Earlier on in my FBI career, before my experiences in Greenville, I had quite an active assignment in Akron, Ohio. Despite the fact that I, along with my partner, made some twenty to twenty-five arrests per month of deserters from the Vietnam War while assigned to the Akron Resident Agency, I never really got to see the inner workings of the Summit County jail system where the deserters were lodged following their arrest. We would simply transport an arrested deserter to either the Akron Police Department or Summit County Sheriff's Office and take his fingerprints, thereafter turning the subject over to the custody of local authorities for subsequent return to his respective military unit. The local jails had an arrangement with the federal government whereby federal prisoners could be lodged in locally approved jails. Since the process was so smooth, there never seemed to be any reason to explore the inner workings of the penal system that took so many of our fugitives. It became a very matter-of-fact procedure for me to make arrests and turn the prisoners over to the custody of someone else. I don't recall having any curious interest in seeing where the prisoner would end up after his or her arrest, or what life was like behind bars in Ohio.

My earlier experience as a police officer with the Stone Harbor Police Department included access to one jail cell located within the police department itself. I cannot recall any occasion of even one prisoner being locked up in that jail, and even if it was used, it was only for one night until the prisoner could be transported to the Cape May County jail. The cell was always kept in immaculate condition, containing a thick oak plank serving as a mattress and a neatly folded drab-gray blanket available for use at one end of the bunk. A clean toilet-sink combination device was also present in the cell. While not the place anyone would want to spend the night, it was clean, tidy, warm, and certainly more than conformed to all standards of decency.

Following my transfer to Greenville, John Neelley advised me that any of our federal arrest subjects should be taken to the local county jails or the Greenville Police Department, until the US Marshals Service could make arrangements to transport the prisoners to appropriate federal correctional institutes. There were no such jails located within the Delta at the time, and once again, the FBI used the services of the local sheriff or chief of police. As in Ohio, the county jails were approved as federal holding cells until a prisoner could be transported to a federal facility by the US marshals.

One day while I was working in the office on paper work, Ron asked me if I was available to go with him the next day to Parchman, or Parchman Farm as it was known in the area. More accurately, it was the Mississippi State Penitentiary, well known by anyone who was ever incarcerated during the past seventy years or so for any felony state crime. The prison farm was located in the northernmost part of Sunflower County, about a seventy-five-minute drive from Greenville. Since Ron was at the time assigned to Sunflower County, he had responsibility for most of what occurred at Parchman. I told him I was available to assist him with his interview, and we made plans to travel up there the following morning.

Earlier in the week, I had spoken with Chuck Wilmore, and he was filling me in on one of the civil rights cases the FBI had worked at Parchman not too long ago. It seemed that the inmates were complaining about the food that was being served at the prison, both in terms of quality and quantity. The inmates filed a civil rights action against the prison for relief, and the case was eventually passed on to the Greenville office of the FBI to resolve it. As Chuck explained it, the prison was told to prepare three food trays, one for each meal of breakfast, dinner, and supper. The trays were to hold a representative example of each normal meal served to the inmates. Once the trays were prepared by the prison staff, FBI investigators arrived on the scene and photographed each tray of food and carefully weighed each portion on the tray. Even the slices of cornbread were measured for size with a ruler. Once the sample trays were fully documented by photography and by size and weight, a system was set up where each inmate in the respective camp would be asked to look at each food tray. Each inmate was asked to comment on every one of the three food trays. The inmates would be asked if each food tray approximated the specific meal served at the prison. Did he get more or less food at each meal, or did the tray look about average? Were the portions larger or smaller than what the inmate would normally receive? Was there anything different on the sample trays of food that would never appear on the actual food trays served to the inmates?

Chuck explained that the interviews were tedious as every inmate was involved in an interview. Most of the inmates had no idea as to why they were being asked the questions and, according to Chuck, most of them identified the food trays as fairly representative of the quality and quantity of food normally given to them. Thus, a huge investigative effort really did not lead to any changes at the prison in terms of the civil rights complaint regarding food service. Or so it seemed at the time. Chuck noted the investigation did show the extent that the FBI would go to in order to investigate allegations of civil rights violations at the prison.

According to information from 2014 on a website hosted by the Mississippi Department of Corrections (www.mdoc.state.ms.us), in 1900 the Mississippi legislature appropriated $80,000 for the purchase of the 3,789-acre Parchman Plantation located in the northern part of Sunflower County. In 1901 four stockades were constructed, and state prisoners who were scattered across the state were moved to Parchman to clear the land for the subsequent cultivation of crops at the sprawling farm.

The prison farm quickly became the only prison in the state where anyone convicted of a state felony would be sent to serve jail time. Subsequently, the prison farm grew to encompass some eighteen thousand acres of land. The prison was built around the concept of various camps spread out on the grounds. The grounds were so vast that escape from the prison was practically impossible. The inmates were put to work in the fields raising cotton, soybeans, and other vegetable crops. Cattle, poultry, and pigs were also bred, raised, and slaughtered on Parchman Farm. A dairy also existed on the prison farm.

The prison camps were initially segregated by race, with separate living quarters for blacks and whites. There was no distinction held between violent offenders and first-time or minor-crime offenders, and they would often be housed in the same quarters. Even the Freedom Riders from the 1960s who were arrested for their efforts were assigned to Parchman to complete minor sentences.

As the prison camps aged, basic human sanitation disappeared from them, and they began to see an increase in rat population and disease. Medical conditions were poor at the camps, as were the drinking water and sanitation facilities. Open sewage flowed in the vicinity of the camps, creating more health hazards. The prison had a policy of placing inmates in positions of responsibility, even going so far as arming trusty inmates and using them to guard other prisoners. Selection of a trusty inmate was done by a paid sergeant, and it usually involved some sort of bribe or payment to him. There were no shakedowns at the prison for illegal weapons, and many inmates were injured or killed by homemade shivs, knives, and guns. Mail was censored on a daily basis by members of the staff. Heating systems were inadequate, and broken windows were often left unrepaired. From all accounts of the prison, it was a true hellhole.

Prisoners who created problems at the prison and broke the rules were often punished in unconventional ways. Some would be completely undressed and then sprayed with water. Large fans would then be turned on them to get them very cold. Some prisoners would be forced to stand on crates for long hours in an odd, uncomfortable position. Others would be placed in the black hole, a six-by-six-foot cell dug into the floor in the maximum-security unit. Their heads would be shaved with sheep wool shears, and they would be put naked into the hole, where they would remain without toilet facilities for up to seventy-two hours. A small, nonflushable hole in the floor would serve as a place to relieve bodily functions. Inmates who broke the rules were also liable to be struck with the whip or lash. Up to seven lashes could be given to an inmate for misbehavior.

Just prior to my arrival in Greenville, Federal District Judge William C. Keady, a native and resident of Greenville, sat on the bench in federal court listening to the case of *Gates v. Collier.* This was a landmark case involving the Mississippi State Penitentiary and a lawsuit filed by Nazareth Gates, an inmate at Parchman, against the prison superintendent at the time, Thomas D. Cook, on February 8, 1971. Cook was subsequently replaced as superintendent by John Collier in February 1972, and it was his name used in the case title. The case was a class-action suit filed by the inmates, claiming that their rights, privileges, and immunities granted to them under the First, Eighth, Thirteenth, and Fourteenth Amendments of the US Constitution had been denied as a result of practices at the prison farm. In addition, the black inmates also claimed that they were discriminated against on the basis of their race in violation of the Equal Protection Clause of the Fourteenth Amendment.

The case was set for full hearings on May 15, 1972, in Judge Keady's court. Once all the hearings were completed, Judge Keady issued his judgment on October 20, 1972. He divided his judgment up into three parts, noting that the State of Mississippi would need time to address all of his findings and to make necessary corrections at the prison. His rulings included immediate, intermediate, and long-term relief. His immediate-relief orders included new rules for censoring mail, corporal punishment, discipline issues, and medical treatment. The judge set dates when he wanted a full and comprehensive plan from the prison addressing his findings. He realized changes of this magnitude could not happen overnight. He recognized that the lash had not been used on inmates since 1965 and responded with praise in that regard. He ruled that only the superintendent could punish an inmate by lash, and then with no more than seven strokes of the whip or lash. He set additional time frames for a response from the State of Mississippi for all of the complaints filed by the inmates. His findings were far reaching and, for the most part, fully supported the complaints as set forth by the inmates. The Parchman prison farm was now on the way to total reform, after seventy years of mistreatment and poor facilities not fit for human habitation. Much of the civil rights work done by the FBI at Parchman over the years, including the food matter that Chuck spoke about, helped lead to the sweeping change for the good, as set forth by Judge Keady in his ruling.

I was ready for my first trip to Parchman with Ron Ott, as I promised him a day earlier. Ron drove, taking Highway 82 east to Indianola, and then taking the two-lane Highway 49 north toward Parchman. The road went past the small Mississippi Delta towns of Doddsville, Ruleville, and Drew. The trip took about seventy-five minutes past some of the most boring road sights around. There was simply nothing but cotton field after cotton field, with an occasional soybean field or rice paddy interspersed within. An occasional decrepit shotgun shack stood like an aging symbol of the past. Along the way, we chatted about our old buddies from training school, wondering how they were making out on the job, all now serving in their second office of assignment like we were doing.

In due time, we finally reached the Parchman farm. Arriving at the administration building, Ron parked the car, and we headed toward the staff building. I was initially surprised at not seeing any fences, high walls, or barbed wire anywhere around me. The concept of a prison farm had eluded me for the moment. We walked into the administration building and walked over to several of the ladies working in a large room. Several recognized Ron as an FBI agent, and he introduced me to them as a new transfer into the Delta. He requested a prisoner record to review, and one of the ladies went to find it for him. She returned with a binder containing the prisoner's full record, including several photographs. Ron copied the information he needed and, after some small talk, told one of the clerks that we needed to go to Camp 8 to interview one of the prisoners. We left the administrative building and headed back to his car.

"Where are all the prison cells?" I asked Ron as he drove into the extensive fields of cotton and soybeans.

"You're about to see more than you ever wanted to see." He laughed.

After ten minutes or so, we approached a red brick building that suddenly appeared like an oasis in the desert. As we got closer to the building, I saw a rusty chain-link fence surrounding the building with a bit of barbed wire running along the top of the fence. It did not look all that secure to me at the moment, and I wondered if it was a minimum-security unit. Ron replied, "It's one of the worst camps in the prison. Camp 8 used to be an all-black camp until Judge Keady desegregated it this year. You'll see what I mean once we get there."

Ron drove up to what appeared to be a security gate located just outside of the main camp building. We were greeted by a guard wearing a casual-style uniform. His trousers were made of white jean cloth and had a light blue stripe running down the outer seam of each leg. He was not wearing a uniform-type shirt, but rather a soiled, common-style buttoned shirt. He approached the window and asked Ron if we were the FBI agents coming to the camp. We showed our FBI credentials to confirm we were the visitors he was expecting to arrive after receiving a call from the administration building. At least there did seem to be some security at the place, I thought. The guard asked if we were carrying weapons, and we said we were. Following Ron's lead, I took my holster off of my belt, leaving my revolver inside it, and handed it out the window to the guard as Ron did. "They'll be waitin' for you when y'all leave," the guard replied as Ron drove through the gate and parked the car in front of what I now knew was Camp 8.

Before we walked inside the camp building, Ron looked at me and asked how I felt about leaving my revolver with a prison inmate. Dumbfounded, I asked him to repeat what he just said to me. "How'd you like leaving your piece with a prisoner? The guy at the gate is a trusty inmate. He got the assignment at the gate, as his sentence is almost up, and he's done some favors for the hired help. They 'trust' him to watch the front gate." I simply could not believe that I just handed my loaded gun to an inmate. For the rest of the time I was at the camp, I fretted that the trusty guard had done some federal time, or that the FBI was somehow instrumental in his conviction, and how he'd like to get his revenge on us by blowing us away. But Ron seemed rather nonchalant about the whole thing, so I just followed him into the building, trying to put the expected carnage out of my mind for the moment.

As we entered the tired and rather dilapidated building, we were met by a sergeant on duty. He was wearing more of a traditional-style uniform, sky-blue shirt and navy trousers, both needing pressing. I hoped he wasn't yet another trusty inmate. We showed him our FBI credentials, and Ron told him who we were there to speak to. As the sergeant walked down the hall to find the prisoner, he told us to take a seat in the dining room at the end of the short hallway.

As we walked down to the dining-room area, I noticed there were built-in metal cages along both sides of the narrow hallway. The cage on the right was larger than the one on the left. At the end of the cage on the left was a small canteen-type shop that sold cigarettes, tobacco, and candy for the inmates. The inmates on the left side in the smaller of the two cages were dressed just like the guard who took our revolvers, wearing white jeans with a light blue stripe running down the outside seam of both legs. However, the inmates in the larger cage on the right side of the building were all wearing blue jeans with a white stripe running down the outer seam of each pant leg. Each of the cages was full of metal cots where the inmates slept together. There were no individual cells present, simply large groups of inmates all penned up together. The place was pretty filthy, with towels and all sorts of clothing draped everywhere. The floors were all made of wood, and there seemed to be nothing one would call a modern convenience anywhere in the building. Even the lighting was dim and ineffective. As we walked down the hall, catcalls of all sort rang out at us. There was no mistaking in their minds exactly who Ron and I were.

We took a seat on the wooden benches that sat along the rows of picnic-like tables that filled the dining hall. Along the back wall appeared to be an old drinking fountain with a kitchen off to the side. A sheet-metal ice bin dripped with condensation along the dirty wall. While we waited for the sergeant to bring the prisoner we requested, Ron explained the difference in the prisoners on opposite sides of the cages we'd just walked past.

The prisoners on the left side in the white pants with blue stripes were the trusties. Their behavior was good, and they were not serving time for more serious offenses. The prisoners in the larger cage were known as "gunmen" and were wearing blue jeans with the white stripe on their legs. They were the more hard-core felons, serving time for aggravated and violent offenses like robbery and murder.

With that, the sergeant appeared, escorting a prisoner to us and then returning to the area of the cages. The prisoner wasn't in handcuffs or leg irons. It seemed as though he could simply walk out the back door and disappear if he so desired. As he sat down at the table with us, we identified ourselves, and Ron conducted an interview of him. He claimed to be yet one more victim of his civil rights being violated at the prison. It was a common thread of complaints from the prison, from inmates who had nothing better to do with their time. He claimed there were no witnesses to his problem, so we finished up the interview, and he simply walked back to his cage. At this time, I was not really aware of Judge Keady's rulings at the prison, and unbeknownst to me, many changes were already being implemented as a result of his ruling. For example, Camp 8 was no longer a segregated camp. However, I noted that several trusty guards were still armed, despite his ruling and my own consternation.

As Ron and I walked back down the hallway and out on the front porch, the sergeant asked me if it was my first visit to the prison camp. I told him it was and that I was somewhat surprised at what I saw. He walked us to the end of the front porch and pointed out a series of trees growing inside the rusted chain-link fence a short distance from the building itself. The trees were old, having a diameter of at least one foot or more. Each tree had a white strip painted in a circumference around the trunk, about six feet off the ground or at about eye level. "Know what that white paint on the trees means?" he asked me. I had no idea. "That's called the gun line," he answered. "If an inmate walks past those trees with the white paint, we can shoot them on sight." I replied that was a very interesting fact and probably explained why there weren't a lot of guard towers around the camp perimeter. I could only reflect back on the movie *Cool*

Hand Luke, starring Paul Newman, which came out in 1967. It was a movie that made me think nothing could be worse than being an inmate in that prison, until I saw Parchman with my own eyes. It made *Cool Hand Luke* look like a Sunday school picnic in comparison.

After our little chat with the sergeant, Ron and I left in the car to return to Greenville. At the entrance gate, we stopped at the trusty guard and retrieved our weapons. I opened and checked my revolver cylinder to ensure that all the bullets were still there. As we drove away from the gate, returning our holsters to our belts, I was very grateful that the trusty inmate guard had no obvious beef with the FBI. I returned to Greenville with lots of stories to relate to my wife later that evening. I'd just had a once-in-a-lifetime experience.

My next trip to Parchman was quite different from the first quick trip with Ron. I had taken over responsibility of Sunflower County, and with that, I had full responsibility for federal investigations at Parchman. Once John Neelley assigned me to the county, I wanted to meet the new prison superintendent to let him know I would be his point of contact for the foreseeable future. With all the changes made following the *Gates v. Collier* lawsuit, the staff at the prison seemed to be changing more frequently than it should. I made arrangements with the superintendent's secretary to meet with him at eleven o'clock one summer day in 1973. I drove alone by the usual dusty, boring route, trying to avoid the dangerously overloaded pulpwood trucks that seemed to be all over Mississippi highways driving in reckless fashion.

Upon arrival, I parked my faded-yellow Chevy and entered the welcomed air-conditioned coolness of the administration building. I made some small talk with the ladies in the records section and then went into the superintendent's secretary's office. I introduced myself, and in a minute or two, the new superintendent came out.

He was a former law enforcement officer who had a worthy reputation in the Delta. He invited me into his office, and we chatted for a while to get to know one another better and gain a bit of trust between us. He mentioned the *Gates v. Collier* case and listed the many things the prison was trying to improve as a result of that case. We chatted about the problems in the prison's past. At one point, he got up and walked to his closet. He removed a black leather strap with a heavy leather handle. The strap appeared to be about six inches wide and about five or six feet long. While the leather near the handle of the strap looked to be a quarter inch thick, or perhaps a bit thicker, the bottom end of the strap appeared to be worn paper thin. He explained to me that this was the infamous "Black Annie" that was used for decades to inflict punishment on the prisoners. He said it was no longer used and was now locked away in his office as a relic of Parchman's past. I couldn't help but wonder about the many men who suffered greatly at the hands of some untrained field boss at the prison who would take the use of the lash into his own hands.

We continued a more civil conversation, and as noon approached, the superintendent asked if I would be his guest for lunch. Being far from any decent lunch facility, and eager to learn more of the prison ways, I gladly accepted his offer.

We left the administration building in his air-conditioned car and drove a short distance to his home on the prison campus. I recall entering a lovely southern-style home, built after the Civil War but not too long after. The house was immaculate as the superintendent walked me into his dining room and offered me a seat at the table covered with a white linen tablecloth and set with fine china and gleaming silver utensils. Several other employees entered the dining room shortly after I did, and the superintendent made the appropriate introductions. After we sat down, a very dark-complexioned black man dressed impeccably in a starched white uniform began to serve the noon dinner. After a salad of fresh greens and tomatoes actually grown on the prison grounds, the main course was served, which consisted of delicious chicken in a rich cream sauce. But the best part of the meal was yet to come. Once we had finished, the waiter cleared the dishes and then returned with dessert. The superintendent explained that dessert was homemade English walnut ice cream, served in frosted silver cups. To this day, it was the best-tasting ice cream I've ever eaten. I still wonder whether prison labor prepared the meal, and suspect that they did. I also think our fine waiter was himself a trusty inmate, or perhaps a paroled man who decided to remain on the job at the superintendent's home. Whatever the truth was, the superintendent lived like a king, if this lunch experience was any guide.

I thanked him for a wonderful lunch and mentioned that I needed to get back to Greenville. He let me know that the prison was doing its best to comply with all of Judge Keady's directives in the *Gates v. Collier* case. He pledged his future cooperation whenever I needed it.

On the drive back to Greenville, I could only wonder just how bad the prison had been for the past seventy years. Actually holding the "Black Annie" was like holding a piece of some of the disturbing history of the old South. Having seen Camp 8 with Ron and having passed several other camps that looked just as dismal, I knew there was a long way to go before Parchman would improve to the standards set forth in Judge Keady's rulings. Still, I found Parchman to be a fascinating place, in part due to its storied history, and I looked forward to handling cases in the future that would be assigned to me. I had no idea what would confront me in the days ahead, and I would grow to regret my current excitement about working cases at the prison farm.

In the weeks and months ahead, I found that I was driving to Parchman almost once a week. It might be to cover a case for another FBI office looking for me to review an inmate's file for leads in locating a relative who was wanted for a crime in their respective jurisdiction. At times, there were requests to conduct inmate interviews for various reasons. It wasn't too long before a new superintendent was appointed to run the prison, and with him came more changes to comply with the federal court guidelines. No longer did I have to leave my revolver with a trusty inmate. Mercifully, the system ended while I was there, and I began leaving my weapon with a professional guard who had some training as a prison official. The camps were no longer segregated by race, with both whites and blacks mixed together in the trusty and gunman cages. Little was done to correct the broken physical condition of the camps, however, or the poor sanitation situation, as that would take more time and money to accomplish. But it was very clear to me that things had improved considerably since Judge Keady's ruling.

Of course, the inmates also took advantage of every conceivable way to get around the new rules. With little or no mail censorship, the inmates began frequent correspondence with girlfriends, gun molls, and unknown women who posted ads in magazines like *Lonely Hearts Club*, allegedly looking for companionship. Sadly, these desperate women were so lonely that even a written correspondence relationship with a prisoner brought them great joy, and with it a willingness to help their poor inmate friend in any way possible.

The lack of mail censorship resulted in a number of scams being perpetrated by the ever-crafty inmates. One popular scam was to have a friend mail a few money orders made out in the amount of one dollar and smuggled into the camp in a tin of talcum powder or other similar container that would conceal the currency contraband while not appearing to weigh an unusual amount. The inmates would then open the cans, obtain the contraband, then dump or return the powder after getting the money orders out. Several of the inmates were clever check forgers who could alter the $1 money order to look like a $91 or a $191 money order. The altered money order would be mailed or given back to someone on the outside to cash.

But the biggest scam of all came from the inmates who got their hands on packs of blank counter checks that were issued by the hundreds at all of the local Delta banks. These blank counter checks were easily obtained by the inmates, possibly through the mail or during Sunday visiting hours with friends and family. The inmates then began a process of ordering from mail-order catalogues like Sears, Roebuck & Co.; J. C. Penny; Montgomery Ward; and others. The inmates would fill out an order slip, then type the amount of the order on a blank bank counter check. The completed order would be placed in the mail. Several days or weeks later, the requested item would be delivered to the prison. While the inmate was not allowed to have the item, the item was made available for him to sell for spending money on visiting Sundays.

The scam seemed to be working perfectly, until one day when one of the security departments of the victim stores followed up on the trail of a bad check they received for an order that had already been sent. The destination of the package was the Mississippi State Penitentiary. Since the bad check passed through interstate commerce, the matter became one for the FBI to investigate. And since I was the point of contact for the Mississippi State Penitentiary, the case was assigned to me. At first I thought that I had a simple case of interstate transportation of stolen property. That wouldn't be too difficult to handle. But slowly, the size of the case grew to what was called an FBI major case, due to the sheer volume of subjects and financial loss involved.

At first, it seemed like it was only one or two inmates involved. Somewhat foolishly, the inmates early on in the scheme used their personal Mississippi State Penitentiary inmate number as their bank account number on the blank counter checks. This act made it simpler to identify the inmate who prepared the bad check and received the merchandise. In addition, they started out using their true names on the checks as well as on the order forms. But as the weeks passed, more and more different inmates became involved in the illegal scam against the mail-order stores. Incredibly, the inmates were ordering items like garage-door openers and home security systems. These items would then be sold to visitors and family members who came to the prison on visiting Sunday.

One inmate involved in the scam was Ernest Charles Lewis. While I would like to make him appear to be just the average inmate check forger, Lewis had a much greater history at Parchman. He was serving a life sentence as a result of his participation in an armed robbery with intent to kill at a local service station in Batesville, Mississippi. Also incarcerated at Parchman was his wife, Lucille, who was serving fifteen years for the same offense as her husband.

On February 28, 1972, Ernest Charles Lewis was one of thirty-three inmates riding on a prison bus returning from a prison blood plasma center. During the trip back to the camps, a prison trusty guard, William Shirley, was killed by a shotgun blast to his back as the prisoners commandeered the bus and drove it off the prison grounds. Thirty minutes later, the bus was stopped by the Drew Police Department, and the inmates surrendered. Inmate William McCollum was subsequently indicted and charged with Shirley's murder. On June 12, 1972, McCollum pled not guilty to the murder charge in Indianola Circuit Court. At the same time, thirteen other inmates, including Ernest Lewis, who had been indicted for "escaping by force or violence," pled not guilty at the hearing.[9]

On May 9, 1972, Lewis and his wife, Lucille, filed a petition in federal court alleging they were not allowed the same conjugal visiting privileges as other inmates. They complained that they were only allowed "one monthly visit and that visit being in the presence at all times of penitentiary officials." According to an article in the *Delta Democrat-Times*, the state penitentiary had long had a policy of permitting male inmates to have conjugal visits with their wives. The policy was recently expanded to include conjugal visits for female prisoners. The Lewis couple maintained they were not given the same privileges as other inmates, charging that the denial of conjugal visits represented cruel and unusual punishment and caused "marital strain."[10]

That was not the last time anything was heard from inmate Ernest Lewis. One month later, on June 21, 1972, the trial started in the murder of trusty guard William Shirley. Then considered a witness for the defense, Ernest Lewis took the stand and blurted out, "It's my understanding that W. L. McCollum has tried to enter a guilty plea. Therefore, I'm going to take the Fifth Amendment." With that comment, circuit court judge B. B. Wilkes immediately declared a mistrial. Prior to his comment, Lewis had been asked by the defense attorney if he would mind telling the court how many times in the past he had been convicted of a crime. Lewis's

---

9. Ed Issa, Staff Writer, *Delta Democrat-Times*, June 13, 1972.
10. UPI, State Briefs, *Delta Democrat-Times*, May 10, 1972.

answer, "Yes, I do mind," came just prior to his outburst comment about McCollum.[11]

The trial date was then moved to October 1972, after my arrival in Greenville. I had yet to visit the Parchman farm or interview any inmates. On October 18–19, 1972, the prosecution presented its case and rested. Testimony from James G. Powell, a former inmate, showed that he saw McCollum shoot Shirley in the back with a sawed-off shotgun. Ernest Lewis was again called to the stand to testify as to what he observed during the killing. This time, he appeared quiet and reserved and answered questions. Following the testimony of four inmates, the case went to the jury at 4:20 p.m. They returned with a "not guilty" verdict one hour and ten minutes later. McCollum, who was serving a sentence for a strong-armed robbery in 1971, was returned to Parchman to complete his original sentence.[12]

But that wasn't the end for Ernest Lewis. On March 15, 1973, Lewis and thirteen other inmates used some sort of hacksaw blade to cut their way out of Camp 8 and disappeared into a heavy rain. All but two of the prisoners were recaptured by noon the following day. Lewis, age twenty-six, and Lester Lee Thomas, age twenty-one and serving a rape conviction, had gotten away. Lewis was white and Thomas was black. Since the twelve inmates arrested never made it off the prison grounds, they were not charged with escape but were to be punished at the prison. On March 19, Lewis was captured while he hid in a barn on the vast grounds of the Parchman prison. His associate, Lester Lee Thomas, remained at large.[13]

Lewis still could not stay out of the news. On August 29, 1973, he and three other fellow inmates filed a lawsuit against state prison officials, charging that the canteen system at the prison facility violated federal antitrust laws. The suit, another frivolous effort by a lifer with nothing better to do with his time, alleged that the canteen, operated by prison officials and trusty inmates, charged excessively high prices because it was

---

11. *Ed Issa, Staff Writer, Delta Democrat-Times,* June 22, 1972.
12. *Ed Issa, Staff Writer, Delta Democrat-Times,* October 20, 1972.
13. *Bill Rose, State Editor, Delta Democrat-Times,* March 16–20, 1973.

a monopoly. They wanted excessive and illegal profits to be returned to the inmates. I was unable to identify any outcome for this particular suit in which Lewis was involved.[14]

As I received the evidence from the security departments of the victim stores, as well as the bad checks that were returned to them, I began keeping a list of the inmates who were involved in the scam. I put the bad counter checks in plastic envelopes to protect any fingerprint evidence and sent the evidence to the FBI Identification Division for fingerprint comparison. A request was also made of the FBI laboratory to examine each document as well for handwriting comparison with suspected inmates. In order to do that with any degree of success, I needed to obtain handwriting samples from the inmate suspects I thought were involved in the scam. That meant more frequent trips to Parchman, and I subsequently began visiting the prison three days a week.

Most of the inmates who were suspected of writing a bad counter check, and who used their true name and inmate number, were interviewed as criminal suspects, complete with their advice of rights read to them before proceeding with the interview. Handwriting samples were taken only if the inmate volunteered to do so. And, surprisingly enough, most inmates did provide handwriting samples. It was as if they were enjoying playing a game, knowing they weren't being released anytime soon and had nothing to lose in the check-writing scam.

Ernest Lewis was one of the first inmate names that appeared on the counterfeit bank counter checks. On one of my next trips to Parchman, I wanted to conduct an interview of Lewis to determine his role in the scam. I arrived at the prison and reviewed his file. At the present time, he was incarcerated in the maximum-security unit on the prison farm. He was also serving a life sentence for an armed robbery complete with intent to

---

14. *Delta Democrat-Times*, August 30, 1973.

kill with assault and battery. His escape record was also in the file. He was obviously a hard-core prisoner with absolutely nothing to lose, and he had demonstrated his total lack of respect for authority during his stay. And it was possible that he had some involvement in the murder of prison trusty William Shirley on the bus just a year or two ago. I was a bit apprehensive as I drove to the maximum-security unit to conduct my interview.

Upon arrival at the unit, I was pleased to see that there was finally a prison building that looked like what I always expected a prison to be. A strong fence secured by both barbed wire and razor wire and manned guard towers surrounded a solid-looking concrete-and-brick building. I parked my car in a visitor spot and entered the main door. I left my gun in a secure gun vault before gaining access to the prison. I was then buzzed inside the first set of steel-bar doors and waited to be buzzed into a second set of secure doors while those behind me closed first. There I was met by a guard who escorted me to a shabby interview room with a small, gray metal desk and two metal chairs with seats covered in green vinyl. I was told to wait there while the guard brought inmate Lewis in to see me.

In a few minutes, Lewis and I met for the first time. He was a bit shorter and thinner than I imagined. But he had a look in his inflamed, red eyes that was a bit haunting, and he perhaps tried to be a bit intimidating. I identified myself to him with my FBI credentials and told him I was there to ask questions about some illegal check writing. I advised him of his rights, and he signed an Advice of Rights and Waiver form, the standard form we used in the FBI at the time. I showed him a copy of the check I suspected him of writing, and he admitted that he wrote and sent the check to a mail-order company for merchandise. The interview was going better than I expected, as I had thought he would not speak to me at all. He even provided some handwriting samples as I requested.

When I asked him why he wrote the bad check, he looked at me and simply said, "Why not. I'm doing life in this place and have nothing to lose. What else can they do to me, give me another life sentence? Besides, it's something to do to pass the time."

He denied knowing any other inmates involved in the check-writing scam and refused to tell me where he got access to the blank counter checks. When it was clear that no more information was forthcoming, I thanked him for his time and summoned the guard to take Lewis back to his cell and me back to the freedom outside. I had my first confession in the case and was looking forward to contacting the assistant US attorney for his prosecutive opinion in this matter.

Many of the inmates involved in the scam freely admitted doing so, not at all worried about additional sentencing as they were already serving a life sentence and had no hope of ever being released, just like Ernest Lewis. The prison officials were handicapped in trying to stop the scam from continuing as they were powerless to begin censoring inmate mail, something that was stopped under Judge Keady's ruling in 1972.

In order to try to eliminate some of the problem, I met with the mail-order security people in an effort to see what they could do to delay mailing merchandise to the prison address, or at least wait until the checks cleared before shipping merchandise to the alleged purchaser. They explained to me that when a check and order arrived at the mail-order facility, the check was examined to see that the amount was correct for the merchandise ordered. The check was then sent off in one direction while the order was sent to the warehouse to be filled and shipped to the customer. There was no waiting period for the check to clear the bank. In most of the cases at the prison, the merchandise was shipped before it was determined that the check was invalid. Hence, the problem continued at the prison with no end in sight.

Fingerprint examination and handwriting analysis began to identify more inmates involved in the scam. However, it was difficult to determine if an inmate identified on a check by his name and inmate number was the actual inmate who prepared the fraudulent check. While FBI laboratory analysis and latent-fingerprint examination were very valuable tools, they did not always positively identify a specific inmate with every fraudulent check written.

I contacted Assistant US Attorney Alfred E. Moreton III and briefed him on the ongoing case. I worked with Al on most of my criminal cases in the Delta. He was an experienced and excellent attorney assigned to the US Attorney's Office, Northern District of Mississippi in Oxford. Al was willing to prosecute those check cases where we would be able to identify the inmate responsible with available physical evidence like fingerprints or handwriting, as well as those inmates who may have confessed to the crime.

The list of potential inmate suspects continued to grow, resulting in more evidence being sent to the laboratory and to the Identification Division. Some inmates, the smarter ones, refused to provide handwriting samples and refused FBI interviews. The case was running at a painstakingly slow pace as I awaited lab results and attempted to identify additional inmates in the scam. The mail-order companies were frustrated in their inability to directly address the problems at their end, and they were seeking immediate relief from the FBI. It was clear that something had to be done to stop the inmates before this matter got much worse. At last, some relief finally appeared on the horizon.

On April 23, 1974,[15] a hearing was held in the US district court in Greenville, with Judge Keady presiding. The hearing had the express purpose of determining whether or not additional censoring of inmates' mail should be allowed, after it had been banned by Keady's original order in October 1972. During the hearing, Mississippi State Assistant Attorney General Jim Ward called upon Internal Revenue Service agents, a postal inspector, a highway patrol investigator, two Parchman security employees, and me in an attempt to demonstrate that the current problems at the prison were the result of the inmates' use of the mail without censure. Ward identified a number of issues, including the forging of bank counter checks, obscene and threatening letters, and illegal drugs, as well as a "refund mill" in which inmates applied for illegal refunds from the Internal Revenue Service. During my testimony, I testified that one

---

15. Ed Kohn, *Staff Writer, Delta Democrat Times,* April 26, 1974.

inmate had already admitted his part in the check-forging scheme. I also testified that to date, the names of thirty inmates had been used to purchase merchandise illegally.

There were lots of lawyers present in the courtroom, and my testimony was often interrupted with objections from both sides of the lawyers' tables. It seemed to me that no one wanted me to talk about my knowledge of the problems at the prison. Frustrated by the constant objections to my testimony, I looked over at Judge Keady and said, "They won't let me answer the question." Judge Keady looked out from the bench and said to all, "Let him speak." I continued with my testimony that to date I had already sent fifty-some checks to the FBI laboratory for examination and analysis. I also testified that merchandise was ordered illegally from nineteen different companies located in eleven different states. The total loss in money to date was $7,800 (1974 dollars) in merchandise. On cross-examination, I had to admit that it was possible that one inmate could have forged all the checks sent to the mail-order houses, even though I was confident that more than one inmate was involved. Following my testimony about the counter-check scam at the prison, I was dismissed and left the courtroom to return to work.

On April 25, 1974, after listening to two days of testimony in his courtroom, Judge Keady agreed to temporarily permit Mississippi State Penitentiary guards to read all of the inmates' incoming and outgoing mail at the prison's seventeen camps, including the maximum-security unit. Quoted in the *Delta Democrat-Times* newspaper on April 26, 1974, Keady said, "If the process slows the delivery of the mail down, so be it. The state has made a convincing showing that some things need to be revised" (referring to his previous court order banning censorship of inmate mail). He ruled that prison authorities have a "routine right to inspect" the inmates' mail for obscenity, extortion attempts, and attempts at fraud.

Following Judge Keady's ruling at the hearing, I was thrilled at the outcome. It simply made no sense to allow the inmates to continue a pattern of fraud and other criminal activities when such activity could be eliminated by a simple review of inmate mail. I hoped that his ruling would bring a sudden stop to the counter-check scam at the prison, even though I knew that enterprising convicts would likely figure out other ways to continue to perpetrate their lucrative scams. I still had many pending examinations by the laboratory and Identification Division to await results, and more inmate interviews to accomplish. The case would continue for some time in the future.

Al Moreton was happy to learn that Ernest Lewis had confessed to his role in the check scam at Parchman. I gave him copies of all the physical evidence I had obtained pertaining to Lewis as well as a report of his confession to the crime. It came as no surprise to either of us that Lewis entered a plea of not guilty to the charges. Why not—as he said to me, "What do I have to lose?" Being at trial was probably more interesting than sitting alone in the maximum-security unit. His earlier confession to me as well as the overwhelming physical evidence tying him to the fraud was pretty much all we needed for a jury to return a commonsense guilty verdict. On June 18, 1975, a jury in the US District Court for the Northern District of Mississippi convicted Lewis of five mail-fraud counts, violations of Title 18 (sections 2 and 1341) of the United States Code. Specifically, these counts charged that Lewis, while an inmate at the Mississippi State Penitentiary, had engaged in a scheme to defraud mail-order companies by ordering merchandise and submitting forged or worthless checks in payment for the ordered items.[16]

In keeping with his high profile as an inmate at Parchman, Lewis wasn't finished just yet. Just one month after his federal conviction for mail fraud, the *Delta Democrat-Times* newspaper on July 17, 1975, reported that Lewis and three other inmates at the penitentiary filed yet another suit against the prison, this time seeking $5 million in damages. This lawsuit

---

16. United States v. Ernest Charles Lewis, No. 75-2707.

charged that inmates in the maximum-security unit were receiving cruel and unusual punishment and being denied due process of law. The suit charged that maintenance of a maximum-security unit was "dehumanizing to both prisoners and keepers." The suit further charged that the prisoners received no hearing or reason before they were placed in the maximum-security unit, in violation of the prisoners' right to due process. The suit alleged that prisoners must spend twenty-three to twenty-four hours a day in a cell with seventeen feet of space (not further identified) without any sort of recreational or rehabilitative program. One of the plaintiffs, Hytze Eugene Evans, claimed he had not seen the light of day since December 1974. The suit also contended that their food contained sand, insects, and filth. In addition, the lawsuit claimed that prisoners in the maximum-security unit were in constant fear of beatings from guards and that prisoners' mail was tampered with and restricted. The lawsuit also asked the court for an injunction enjoining the prison from harassing and punishing the plaintiffs because of their participation in the lawsuit.

How interesting is it that an inmate, given mail privileges and privacy by a federal judge in October 1972, used the freedom to his advantage by getting involved in a large mail-fraud scam as soon as possible. And then, on the heels of his conviction for mail fraud, filed a $5 million lawsuit, again alleging that in part, prisoners' mail was being tampered with and restricted. Like he told me, "I have nothing to lose."

Of course, Ernest Lewis filed an appeal to his federal sentence for mail fraud at first chance as well, claiming two issues. First, he claimed the trial court erred in allowing a witness to respond to questions concerning an independent investigation of money-order fraud at the prison, on the ground that this constituted inadmissible evidence of his possible commission of a separate and distinct offense. The challenged testimony was merely designed to correct the defense's insinuation during cross-examination of the witness that the defendant had already been subjected to prison disciplinary measures because of the offense for which he was being charged. The Court of Appeals for the Fifth Circuit found that a defendant cannot complain on appeal of alleged errors invited or induced by himself, particularly where, as here, it is not clear that the defendant was prejudiced thereby.

Lewis's second contention was that admissions attributed to him by an FBI agent (me) were obtained as a result of the "coercive atmosphere that pervades the maximum-security unit" at Parchman. He claimed he was promised by Eugene R. Mailly, assistant chief of security at Parchman at the time of his trial, that he would be released from the maximum-security unit if he confessed. The trial court's contrary finding, after a midtrial suppression hearing held out of the presence of the jury, that Lewis's confession was voluntary, is not clearly erroneous. Not only does the record contain Mailly's testimony that no such promise was made, but there is additional evidence that at the time of the alleged coercive bargain, Mailly was merely an internal security investigator, had only been at Parchman fourteen days, and lacked authority even to suggest such an arrangement. Moreover, the time and circumstances suggest that Mailly would have had at best minimal advance notice that the FBI agent who received the confession would be interviewing Lewis on the day when the admission occurred. Thus, on December 17, 1975, the Court of Appeals for the Fifth Circuit affirmed the defendant's conviction. That would thankfully be the last dealing I had with Ernest Charles Lewis.

Al Moreton and I secured the conviction of another inmate on fraud charges. In fact, he seemed to be responsible for writing more of the fraudulent checks than most of the others involved in the case. Those two convictions, coupled with Judge Keady's review and subsequent revised order again allowing inspection of the inmates' mail by prison authorities, seemed to stop the ongoing bad-check scam. In an effort to resolve all remaining open cases, the FBI laboratory and Identification Division continued their efforts to positively identify any other inmates who were responsible for writing fraudulent checks. Another new prison superintendent along with a better-trained and professional prison guard force helped reduce a lot of the problems that had existed for years at Parchman. I was certainly thankful for that, and I suspect many of the inmates who were looking forward to doing their jail time and being released were thankful as well. Civil rights complaints continued to emanate from the prison with their usual frequency, but most of them seemed to be without any substance. I still usually made a weekly trip to the Mississippi State Penitentiary but was pleased that the greater problems had finally been addressed and corrected as best they could be, until a new, more modern prison facility could be constructed at some time in the future.

CHAPTER 17
THE BLUES

I would sit on the street corners in my hometown, Indianola, Mississippi, and I would play. And, generally, I would start playing gospel songs.

—B. B. KING

As surprised as I was to learn about country-western music when I first attended those Friday evening dances held at the Downtowner hotel when Donna and I arrived in Greenville, I was even more surprised that the Mississippi Delta had a music genre it could call its own. The style of music known as "the blues" has reportedly grown out of several southern states, including Mississippi, Louisiana, and Texas, from sometime after the Civil War, as early as the 1890s. The music has a signature style of its own, and not one being familiar with music style, I cannot explain its exact notation and the note sequence that makes the music distinctly the blues. Suffice it to say, the words written and sung to blues music often originated from the black populations working in the fields. Much of it refers to hard times spent in slavery or working as sharecroppers during those difficult years. Stories of love and relationships made and broken, and stories of lives torn apart by stints in prison and other tales of the drudgery of life fill the blues music with a history of the persecuted black worker. At times the songs reflect hope that a new day and promise of deliverance is about to dawn. Many of the songs were developed out of popular Christian hymns, African-American spirituals, or were verses made up during a prison stay. Truth be told, during the early 1970s while I was assigned in Greenville, I rarely heard any blues music and had little interest in it.

Some of the more notable Mississippi native bluesmen were Muddy Waters, who was born in Rolling Fork, Sharkey County; David Honeyboy Edwards, born in Shaw, Bolivar County; and John Lee Hooker, born in Clarksdale, Coahoma County. Other famous Delta bluesmen were Robert Johnson, Charley Patton, Howlin' Wolf, and Son House, all from Mississippi. The most famous of all, B. B. King, was born on a cotton plantation in Berclair, in Leflore County, near Greenwood. However, King claimed Indianola as his home.

About all I knew of the blues was that Elvis Presley started his career after growing up in Tupelo, Mississippi, and listening to local blues music as a boy. I knew some of his songs incorporated blues lyrics, and that he added his own signature style of rock and roll to his music. I've since learned that almost every genre of popular music has its roots in blues music, with the exception of classical music, which far predates the blues. It did not seem to me like there was any place to go to listen to blues music in Greenville, or for that matter, anywhere else in our six-county area, unless some local honky-tonk or juke joint in the black section of town had someone who was entertaining there. Of course, there was never any advertisement in any local newspapers or on television for such a concert or performance. Such programs would only pass by word of mouth through the black community and would be attended by blacks only living in a black section of town. That's just how it seemed to be back in the day.

Even if I wanted to explore blues music, I had no time to learn or appreciate the genre of the blues, as I had no familiarity with it at the time. There was little to offer from a cultural standpoint in Greenville that was openly available to all citizens at the time. And I was still busy with my family responsibilities and my job. In fact, things stayed fairly interesting at work.

On Friday, January 19, 1973, a few of us were sitting around in the office at about noon, wondering where we would go for lunch. It was a relatively warm day in Greenville, unlike the often damp, chilly Delta days of winter. As we discussed restaurant options, the telephone rang in John Neelley's office. A minute or two later, he announced to all that lunch would have to be put on hold as there had just been a bank robbery at the Bank of Hollandale in Glen Allan, Mississippi. Glen Allen was the farthest town in the southern end of Washington County, bordering on Issaquena County. It would be John's case to handle. He asked Joe Lattus and me to drive together, and he took Ray Mislock with him. The other agents were out of the office at the time of the call. We quickly grabbed our gear, including the Speed Graphic camera, packed up, and headed out. This would be my first bank robbery investigation since arriving in Greenville, and bank robberies were always exciting to work.

Joe and I arrived at the bank about the same time John and Ray did. Harvey Tackett, Washington County sheriff, had already arrived with a deputy or two. We entered the bank and began with our investigation, conducting an interview of the victim teller, the only person present in the bank at the time of the robbery, and conducting a crime-scene investigation, dusting for latent fingerprints and checking to see if the bank had any surveillance cameras. Following John and Harvey's interview of the victim teller, they shared the details of the case to date.[17]

The teller described the robber as a black male wearing a white gauze patch over one eye, a pair of sunglasses, and a long, gray overcoat. He was carrying a small revolver, and she thought he was going to kill her. The robber said to her, "I'm sorry about this, but someone in Chicago is forcing me to do this, and y'all will catch the people who are responsible." The teller asked him to put the gun away once, and she twice asked him to point the barrel away from her. He replied, "Just do what I say, or I'll kill you." He then told the teller, "There are seven or eight people outside watching you, and if you move, they will come in and kill you. Just stay where you are, and in a few minutes, someone will come in and tell you what to do."

Once the bank robbery had occurred and been reported, the sheriff's office, Greenville Police Department, Mississippi Highway Patrol, and the Hollandale Police Department set up roadblocks throughout the county. I don't recall for certain how we actually came up with a suspect so fast in this bank robbery, but within five hours of the robbery, we had identified a suspect and responded to an address where he resided with his sister near Glen Allan. But if I'm not mistaken, I believe that Jimmy Lee, the suspect, actually wrote a brief demand note on the back of a piece of paper that he first handed to the teller. It was not a complete message, and when she looked up at him to decipher the short note, that's when he announced the robbery. Jimmy Lee's biggest mistake was that he wrote his robbery demand note on the back side of a personal bank check that contained his preprinted name and address on the front side.

At about eight that evening, after obtaining warrants for a search of the residence and his arrest, FBI agents and sheriff's deputies entered the house. Jimmy Lee, a thirty-three-year-old tractor-trailer truck driver was arrested at the scene for the bank robbery. He had been living with his

---

17. *Delta Democrat-Times*, January 21, 1973.

sister since separating from his wife and three children in 1967. His family also lived in the Glen Allan area. Lee was a truck driver making runs to Louisiana and to South Carolina. A search of Lee's sister's residence resulted in the recovery of most of the money taken from the bank, a total of $4,500. Lee admitted that he only earned $200 a month for his truck driving.

John Neelley ordered Joe Lattus and me to put Lee in handcuffs, place him in the rear seat of John's FBI vehicle, and watch him until John was ready to return him to Greenville. After doing so, as we waited for John to take the prisoner away, Lee's sister came outside and approached the car. When Jimmy Lee saw her, he apologized to her for robbing the bank. His apology was overheard by Joe and me. John and Ray Mislock eventually took Lee to the Greenville City Jail, where he was lodged for the night until he could be brought before a magistrate for a bond hearing.

The following morning, Lee was brought before Greenville Federal Magistrate David Orlansky for a bond hearing. The magistrate set bond for Lee in the amount of $25,000 and remanded him to the custody of the Greenville City Jail in lieu of bail. He told Lee that he would find a court-appointed attorney for him on Monday, and he set a preliminary hearing date for Lee for Friday, January 26, 1973.[18]

On the day of Jimmy Lee's preliminary hearing, things got a bit more interesting in the case. Joe Lattus and I were the only FBI agents called to testify, mostly because we overheard him apologize to his sister for committing the bank robbery. Al Moreton was the assistant US attorney who presented the government's case to Magistrate Orlansky. Joe Lattus was the first to be called to testify as to the confession he heard from Jimmy Lee. During cross-examination by Lee's court-appointed attorney, James E. Upshaw, Lattus became frustrated on the stand. In fairness to Joe, he was not aware of a lot of details in the case, as all he was there to testify to was the confession he heard. However, Lee's attorney continued to press Lattus as to why he didn't advise Lee of his right to remain silent, and why he couldn't answer a lot of the questions posed to him. Following

18. *Delta Democrat-Times*, January 26, 1973.

Joe's testimony, and not having heard any of the difficulty he was having as a result of being kept out of the courtroom, I had less trouble with the defense attorney. I simply stated that while standing next to the subject as he sat in the FBI car, I heard him apologize to his sister for robbing the bank. I suppose the defense attorney made his point with Joe and didn't want to go over it all again with me.

When I finished, the defense attorney stated that the most obvious person who should be at the hearing was the victim bank teller. However, after all of the attorney's ranting about what he saw as the FBI's handling of the case in a "rather shabby, shoddy manner," Al Moreton reminded him and the court that Jimmy Lee was not on trial, and that he was merely seeking enough evidence to bind him over to the grand jury. Magistrate Orlansky advised Lee's attorney that hearsay evidence and questionably obtained information were permitted as evidence in a preliminary hearing, according to a new federal rule for criminal procedure. The hearing ended, and Lee was again remanded to jail in lieu of bail.[19]

Following the hearing, as Joe and I went back to the office, he told me how badly he had been grilled by Lee's defense attorney. I had to laugh, as Joe was the largest man in the office, and a guy we always wanted with us on any kind of raid situation. It was funny to see such a tough guy get beaten up by a defense attorney. But, I suppose, better Joe than me.

On March 30, 1973, before Federal District Court Judge William Keady, Jimmy Lee pled guilty to robbing the Glen Allan branch of the Bank of Hollandale. Assistant US Attorney Will Ford reviewed the government's evidence before Judge Keady accepted Jimmy Lee's guilty plea. Lee admitted the robbery but denied making any threats to the bank teller. All of the $4,500 taken from the bank had been recovered from a bag found hidden in Lee's sister's attic. Judge Keady scheduled sentencing for April 27, 1973.[20] Despite my best efforts, I have not been able to locate the sentence given to Jimmy Lee by Judge Keady.

---

19. Penny Jenkins, Staff Writer, *Delta Democrat-Times*, January 28, 1973.
20. Bill Vaughn, Staff Writer, *Delta-Democrat Times*, April 1 1973.

The Blues

Things weren't always that exciting in the FBI resident agency. I'm highlighting some of the more interesting cases, assignments, and experiences I incurred during my time in Mississippi. In the downtime in the office, it would be prudent to catch up on dictation, look through cases that hadn't received much attention, and try to keep them up to date. It was also a good time to meet with informants who were developed by the individual agents.

Informants were the heart and soul of the FBI in terms of cracking cases. There was constant pressure by the supervisory staff for each agent to develop quality informants as a significant part of an agent's assignment. There was no doubt about the effectiveness of informants. One only has to look at all the successes the FBI had in the early rounds of fighting racial injustice in Mississippi. In many cases, it was an informant who broke the major cases involving lynchings, bombings, and murders in the 1960s. It wasn't easy to develop quality informants, but the agents persisted and did so. As time passed, and the size and activity of hate groups waned, so did the availability of those types of quality informants. But it was still important to have sources who knew what was going on in the small Delta towns.

For me, having good informants meant knowing decent folks in all of the towns and counties where I was assigned. They didn't have to be part of the Ku Klux Klan or members of a black extremist group, just an informed group of citizens of the town in which they lived, willing to sit down with me over a cup of chicory coffee and talk about what was going on. Maintaining quality liaison with local law enforcement officials was a big part of keeping abreast of developments in the counties I was assigned to as well. A lot of agents struggled with informant development, but I found it somewhat enjoyable, as long as I didn't expect spectacular results right away.

One of my best informants at the time developed out of a small kindness to a young child and the subsequent soft pressure with his parent to assist in locating a dangerous fugitive who was about to be placed on the FBI's Ten Most Wanted Fugitives list. All I really did was prevent the child from choking on a twist tie that got stuck in his throat. I was sitting close enough to him to hear him start gagging, and I reached into his mouth to retrieve the twist tie.

The particular fugitive in question, Curtis Ray Michelson, a white male, was wanted in connection with the robbery of the First National Bank of Nevada in Reno on September 27, 1974. He and three others were suspects in this bank robbery. Michelson was also wanted for escape from the federal prison camp at McNeil Island on January 15, 1973, where he was serving a sentence for bank robbery with assault. Michelson was considered an armed and dangerous fugitive bank robber. My informant had a small piece of information that, when forwarded and put together with information from other sources, coupled with FBI investigative efforts throughout the country, resulted in the safe apprehension of Michelson, without shots being fired. As I recall, Michelson had vowed that he would not be taken alive.

This small example, spread out among Americans living all over the United States, shows how valuable the common citizen can be. Without a doubt, the good citizens of the United States, in cooperating with local, state, and federal law enforcement agencies, are what make those agencies great at succeeding at their jobs.

As more time passed, our local Greenville Resident Agency began to change as well. Joe Lattus, the only single agent in the office, was given a transfer to the Oxford, Mississippi, Resident Agency. I don't recall why he wanted to leave Greenville, with the possible exception of the availability of the University of Mississippi for additional education opportunities, as well as the greater possibility of more contact with single co-eds, which may have helped his decision. Once Joe left, he was not replaced, and we were down to just six agents.

The next guy to go was Ray Mislock. Since Ray was a first-office agent, we all knew he would be transferred to a second office after a year or so. As it was, Ray stayed on a bit longer than a year, actually completing an eighteen-month tour of duty. Still, his transfer was a bit of a blow to me, as he was a good friend, great coworker, and fellow golfer and poker player.

His wife and mine got along well, and we had very young sons nearly the same age. Ray's transfer came in, and I think he was very happy to find he had been transferred to the Los Angeles office. From the rural Mississippi Delta to one of the largest offices in the FBI, his transfer would bring on many new challenges and experiences. For sure, there would be no shortage of interesting work in Los Angeles. Again, once Ray left, our office became smaller yet again, as he was not replaced with another agent in a first office assignment.

On October 18, 1974, I was headed to Indianola. The last of the cotton crop had been harvested for a second time to gather the remaining bolls that survived the first harvest. The fertile fields were mostly brown now, with just a scattered, flimsy cotton boll to be seen clinging desperately to its mother plant, refusing to surrender to the combine looking to pull it away. It was a nice day, as fall was one of the nicest seasons in the Delta, with lower humidity and pleasant temperatures than most other seasons. I was asked to travel to the Sunflower County Sheriff's Office in order to take fingerprints from a subject the county had in custody. He was a suspect in an interstate stolen car matter, a federal offense. Cole David Hammontree, age twenty-one, of Atlanta, Georgia, had been arrested a week earlier for attempted assault on a woman he was visiting in Indianola, and she made the complaint against him. While investigating the matter, the woman told the Indianola police officer that Hammontree had stolen a gun from her residence and likely had it in his possession.

Hammontree was subsequently located and arrested by Patrolman Bob Atkinson of the Indianola Police Department while driving in his car. Hammontree granted Patrolman Atkinson permission to search his vehicle. During the search, Atkinson found the stolen handgun in the trunk of the car, along with a small amount of marijuana in a bag. He then transported Hammontree to the county jail, where he was being held on the assault charge. A subsequent check of Hammontree's vehicle through the National Crime Information Center (NCIC) system determined that the car in his possession had been stolen in Mobile, Alabama. I was dispatched to the county jail to fingerprint Hammontree in connection with the alleged theft of that car and subsequent interstate transportation of a stolen motor vehicle.

After arriving at the Sunflower County Courthouse, I stopped into the sheriff's office and met with Sheriff Sessums. We talked about a variety of topics before I asked him to take me upstairs to the jail on the third floor so I could fingerprint Hammontree. We walked up the steps, and the sheriff asked the jailer to bring Hammontree to the fingerprint processing area. A few minutes later, the jailer appeared with Hammontree and a deputy who removed his handcuffs so he could be fingerprinted. I had already rolled out the black ink on the glass plate and prepared two sets of federal fingerprint cards to use. Hammontree was very compliant and was easy to fingerprint. When I had finished, I handed Hammontree some cleaning solution and a couple of paper towels so he could wipe the ink off of his fingers. The jailer and deputy remained with me during the entire time I took the fingerprints.

As Hammontree tossed the dirty paper towels into a waste container, while in the custody of the jailer, he suddenly bolted from the room, running across the next room to a small, open doorway. He must have seen the open doorway on his way in to be fingerprinted, as he was quickly outside the door and onto the roof of the courthouse. By the time the deputy, jailer, and I reached the open door, Hammontree, perhaps thinking he could fly, had leaped off the roof in a failed attempt to escape. Perhaps he was not aware he was on a roof three stories high. Or maybe he did know that and thought he would survive the three-story fall and be able to run off. In either case, he was sadly mistaken. As we reached the edge of the roof and looked down on the ground, Hammontree lay sprawled facedown on the grass surrounding the building. An ambulance was summoned, and Hammontree was taken to the University Medical Center in Jackson, where he was listed in stable condition. I prepared a statement of the incident for the sheriff and returned to the FBI office with the fingerprint cards. They would need to be sent to the FBI Identification Division in Washington, DC, for classification and examination. It had been a very unusual morning to say the least.

Indianola Police Chief Herman Steed later advised that the assault charge against Hammontree was dropped by the victim of the attempted assault. Hammontree was being held until his health improved so that he could be turned over to the Mobile, Alabama, authorities on the auto-theft charge. Steed informed us that although Hammontree was suffering from a dislocated vertebra and a cracked pelvis, he was in stable condition.[21]

Just as I was beginning to adjust to life in the office without Joe and Ray, we were hit with yet another transfer. This time it was Ken White-Spunner who received a transfer to the Gulfport, Mississippi, Resident Agency. Apparently Gulfport needed agents more than Greenville did because Ken was not replaced. That left only John, Chuck, Ron, and me to cover the entire six-county Delta territory. Ken was another fine man, a great friend, and an experienced FBI special agent. His presence would definitely be missed in the office, and we were all sorry to see him go, yet happy for him for a transfer of his choosing.

With the transfer of almost half of the office, I was beginning to wonder if I was going to be assigned to Greenville for the rest of my career. A few months earlier, I had asked for a transfer to the Jackson office to serve as a relief supervisor in an effort to see if administrative advancement was something I would consider for my future in the FBI. It was also an effort to move to a more populous city and escape some of the boredom of the Delta. My wife was looking forward to having better shops and stores, and we hoped the school system in Jackson and its surrounding suburban communities would be somewhat better than what we knew existed in Greenville. My wife and I began growing tired of our stay in rural Mississippi, and we were considering other options available to us.

The transfer-to-Jackson option did not pan out as I had hoped it would. I was advised that there were simply no openings in Jackson for any transfers into the office. My request for relief supervisor would therefore have to be put on hold. At about the same time I made my transfer request, one of the agents assigned to the Greenwood, Mississippi, Resident Agency

---

21. *Delta-Democrat-Times*, October 22, 1974.

had decided he'd had enough of the Delta and requested a transfer to New York City. At that particular time in the FBI, the New York City office was the largest in the entire country (and still remains that way today). Any agent crazy enough to ask for a transfer to New York City was guaranteed to get it in a matter of a few short weeks. The cost of living in New York was the highest in the nation, and there was no cost-of-living adjustment made to an FBI agent's pay based upon his office location at the time. So a transfer to New York City would result in the same paycheck with a ton of increased expenses, taxes, and a very costly mortgage.

Before Donna and I ever reached Greenville, we had discussed an assignment so far from both of our homes. We had hoped to rent an apartment for a year, and if we did not like living in Greenville, we knew we always had that one option to ask for a transfer to New York. After being unable to find a suitable apartment for rent upon our arrival, we ended up purchasing a home, which did turn out to be a good financial move for us. Coupled with the addition of our first son one year later, we really did not have any time to think about a transfer out to New York City. And we were enjoying newfound friends and new activities. But we began spending all two weeks of my vacation time returning home for visits. Two different trips, one during the summer and one at Christmastime, depleted all of my accrued annual leave. Donna would fly home to Ohio a week before me with our son to visit with her folks. I would fly up the following Friday evening and visit until Wednesday, the middle of the week. Then we would fly together to my parents' home, where I would stay until Sunday evening before flying back to Greenville.

Donna would remain another week so the grandparents could have more time with their firstborn grandchild. It was hard on everyone to be so far away and to have so little time to be together. A transfer to New York City would have us only a short drive to all of our relatives, and just a two-hour trip to the Stone Harbor, New Jersey, seashore.

With the transfers of Joe, Ray, and Ken, and Marty's transfer from Greenwood to New York City, we both began to feel those other kind of blues to some extent. It did not seem like there was any realistic way we would ever be transferred out of Greenville to another office. We began to contemplate the actual possibility of asking for a transfer to New York City. If not that, were we ready to spend the rest of our lives in the Mississippi Delta? Just the thought of such a radical change in lifestyle began to affect my health.

Shortly after our arrival in Greenville, we'd met a couple, Bill and Margie Leunig, who were living in Greenville but came from New York City. We spent a lot of social time with them in Greenville and enjoyed their company. They were a great resource to have as we talked about a possible transfer to New York. During one of our vacation trips to Cheltenham, Pennsylvania, Donna and I drove to New York City and met with Bill and Margie. They took us on a lengthy tour of the city. As we crossed the Brooklyn Bridge heading into lower Manhattan at night, the lights of the city were simply breathtaking, especially knowing there were no visible lights anywhere in the Delta at this very time. Was all this glitter and glitz of the famed Big Apple really the answer to our boredom in the Delta? That was something we would continue to discuss as the days passed by in the oppressive Mississippi heat of early spring.

Working at my desk, Greenville Resident Agency, 1973

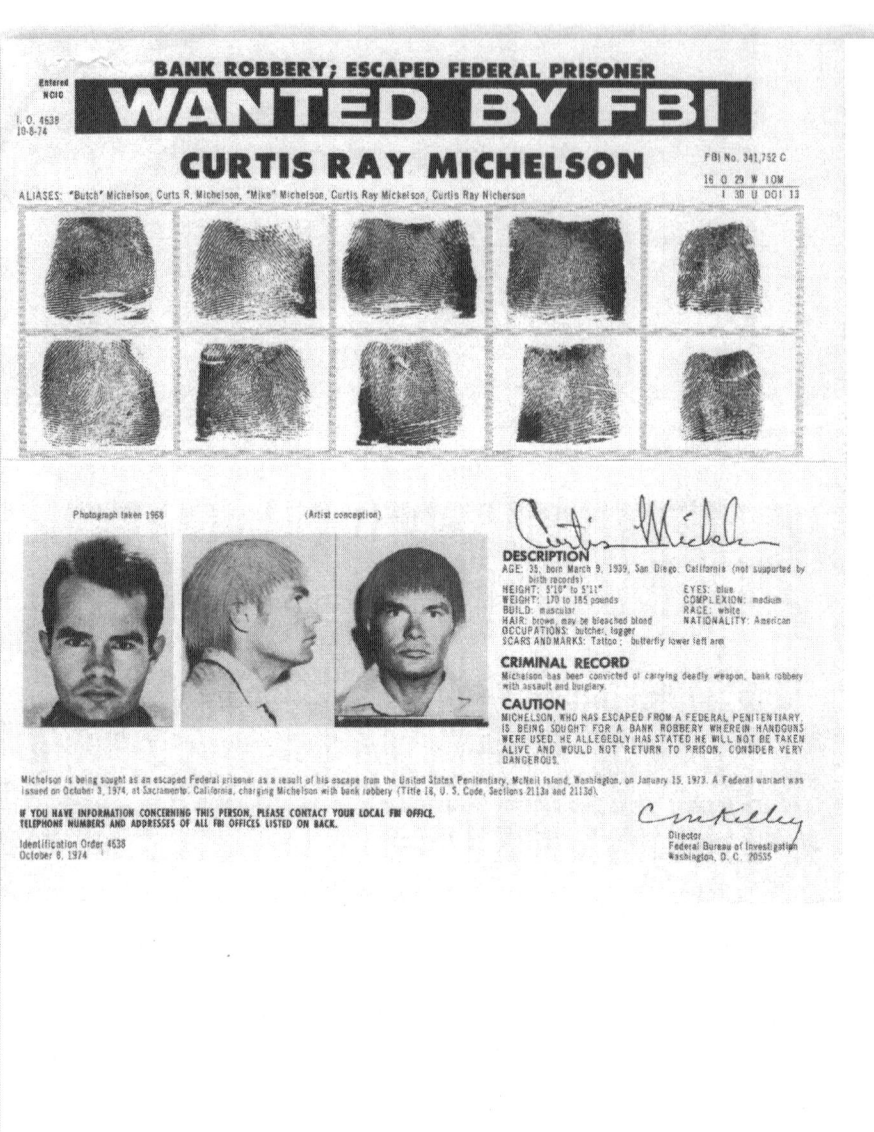

FBI identification order for Curtis Ray Michelson, 1974

CHAPTER 18
Y'ALL COME BACK

*Could we see when and where we are to meet again,
we would be more tender when we bid our friends good-bye.*

—OUIDA

I'm not sure where dangerous fugitives, highwaymen, and other undesirables obtain their training for their criminal enterprises, if any such training actually exists. But I do suspect I know how they learn how to avoid detection by law enforcement once the inevitable chase is on. When I think back to my "deprived" childhood when no computer or other electronic games existed, we had to play in the dangerous outdoors. We filled our playtime riding bicycles with friends (even in city-street traffic), playing pickup sports of all kinds, and inventing different games, like cops and robbers, cowboys and Indians, or tag. Often we played the timeless game of hide-and-seek. And it must have been there, in the midst of those hide-and-seek games, that the future criminal element learned to become invisible from their law enforcement pursuers. A few cases in point.

Even before my transfer to Mississippi, while still serving in Akron, Ohio, the office was looking for a murderer wanted for unlawful flight to avoid prosecution. The case agent had received some information that this dangerous fugitive was living at the home of a friend or relative in a rural location in Kent County. I was asked to join the group of five or six other agents to participate in my first fugitive arrest. Needless to say, I was extremely excited to be asked to participate in the arrest scenario. Being the FBI agent most recently out of training school, and therefore believed to be the most familiar with the use of the shotgun, I was assigned to carry the shotgun on the raid of the home. The teams left the office garage and proceeded early one morning to the potential address housing the fugitive. I sat in the rear seat of the FBI car, behind the front passenger seat. After a thirty-minute trip as my heart rate rapidly increased, we arrived at the suspected location.

The driver quickly pulled off to the side of the road, tires crunching in the gravel. The agents rapidly exited the vehicle, as did I. Unfortunately, as I jumped out, I didn't see that the car was parked on the very edge of the roadside, with a three-foot drop just outside my door. I went tumbling down the short drop, head over heels, doing my best to keep the shotgun from discharging into the air, or worse, into one of my colleagues. It was quite an embarrassing moment for me, but fortunately it went unobserved by the others as they were hustling to the front and rear entrances of the house. I quickly gathered myself together, climbed up the rise, and got to the front door just as the lead agents were pushing their way in past a somewhat reluctant homeowner. A quick search of the house failed to locate the fugitive, until a noise from the attic revealed someone was hiding there.

Just like the old hide-and-seek game, one of the agents called out to the fugitive now believed hiding in the attic. "Come down with your hands up, or we're coming up after you," he yelled out. I was ready with the shotgun, even though I didn't really want to be the first one up the attic stairs. I racked the pump action, creating the sound that means the shotgun is ready to go as a round is now in the chamber, ready to be fired. It's quite an intimidating sound to the person not holding the weapon. In another moment or two, a meek voice said, "I'm coming down, don't shoot!" and just like that, the hide-and-seek game ended in his arrest. He was quickly put in handcuffs and taken off to jail. I returned to the car and safely unloaded the shotgun for the trip back to the office.

Even though the hiding antics of the murderer seemed silly to me, the danger in seeking a violent fugitive was very clear. Probably the most dangerous thing for an FBI agent to do was step up into a dark attic or go down into a dark basement looking for someone who might possess a weapon and be willing to use it. It is the most vulnerable situation one faces in a search for a fugitive. Fortunately no one was hurt, and the arrest was successfully made. I made a mental note to myself to check the landing before jumping out of an FBI car in the future.

Back in Greenville, and prior to Ray's departure for Los Angeles, we received a call that a deserter from the military was residing at a relative's home in Leland, Mississippi (Leland was the birthplace of Jim Henson, creator of Kermit the Frog). Ray and I left the office early one morning to check out the report of this deserter. Upon arrival at the home, Ray went to the front door, and I went to the back door to keep the potential deserter from fleeing that way. Once Ray had made entry into the house, he let me in the back door. We spoke with a woman who claimed that the deserter was not there, but he had been there a few weeks ago. She protested that he wasn't there and told us to feel free to search the house. We did just as she asked.

This house, built like most of the homes in the Delta, on a concrete slab without basement or attic, proved to be a much easier search. We saved the master bedroom for last, and a quick peek under the bed revealed the hiding spot of the deserter. After being ordered to slide out from under the bed with his hands spread apart, he reached up with one hand and placed his loaded Magnum on the top of the bed. He slowly crawled out from under the bed, hands raised in the air, and was placed in handcuffs for an eventual return to his military unit. I suppose he was one of those kids who was always found early in the childhood hide-and-seek games. We were lucky that he decided not to try to use his gun. So was he.

Not to be outdone by these two clever fugitives, another fugitive in Greenville tried out yet another crafty hiding place. One afternoon, John Neelley received an anonymous telephone call from a black woman, indicating that a man wanted for murder was currently living in her house in Greenville. John told the woman that he would check out her information on the wanted man, and if there was an outstanding warrant for his arrest, then we'd be over shortly. She told John that she didn't want the man to know she was the one who called. John contacted the Jackson Division and had the NCIC operator check the name he had been given for any outstanding warrants. In seconds, the computer spat out information that the subject in question was indeed wanted on an unlawful flight to avoid prosecution federal charge for a murder committed in a midwestern state.

Since only Chuck, Ron, and I remained in the office, and the information was that the subject was there, we all quickly left the office and proceeded to the address in question. Chuck and Ron went to the rear of the house as John and I knocked at the front door. A black female answered the door. We identified ourselves as the FBI and announced that we had a warrant for the arrest of a subject believed to be at her home. She quietly opened the door, and we walked in. John went to the back door to let Ron and Chuck in to begin the search. I whispered to the woman, asking where the subject was located, assuming it was she who called us with the information. She pointed to the next room. I asked her if he was armed, and she replied that he was not carrying a weapon.

As the four of us congregated into the room where the fugitive was hiding, there was only one place he could be. The very favorite hiding place of the hide-and-seek aficionados, the closet! I pointed to the closed closet door, looked at the woman, and she nodded in assent, as she quietly walked into another room, so as not to play any role in the arrest. John pulled open the door as Ron, Chuck, and I pointed our revolvers at the inner sanctum of the closet. There sat our fugitive on a small stool, doing his best to win at the hide-and-seek game. He was placed in handcuffs and taken to the Greenville City Jail to be held until the US marshals could make arrangements to return him to Indiana for trial.

Other than these few arrests, things remained rather quiet for the most part in the office, despite the fact that we were down to only four agents. I suppose someone in higher authority than me had access to case numbers, crime statistics, and other personnel information, showing that Greenville simply could not have or did not need more manpower, and the earlier manpower that existed was needed in different locations. All four of us pretty much had to work our responsible counties alone, as there was simply too much geographic area to work and team up together at the same time.

On one occasion, a bank robbery occurred near Holly Springs, Mississippi, and Ron and I were sent to help out in the investigation. We arrived at a rather rural site as directed by the case agent. The investigation had determined that the robber apparently fled into a wooded area, and they were beginning a search for any evidence he may have left behind. As we arrived at the site and exited the car, I noticed a cottonmouth snake writhing on the ground. Others standing around seemed to take no notice of the snake. He looked alive and well to me, and I immediately announced that there was a live cottonmouth just behind the area where the agents were standing. One of the FBI old-timers, a good ole Mississippi boy, informed this city slicker that the snake was dead as his head had been crushed. I looked at the snake and noticed that his head was bloodied to some extent; yet it continued to slither about. "Boy, I guess you don't know nothin' 'bout snakes. He's dead for sure, but he won't stop movin' till sundown." I don't know if that is a scientific fact or just some local legend about snake behavior, but that snake did stop moving at sundown.

Ron and I helped search the area for the bank robbery money, exploding dye package, and any clothing or mask that may have been discarded by the robber during his getaway effort. We were unsuccessful in that attempt. Due to the lateness of the day, and in the event we would be needed the next day, we spent the night in a local motel. During some downtime, I learned that the cottonmouth had been dangling from a tree when it was found. When the rivers and creeks rise due to flooding in Mississippi, snakes are often found to take shelter in tree branches. And here I thought they could only be found in the rivers.

We returned to Greenville the next day as there was no more work to do at the crime scene. On the way back to the office, Ron and I talked about our boredom and life in general in the Delta. We both wanted to get out and to live in more familiar-type surroundings. But it wasn't easy to do so. I kept hearing from Marty, who claimed he was very happy that he made the move out of Greenwood and into New York City. Ron wanted no part of New York, hoping to get back somewhere close to his home state of Nebraska. But Omaha was a small office, like Jackson, and there were simply too few openings to be considered for a transfer anytime soon. I simply couldn't see spending the remainder of my career in the Delta, mostly because of the school situation that would soon face my son in two or three more years. And I kept thinking that I'd only be a two-hour drive from the Stone Harbor seashore no matter where I lived if I worked in New York City. But this had to be a decision both my wife and I made, and we continued to contemplate it.

As the days passed, and the decision whether to stay or go weighed heavily on my mind, there was still a little work to keep active to some extent. And there was plenty of time to keep up on meeting with area informants. One day I received a new case about an escaped federal prisoner and leads to conduct an interview with a relative in Sunflower County, with the intent of trying to find additional relatives or friends of the prisoner who could eventually lead to his apprehension. With nothing better to do one morning, I decided to head out to locate and interview the relative mentioned in the lead. There was no reason to believe that the escaped prisoner was in Mississippi—simply that a distant relative lived there who might have some information that could lead to his whereabouts. There was no one available to take with me as everyone else in the office was out working in their own territories. And if I really needed help or assistance in any way, I could always contact the Sunflower County Sheriff's Office. So off I went to cover the lead for another FBI office.

I arrived at the residence noted in the lead communication after about a forty-minute trip through a rural part of Sunflower County. I continued to be amazed at the vastness of the endless fields of cotton and soybeans even though that was all I'd seen for the past three years. There was a peacefulness in the Delta that permeated the area as the crops grew silently, unaware of the racial torment of years past. Racism issues seemed to have disappeared almost completely in the Delta by now, with the exception of an ugly singular event on occasion.

I thought about a transfer and how completely different my home life and working life in New York would be from what it was in the Delta. It would be as different as night is from day; I couldn't think of one similarity between the two places to live and work, with the exception of the FBI employees. I knew that would be the one common ground of a transfer to a place so vastly different from where I now worked. I was quickly brought back to reality as I arrived at the address I was seeking on my journey.

I exited my vehicle and walked up to the house. After I knocked at the door, a small black woman answered. I introduced myself, told her I was a special agent of the FBI, and said that I needed some information from her if she was able to provide it to me. She invited me into her home and offered me a chair. I sat down and opened my notebook and began asking questions about her relative, the escaped federal prisoner, and where she might think we could look to find him. She replied, "Well, he's right here!

I'll go fetch him for you." Shocked, I stood up as she left the room, closing my notebook and pondering my next move, which would have to be an arrest of the subject. In less than a minute, the lady returned with the subject. Putting on my kindest and least-threatening smile, I introduced myself to the escaped federal prisoner, wondering what he was thinking at the same time. We shook hands, and I asked him if he was indeed the fellow I was looking for. He said that he was the guy, but that he had been released from prison and couldn't be wanted for escape.

I had to make a decision and make it fast. I didn't see a need to place this guy under arrest immediately, as he seemed nonviolent and genuinely surprised at the fact that there was a warrant out for his arrest as an escaped prisoner. But I wanted to get him to jail and then sort out the problem, thinking he could be released if, in fact, he was telling the truth. I simply had no way of knowing what the truth was at the moment.

"I'll tell you what we'll do," I said to the subject. "If you agree, you can ride with me to the sheriff's office in Indianola, and we can check computer records there and try to see what this warrant is all about. If it's like you say it is and just a mistake, I'll bring you right back home." The subject thought that was a reasonable idea and agreed to go with me.

Now I had to decide whether to put him in handcuffs or trust my judgment and skill and have him sit alongside me in the front seat of the FBI car. I knew he couldn't get to my gun as it sat on my left hip, away from his reach. I felt pretty confident that I could get him safely to the sheriff's office without incident. Based upon the clothing he was wearing, it did not appear that he had a concealed weapon. And to be perfectly honest, he didn't appear to be anything like what I would take for an escaped federal prisoner.

"Okay," I said, "Let's go and get this thing checked out." With that, and a good-bye to his relative, he entered the passenger side of my car, and I drove to the sheriff's office. Along the fifteen-minute ride, the subject admitted that he had been assigned to a halfway house, considered to be a federal correctional facility, as it was part of the prison system. It may have been possible that records were incorrect coming from the halfway house.

In any case, I wanted to get this guy into custody as quickly and easily as possible. There would be time later to verify his claim of innocence in the matter.

We arrived without incident at the county jail in Indianola. I walked with the subject to one of the deputies and told him there was a federal warrant for his arrest as an escaped federal prisoner. I asked the deputy to process the fellow while I contacted my office to try to verify whether or not the warrant was still active for the subject. I wished the subject well and told him I was going to check the records. I would be back to get him and take him home if there was a mistake. As he walked off with the deputy to be processed for fingerprints and photographed, it was the last time I saw him.

I contacted the office in Greenville, but no one was there to take my message. I called the Jackson office and had the NCIC operator again run the subject's name to confirm the existence of an arrest warrant. Within moments she replied that the warrant on file was still good, and that the subject should still be considered to be a federal fugitive. I passed the information on to Sheriff Sessums and eventually returned to Greenville. There, I sent a communication to the office of origin advising of the arrest and all the details. It would be up to them and the US Marshals Service to resolve anything further about the case.

Looking back on the entire day, I realized I was fortunate to not have experienced any problems during the transportation of the prisoner, unrestrained, to jail. However, law enforcement personnel usually depend on a sixth sense, a sense obtained from training and experience. Fortunately, that sense worked fine for me that day.

When I arrived home that evening for dinner, my wife presented me with some more disappointing news. Our friends from New York, Bill and Margie Leunig, had been transferred out of Greenville. Bill was an engineer who worked for the Bechtel Corporation and had been assigned to Greenville to build a large power plant for the area. His work now complete, Bill was being transferred to a new project in Saudi Arabia. We had grown close to the Leunigs, and our children were playmates. This was just one more disappointment we felt in the ongoing group of transfers from the area, taking our best friends away. That started yet another discussion between us about the viability of seeking a transfer to New York City.

Even though overt racial hatred seemed to have pretty much disappeared in most of the Delta, there were still reminders of the hidden distrust and dislike of those of different-colored skin. One evening, as I attended our weekly Boy Scout meeting, one of the younger scouts approached me and asked me a personal question. He wanted to know if his friend, whom he described as a black kid he knew in school, could join the scout troop. Knowing we were interested in enlarging the size of the troop, and since we encouraged the scouts to invite friends to join, I told him it was fine and that we'd love to have his friend. Later that evening, after the meeting had ended, I mentioned the scout's request to the scoutmaster. I told him that I said it would be fine to let the scout invite his friend to join, noting that he was black. When I told the scoutmaster that the boy's color didn't matter to me, he replied, "Well, it matters to me." Sadly, the new potential scout was not invited to join the troop.

    I was completely taken aback at this event, as I never noticed any prejudice on behalf of the scoutmaster before this incident. He seemed to be a great guy who had the best interests of the scouts at the forefront. I began to wonder how wrong I had been, thinking that racial hatred had mostly disappeared from the Delta region. Perhaps it hadn't really disappeared at all; rather it still remained, as strong as ever, buried and hidden from public view.

    I knew at that moment that I could not in good conscience remain a permanent resident in Greenville. I'd never known racial hatred and was not raised in any way to dislike anyone for any reason, including the color of their skin. I returned home that evening and told my wife what had occurred, saying that I was going to resign as assistant scoutmaster as I didn't want to be a part of what I saw happening. I knew it was not a policy of the Boy Scouts of America, but rather a continuation of a 150-year racial problem. Here I spent the last three years of my life trying to bring more justice and humanity to a people who had been persecuted for so long, only to see the same persecution happening in different ways. It was time to make a change. I simply needed the courage to put in for the transfer.

A few days later, I traveled to Humphreys County to examine a truck that was reported stolen and had been recovered by the Belzoni Police Department. On the way to the police department, my stomach churned with the thought of possibly leaving Mississippi. There were lots of positives in connection with such a move. We'd be much closer to our families and the lifetime friends we left behind upon moving to the Delta. The public schools would be the same kind we attended, racially diverse and with a quality education afforded to each student. There would be sporting events, shopping, and cultural events of all kinds, unlike the Delta where few such events or programs existed. Availability to the Atlantic Ocean and white-sand beaches, or the mountains with their vast lakes and prime fishing and boating areas was another great plus. So why, I wondered as I drove, was the decision so difficult?

The decision was so difficult because I knew that even though the cost of living was relatively low in the Delta, I was still living paycheck to paycheck. There wasn't a lot of money left over each month to spend on the finer things of life. Granted, we had joined the Greenville Golf and Country Club as it was quite a bargain. I knew I'd likely never be able to join a country club in the New York area. But was this a reason to stay in Greenville forever? I would miss all the FBI personnel assigned to the Jackson Division. In three years' time, I knew every FBI employee in Mississippi, and they were all wonderful people. I would miss all of them if I left the area. But the biggest problem would be the increased cost of real estate and taxes if we moved there. I wasn't sure that we could swing it financially.

Taken from my thoughts as I arrived in Belzoni, I met with the chief, and he took me to the stolen truck. I took some fingerprints from the surfaces of the truck, which likely contained areas touched by the thief, and lifted the latent prints for forwarding to the FBI Identification Division.

I chatted a bit with the chief and then went to see the sheriff, just to complete some liaison responsibility.

I met with one of my informants before returning to the office, again pondering my transfer to New York. Marty continued to call from New York, professing his happiness about being out of Greenwood. With each telephone call, he was convincing me that this nerve-racking transfer was actually something that could be done. On the way home, I decided I would ask for the transfer, if my wife wanted to go and was willing to endure the expected hardships that would accompany a transfer to New York City.

I arrived at home just in time for the usual wonderful dinner prepared by my wife, who was quite a cook. As we ate, I told her I'd made my own mind up to put in for the transfer to New York City. Even our local Greenville friends, Sally and Ken Ibsen, who recently married, had been transferred to Houston, Texas. I was beginning to wonder if I'd be the last remaining person in the Delta. My wife was ready to take the transfer to New York and agreed with me to put in for the transfer. I knew the great shopping opportunities, the proximity to the beach, and a nearness to her family were the deciding features. She was willing to deal with whatever financial hardships we'd need to endure upon our arrival. We both realized a lot of agents were working there who were making less money than we were at the time, so we didn't think it'd be all that difficult. Our minds finally made up to take the move, I thought I'd finally get a good night's rest. I didn't.

It was April 1975, and after my first cup of coffee that morning at the office, I typed up a request for transfer to New York. If I didn't do it right away, I might have stalled and never got around to it. I was scheduled to attend the organized-crime in-service training at Quantico, Virginia, the following Monday, April 13, 1975. I thought that would be a great opportunity to get to know some of the FBI agents from New York who worked organized-crime cases against the five major La Cosa Nostra families. I was excited about moving up from working the few small-time football sports parlors in Greenville to major organized-crime figures in New York, with the likes of Carlo Gambino and Joe Bonanno. I made plans to visit my family over the weekend following the in-service course, and I would fly back to Greenville from Philadelphia. I would tell them the news that I'd put in for a transfer to New York and knew they'd be quite happy.

That next Sunday, I left Greenville en route to Washington, DC. Upon my arrival, there was a bus supplied to take agents who arrived by air to the training base at Quantico. While there for the week, I tried my best to meet the agents from New York so I could try for an organized-crime assignment upon my arrival. Most of the agents were surprised that I asked for a transfer to New York, but when the Delta was described to them, they seemed to have a better understanding of my motives. Most of the New York agents were originally from that area of the country and wanted no part of a transfer to the Deep South. When the in-service class ended on Friday, I felt I had made some good contacts in New York and was looking forward to an assignment on one of the squads that investigated the five big mafia families.

I took the train from Washington, DC, and spent an enjoyable weekend with my family in Cheltenham. On Sunday morning, a friend of my sister's arrived at our home for a visit. She brought with her a small black-and-white puppy, only about six weeks old. She was a mixed breed, possibly some border collie and spaniel. Our guest was looking for a nice home for the dog, and she was placed in my lap. I hadn't had a dog since before I was married, and I fell in love with this one. I called my wife and told her I had a nice surprise for her. She asked if my transfer had gone through, but I told her it was a nicer surprise. I just got a puppy, and if she didn't mind, I was bringing her to Greenville with me. While not thrilled about the prospect, she agreed to accepting the pet. With that, my dad and I went to the store to purchase a travel carrier for the dog to take her on the airplane. All was finally in order. I said good-bye to my folks, telling them I hoped to be back permanently very soon.

The trip to Greenville was difficult for the puppy, and she never had a chance to be walked. She traveled about ten hours with stopovers and never messed in her carrier. I knew I had a great dog by the time we arrived in Greenville. We decided on a name for her the next day. We selected "Missi" for obvious reasons, and she was a wonderful pet.

I had to get our backyard fenced in to give her a place to run and play. I knew we might be leaving for New York soon, but there was no guarantee that I'd ever get the transfer letter. Missi grew every day, just like most puppies do. She liked to sleep in her travel crate but was beginning to grow out of it. I had to look into buying another one for her so she could fit comfortably in it at night.

And then it happened! Upon opening the morning mail one day in late May 1975, John Neelley saw my transfer letter. Walking out to my desk with the letter in his hand, he said, "Well, John, looks like the bureau granted you your wish. I hate to see you go, but I wish you all the best in New York."

To be honest about it, the transfer arrived much quicker than I realized. It was over at last, all the agonizing about whether to leave the Delta or stay. The decision had been made for me by a higher authority, and all I had to do was make plans for a smooth transition for my family.

After I arrived home that evening, my wife and I made some telephone calls to put the move into motion. She would live in Stone Harbor, New Jersey, with my parents and enjoy the beach for the summer. If needed, she and our son could remain there throughout the fall, until we were able to find a new home. I would be required to find immediate temporary housing and begin my commute to New York City. I had a cousin who was living in Avenel, New Jersey, with his wife, and he graciously allowed me to use his spare bedroom until we found a permanent home. We also contacted our original realtor, Bob Jones, and put our house on the market.

Somewhat unfortunate for us was that new construction was taking place directly across the street from our house, where a grove of pecan trees once stood. That would make selling our used home a bit more difficult when new housing of a similar style was available for the same price. We had to list our home at a reduced price in order to interest local buyers. It all worked out pretty well as we were able to sell our home rather quickly for a small but important profit. We would certainly need the money to buy a place in or around New York. We also made arrangements to fly our dog home to Philadelphia, where she would be met by my dad at the airport. It was a good thing we bought the larger dog carrier as she had fully outgrown the first one.

I spent the next two weeks in the office trying to close or reassign the remainder of my cases. Thanks to Judge Keady's review of his original order, again allowing prison officials to read inmate mail at Parchman, the long-running fraudulent-check case had ceased to exist. I did receive word that a fingerprint I had recently lifted and sent to the Identification Division from the stolen truck in Belzoni had been identified as belonging to the suspect in the theft. He would subsequently be convicted of interstate theft of a stolen motor vehicle and incarcerated in a federal penitentiary. Little did I know at the time, but that would be the last fingerprint I would ever lift in my FBI career.

I traveled to the Jackson office and spent two days finishing up my case dictation and having my final file reviews with the supervisory staff. I said my good-byes to the agents and support personnel, not knowing if I'd ever see any of them again. Parting was indeed bittersweet; I was looking forward to exciting work in the big city but would miss the friends and good times we shared together the past three years. The trip back to Greenville was sad and lonely. Had I really made the right decision? I was beginning to wonder.

I spent a final day in the office with John, Chuck, and Ron. I knew Chuck and Ron wanted to leave as well, but the option of New York, while available to them, was not beneficial enough to make the move. They'd just have to figure out different ways to return to the area of the country they hoped to see. John seemed content to remain in Greenville. He'd been there for some time and had developed a reputation with law enforcement and the community in general as a gentleman and the man in charge of the FBI. He'd had plenty of other transfers in his career and seemed to want to settle down where he was. I did visit with my law enforcements contacts and said my good-byes, thanking them for their assistance to me as well as their friendship. There was never a bad word spoken between us, and I knew in my heart they were a group of professional law enforcement people with the best interests of the citizens in mind.

Moving day finally came, and we were packed and gone within one day. It was sad leaving our first home, yet we had a lot to look forward to in the future. With our dog, Missi, shipped off in the airplane, we were allowed three or four days' drive to get to our destination in New York. We enjoyed the motel swimming pools along the way, until finally reaching Stone Harbor, New Jersey, our destination. After spending the weekend there and leaving my wife and son with my parents, I left for Avenel to prepare for my first commute to New York. Our lives in the Mississippi Delta were gone forever.

Conducting investigation in the Mississippi Delta, 1974

Crime scene investigation of stolen truck, Belzoni, MS, 1975

CHAPTER 19
THE BIG APPLE

Give me your tired, your poor, your huddled masses yearning to breathe free.

—STATUE OF LIBERTY INSCRIPTION

I arrived at my cousin Richard's apartment late on a Sunday evening, wondering what to expect the following morning. My family would be able to enjoy the entire summer at a beautiful beach location while I adjusted to life in New York City. I sat with Richard, and he gave me directions to find the Avenel train station where I would catch a local commuter train to Penn Station on Thirty-Fourth Street in Manhattan. Unfortunately, that would not signify the end of my trip to the new office. The New York FBI office was located on Sixty-Ninth Street at Third Avenue, across town from Penn Station. Rich told me I would have to take an additional three subway trains to arrive at my destination. I was so excited to begin my work in the largest city in the nation that I didn't give the upcoming commute any thought. Since I had to arrive at the office no later than 8:15 a.m., Rich suggested I catch a 6:30 a.m. train. That meant I had to get up, shower, shave, eat something, and arrive at the train station before 6:30 a.m. The thought of it gave me pause to reflect upon what I'd just given up in leaving Greenville and my five-minute commute to the FBI office there in a government-owned vehicle. But the lure of working in the Big Apple won me over, for the moment at least. I went to bed, excited about my future in the FBI.

After a totally sleepless night, I arose at 5:30 a.m. and got myself ready for work and my trip to the train station. My cousin and his wife were still asleep, so I tried to maneuver as quietly as possible. I made it to the train station in time to catch the 6:30 a.m. local to New York and arrived as scheduled at Penn Station. It was there that the fun began. Inside the station was a labyrinth of rail tracks leading in all directions, located on multiple floors. For the first time in a long while, a complete feeling of helplessness overcame me. I figured it would be better to ask someone where to locate the subway platform and the train that went north to Forty-Second Street. Little did I know at the time that the sign would merely read Uptown.

Once safely positioned on the correct platform, I knew I only had to travel one stop before arriving at Grand Central Station. So far so good. The subway train arrived, packed full of morning commuters. I quickly realized any southern politeness I had acquired in the Delta would soon evaporate, as none of the riders made any effort to open space on the train, and those detraining and boarding pushed and shoved their way past each other. I was fortunate to get aboard the train before the doors tried to close on the slower-moving passengers.

My arrival after one stop at Grand Central Station was more terrifying than my arrival at Penn Station. This station, opulent in its architecture, was seemingly more confusing than Penn Station, with more tracks and platforms. Again, I realized my best course of action was to simply ask someone for directions. Not quite as easy as it sounds, as commuters were scurrying about faster than I could catch up with them, but I finally located a New York City policeman and sought his help. I'd heard a lot of bad things about New Yorkers in the past (like everyone from Philadelphia), but the cop seemed like a friendly guy who sent me off to the crosstown train for a two-stop trip. He told me that once I arrived at Forty-Second Street and Lexington Avenue, I should look for the uptown Independent Rapid Transit (IRT) subway line. There would be a stop at Sixty-Eighth Street and Lexington Avenue, two blocks away from the office.

Now that a few more minutes had passed since my last train ride, more and more commuters began filling the station and the trains. I pushed my way aboard the crosstown train, completely crammed with commuters. There was no reason to hold on to the overhead straps or steel poles for balance as there was simply no way to fall down with the cars as full as they were at the time. Everyone exited at the second stop as the train was merely a shuttle crossing from the west side of the city to the east side. I eventually found the IRT and the signs for uptown.

Boarding my last train for the final leg of my journey to the office, I was already feeling the strain of a lousy night's sleep and a bone-weary commute. I'd still be having breakfast at home if I were living in Greenville. I'd already been up for more than two hours and hadn't made it to the office yet. Still, I had the excitement of working in New York to carry me through. As the IRT stopped at Sixty-Eighth Street, I exited the train, hoping that I'd remember the reverse route to get home later that evening.

Upon reaching the surface of the city street, I was hit with the heat and humidity of July in New York City. I remember thinking that it really wasn't that much hotter in the Delta than it was this particular morning. I needed to get my bearings to determine which way was north, in order to find Sixty-Ninth Street. Finding east would be easy after that. Walking, I finally arrived at the FBI office.

Upon entering the revolving door, I saw there was a bank of elevators, some cordoned off for use only by certain people. At a front desk, two FBI employees checked identification and allowed FBI personnel to use the elevators reserved for the FBI space. I was to learn that the office began at the sixth floor and went up to the roof or the fifteenth floor. It was a great deal larger than any of my previous FBI assignment buildings.

I exhibited my credentials to the employees at the front desk and explained I was a newly assigned agent. They told me to take the elevator to the sixth floor, where I'd find the administrative offices, in order to sign in and be assigned to my squad. I followed their instructions and met with one of the administrative secretaries on the sixth floor. I was welcomed to New York and advised that I was being assigned to Squad 34, a squad that was a part of the Soviet Counterintelligence Division in the office. I thought there must be some mistake here, as I was a SWAT-trained, organized-crime-trained FBI agent with a lot of criminal experience in both Mississippi and Ohio. The secretary told me that an agent from the squad would be coming down to get me and take me to the squad. I thought I'd wait until I met my new supervisor before trying to get to a criminal or organized squad best fitting my personal qualifications.

In a few minutes, an agent from Squad 34 came to get me. Our division was located on the ninth floor, accessible either by elevator or back staircases. We walked up the stairs to the squad area. I was introduced to a couple of the agents who were present on the squad as we walked to the front of the office where the supervisor sat in a small glass-enclosed office. "John, this is our supervisor, Lew Barra," my escort exclaimed. "Lew, meet our newest squad member, John Whiteside." Lew offered me a seat and welcomed me to New York.

We had a lengthy discussion about the responsibilities of my new squad and the kind of work I'd be involved with here. With the presence of the United Nations in New York City and a large presence of Soviet diplomats, KGB intelligence officers, and visitors, the intelligence threat to the United States was great, and we were one of many squads assigned counterintelligence responsibilities to keep the Soviets in check. After all, we were in the height of the Cold War at the time.

I mildly protested to Lew that I was better trained and much more qualified to work organized-crime or general-criminal cases, but I didn't push it as I hoped I still had an ace in the hole. Lew essentially informed me that all incoming agents under transfer to New York were first assigned to work on one of two counterintelligence divisions, and that I was no exception. He told me that unless I knew someone in high places, I'd just have to do my time until making a connection for a transfer. He thought I'd enjoy the work and told me that there were lots of experienced agents on the squad who'd lend a hand. With that, he showed me to my desk and showed me the workbox room where I'd keep my files and cases at night. My New York FBI career had begun.

My "ace in the hole" was a special agent in charge, (SAC) Jim Ingram, who was assigned to the counterintelligence division that was responsible for the rest of the world, not including the Soviet Union. I had no desire to work in his division either. But I was hoping that a couple of personal similarities might get me to either organized-crime or criminal-division work.

When I started my career in Cleveland, Ohio, one of my first cases was to work a matter involving a federal train-wreck statute. I went on a road trip from Cleveland to Lima, Ohio, along with several other agents, including Gary Ingram. Gary Ingram was Jim's younger brother. Gary was a wonderful special agent and a fine gentleman. I believe he was in his second office and was an experienced agent as I was just getting my feet wet. He was a good friend and remained a close associate of mine during my stay in Ohio.

Jim Ingram was a legend in the FBI, especially in the Jackson Division. Following his first office experience in Indianapolis, Indiana, Ingram was transferred to New York in 1959. In his book *The Hero among Us: Memoirs of an FBI Witness Hunter*, Ingram discusses the difficulty of raising a family and his finances while serving in New York. While still serving in 1964, Ingram had been assigned to and was working in the New York office at the same time that the Jackson Division was being opened to fight the racial violence that had grown out of control in Mississippi. Many of Ingram's friends from the New York office had been transferred to Jackson, as most of them were from Mississippi. His friends were urging him to transfer to Mississippi to get to a more affordable place to live. Ingram was subsequently transferred to Jackson in 1964, where he served with distinction until 1970. He served in a supervisory role during his last year or two in Jackson prior to being transferred to FBI headquarters in Washington, DC.

When I worked in Greenville from 1972 to 1975, I heard about this wonderful man who was formerly assigned there named Jim Ingram. It wasn't long before I learned he was the older brother of Gary Ingram, my pal from Cleveland. Nearly everyone who'd been assigned to the Jackson office and knew Jim Ingram spoke in the highest terms about him. While I never met the man, I felt like I knew him from all the nice things said about him. It was always said that he would help you out if he could.

Thus, I called his secretary and asked if I could meet with him, noting that I was in from Greenville. She asked me to come to his office right away on the tenth floor. I found the staircase and walked over to Jim's office. His secretary invited me to take a seat and poured me a cup of coffee. I could only think this was his southern-hospitality style, and I was really looking forward to meeting this Mississippi legend.

Jim Ingram came out of his office wearing a broad smile and introduced himself to me. I rose to meet him, standing well below his shoulders. Jim was a tall, strapping man with a constant smile. I introduced myself, and we sat down for a bit. I told him I'd worked closely with his brother Gary in Cleveland and had heard much about him during my tour of duty in Mississippi. After chatting a bit and discussing common friends from Jackson, I told him I was there to ask a favor of him. I explained my training and experience from my days in Greenville, and how I thought I was sent to organized-crime school in order to work organized-crime matters. I also told him I was a member of the Jackson SWAT team, and that we were told that transfers to different offices would automatically keep us on a SWAT team. I then told him that I thought my talents and skills were being wasted in the Soviet counterintelligence squad to which I'd been assigned. I asked him if there was anything he could do to get me to an organized-crime or general-criminal squad. He looked at me with a warm, fatherly countenance and said that if there was anything he could do for me, he would do it.

However (that dreadful word), he said that if he were to transfer me to either the organized-crime or general-criminal division, he would have a thousand angry FBI special agents at his door demanding transfers as they had seniority over me in New York. The best he could do for me was a transfer to his division, the other counterintelligence division in the office. Not wanting to show my disappointment, I thanked him for his offer and told him I'd try out my current assignment. We chatted a bit more about Mississippi before I took my leave from his office.

I would not run into Jim Ingram at any time in the future. My "ace in the hole" turned out to be a losing hand. It looked like I was stuck being assigned to the Soviet counterintelligence squad, where I had no experience and little interest at the moment. I did return to the administrative secretary in order to be sure she knew I was a member of the SWAT team in Jackson and wanted to be added to the New York team roster. She assured me that would happen, and that I'd hear from the SWAT team leader as to how to proceed in that venue. I returned to my squad and my desk, wondering what the future would hold for me in New York.

I left the office at the end of the day at about five thirty. I had no pressing work and no need to stay any later. I wanted to try my hand at the return trip. I made it back to my cousin's apartment at about a quarter past seven. They were hungry as they had waited on me for dinner, being used to eating at an earlier hour. I explained to them that it didn't look like I'd be home much earlier than I was that night and to go ahead and eat without me. But they were kind enough to change their normal routine to accommodate their new guest and always waited on me to arrive home. My day had been simply overwhelming, and I was completely exhausted. I went to bed early that night hoping for some better rest, as I knew five thirty would arrive much too soon.

After two months of working, I began to miss a lot about my job in Greenville. My new squad, consisting of about twenty-five special agents, only had one government car to share among us. That car was used exclusively for the surveillance teams. Any necessary travel to complete a lead or conduct an interview was done via public transportation. And while I used to hate that long commute to the Parchman farm in Sunflower County, a trip by public transportation to Brooklyn, Queens, or the Bronx could take just as long, minus the country solitude. The peace of mind and fertile fields of the Delta simply didn't exist on the subway system in the city. In fact, the filth on the city streets and inside the subway tunnels was disgusting. The first time I'd ever seen a live rat was while waiting for a subway train and looking down on the tracks. Not one but several huge rats were seen scurrying along the track beds.

I found I had little free time at home after work, as it was nearly bedtime after a late dinner. There was no time for any volunteer work of any kind. It really was dog-eat-dog every day. And the cost of lunches in New York was much higher than it was in Mississippi. Had I made the right move? I wondered. I kept thinking my situation was exactly opposite from that of Jim Ingram. He was in New York, suffering from financial issues, with friends urging him to come south to enjoy easier, cheaper living. I was in the South, with friends in the North, urging me to come up to escape easier, cheaper living and step into the area with the highest cost of living in the nation. I kept thinking, What's wrong with this picture?

By September, my wife had made a few trips up to north and central New Jersey and was looking at homes. She finally located a lovely house I thought I could barely afford in Hazlet, New Jersey, about forty-five miles southeast of New York City. It had a nice fenced-in yard for the dog with a large, above-ground swimming pool. Much larger and twice the price of our ranch-style home in Greenville, this house was a split-level design. The neighborhood elementary school was one block away, and the high school was within walking distance. We were located only about twenty minutes from the Atlantic Ocean beaches at Sandy Hook and only a few minutes from the beaches that lined Raritan Bay, where we could easily enjoy the view of the World Trade Center and the entire Manhattan skyline. Our new community would support boating, sailing, and fishing, assuming one could find the time and money to enjoy those outdoor hobbies. All of my future neighbors commuted to New York City, so we knew we'd found a pretty good location. We moved into our home in late September and began to settle down as a family once again.

The first change for me was a different commute into the city. I was now somewhat more distant from a local railroad line, and the most efficient way to get to the city was by bus. There was a bus stop only two blocks away from my home. By taking the bus to New York City, I would avoid one extra subway ride, as the bus stopped at Grand Central Station. I only needed to catch the crosstown and the uptown IRT subway. At least this new way would be a bit of a time-saver. The bus tickets proved to be expensive and a drain on the budget, and that, while not a surprise, became a troubling reality.

The commute initially was not too bad as there was plenty of time to read on the bus ride. However, as fall slowly turned into winter, and the wait at the bus stop often was accompanied by cold, rain, sleet, or snow, things got much more annoying. Riding into the city with wet feet and clothing was no picnic. Nor was it any fun to ride sitting next to an overweight male coughing up a recent virus he had acquired and spreading it to his fellow commuters. On a good day, the heat system on the bus was operational; oftentimes it wasn't. Those same discomforts accompanied hot-weather travel as well if the air-conditioning system wasn't working properly. It always seemed like at least one passenger was sick with some sort of communicable ailment. It was definitely the worst part of the day, commuting back and forth to and from work, some four hours every day.

With the move to New Jersey from Mississippi, all my insurance coverage for my home and my car doubled in price. Coupled with the cost of commuting, I found I had little money to afford to buy lunch in the city, even though there were many reasonable places to eat. I began taking my lunch in a brown bag and ate it while sitting at my desk. I kept thinking about all the nice lunches I had every day in Greenville or on the road in my rural counties and badly missed those times. No more southern-fried catfish for me. I remembered my easy commute to the office, never in the snow or sleet, and always arriving in dry condition. To make matters worse, the squad on which I was assigned was mostly filled with old-time New Yorkers who had all the good counterintelligence cases assigned to them. My cases involved low-level Soviet workers who were not even suspected of being involved in any intelligence operations. I became bored to death at work and continued to wonder what I had done with this career move. I needed to make a change of some kind; I just didn't really know what to do.

I finally decided to subscribe to *Police Chief Magazine*, a publication produced monthly by the International Association of Chiefs of Police. I knew that the magazine had want ads in it for the position of police chief in different regions of the country. I was hoping to find a place that would be more economical to live in, as well as an open police chief position in a small- or medium-sized police department where I would feel qualified to work. Knowing the sheriffs and police chiefs in the Delta, I was confident I could easily handle that type of job. The search was on every month that the new edition of the magazine was published and delivered to my door. Yet month after month, nothing appeared that seemed to be worth pursuing. It was beginning to look like I was stuck forever in the nonstop world of commuting at least four hours or more every working day of my life.

We did enjoy our home in Hazlet and our local neighbors. Weekends became a most important part of our lives in the metropolitan area. Work was indeed a drag, but frequent summer weekend trips to the seashore eased some of the pain. After a while even the commute became more automatic and less of a hassle. I guess one can grow used to anything if it happens long enough. Small pay raises somewhat lessened the financial burden of living in the area, although bus fare increases usually seemed to coincide with my small raises. We would have our second child, a daughter, in the fall of 1976. We were happy knowing the elementary school was nearby, and it was more in the manner of education in which my wife and I were raised in the North.

I eventually made a contact with a supervisor who was responsible for investigations of the Genovese organized-crime family. He had an opening for an agent on his squad and put my name in for the position. After two years in counterintelligence, I was finally transferred to an organized-crime squad. My dream had come true at last.

But like many dreams, this one wasn't real. The squad did have more available cars, and I was able to join a carpool, ending my bus-and-subway commute forever. I worked with another great group of dedicated agents and enjoyed the possibilities of my new work targeted against La Cosa Nostra. But in spite of my newest experience in the FBI, nothing ever measured up to my experiences in the Mississippi Delta. I would only make two more arrests in my entire FBI career from the time I left the Delta. One of those arrests would be of a mentally disturbed man whom I arrested while serving on guard duty in the lobby of the New York office one weekend.

That day, a Latino man walked into the lobby asking to speak to an FBI agent. He mumbled something about his concern for his missing daughter. He was carrying a half-empty bottle of intravenous solution with the accompanying supply lines attached to it and dangling down by his side. I suspected from the outset that he was mentally disturbed, although he spoke as if nothing was wrong with him. I told him to put the bottle and the IV lines, along with a bag he was carrying, on the ground. After he complied with my request, I began to escort him to the rear of the lobby floor, where the agents who took complaints sat. It was there that they would listen to his complaint, and if it involved a valid crime that the FBI investigated, a complaint form would be written up and sent to the appropriate squad for investigation.

As the man approached the agents, he suddenly withdrew a small-caliber handgun from his pocket, pointing it very briefly toward the complaint agents and then instantly raising it to his head. This all taking place in less than a second, I was drawing my Magnum to shoot the unknown subject as he pulled the trigger of the gun. I flinched to avoid what I expected to be brain matter and blood splattered all over me. Quickly realizing that his gun did not fire, I grabbed the man and disarmed him. The complaint agents and I handcuffed the man, who now seemed to be growing somewhat incoherent. His gun turned out to be a toy gun that would not have hurt anyone. He was lucky he was not shot and killed by one of us.

I contacted a duty assistant US attorney and explained the circumstances of the unsettling event to him and told him that the subject was in handcuffs and in our custody. The attorney authorized us to charge the subject with assault on a federal officer, and we then transported him to the local federal holding unit. I never had to testify in connection with this assault matter and can only assume the subject was eventually committed for mental evaluation and treatment as I never heard anything more of the incident.

The last arrest in my FBI career would not occur until February 23, 1996, long after two more transfers in my FBI experience. At that time, I had the occasion to arrest Robert Stephan Lipka on a charge of conspiracy to commit espionage. Lipka, who had been assigned to the National Security Agency as a soldier in the US Army, walked into the Soviet Embassy in Washington, DC, in September 1965 and volunteered to sell classified National Security Agency information. He subsequently sold two hundred top-secret documents over a two-year period, earning $27,000 for his efforts. Information obtained from former KGB Intelligence Officer Vasili Mitrokhin in 1992 initiated an espionage investigation of Lipka. Following that investigation, his arrest and subsequent sentencing in September 1997 were the culmination of the longest-running espionage case ever brought before the US courts. The case story is fully documented in my first book, *Fool's Mate: A True Story of Espionage at the National Security Agency.*

I would eventually return to the same counterintelligence squad I started with in New York in early 1979. I simply was not the type of special agent who could sit and listen to court-authorized wiretaps for months at a time, which I found myself doing on my organized-crime squad assignment. That's just the nature of the work against big mob targets, but work I didn't particularly enjoy doing. It was much more fun collecting overt evidence of gambling activity in the Delta without the troublesome wiretaps involved. And I would complete my thirty-year FBI career from 1979 on working foreign counterintelligence and espionage cases in New York City, at FBI headquarters in Washington, DC, and in the Philadelphia, Pennsylvania, Division. Once I left Greenville, Mississippi, I would never lift another fingerprint from a crime scene or investigate another criminal case with the exception of the Lipka case.

There was one big change in the FBI by the time I left the New York office. I had the good fortune to work with black agents and female agents assigned to the various squads in the office. The minority contingent of special agents in the FBI would continue to grow during the years to come, with minorities eventually holding some of the highest positions of responsibility in the FBI and doing a great job. I was hopeful that the addition of minority special agents would be a great help in the Mississippi Delta in achieving the trust of the black community that had been distrustful of the FBI for so long.

CHAPTER 20
DIXIE AGAIN

There is nothing like returning to a place that remains unchanged to find the ways in which you yourself have altered.

—NELSON MANDELA

Once my wife, son, and I left Greenville on that sticky June day in 1975, I thought I'd never look back or see any of the friends we'd made in the South. But I found that I was quite wrong about that. No sooner had we purchased and settled into our new home in Hazlet, New Jersey, than I received a telephone call from the US attorney's office in Oxford, Mississippi, telling me that I was needed to testify in court in a mail-fraud case that I had worked in the past. The trial was being held in Jackson, and I was directed to fly there and be ready to testify. After purchasing a round-trip ticket, I was contacted by the Jackson office and was told that I would need to cancel my return flight back to New Jersey. No, they weren't transferring me back to the Delta; I was still enjoying my new assignment up north at the time. Rather, the Jackson Division had an extra FBI automobile that was not in use, and it was subsequently designated for reassignment to New York. Since they had the opportunity for relatively free transportation to New York by virtue of my visit, I was designated to drive the car back on my return trip. It seemed I simply couldn't escape commuting no matter where I went.

I arrived as scheduled at the Jackson airport and was met by an agent from the Jackson Division who drove me back to the office. It was nice to see some of my fellow agents again, although I hadn't been away but for a couple of months. I wouldn't see them that frequently when I was actually working in Greenville. A few of us had a couple of beers together after work, and I answered all the questions about the New York office and whether or not I'd made a good move. None of the agents I was with had any intention of transferring to New York. It was their amazement at my monumental move that incurred lots of questions about my new assignment. After a quick supper, I settled into my motel room for the night.

The following day after returning to the office, I was contacted again by the US attorney's office and was told the subject in the case I was there to testify against had just pled guilty, and my testimony would not be needed. Thus, in a matter of minutes, I became a valet for the FBI.

It was early enough in the day that I could begin my return trip home to New Jersey/New York. Once again, I bade farewell to my friends in the Jackson office, obtained the vehicle that I was to take to New York, and began my lonely return trip home. It was only a few months ago that I'd taken this same journey with my family. I was allotted three days and nights for the travel, based upon the mileage required for the trip. The ride was rather boring when driving alone, and I spent a lot of time reflecting on the move I'd made several months earlier. Was it really worth it? Would it have been better to remain in the Delta and learn to enjoy the sleepy southern lifestyle? Lots of provocative thoughts and no answers came to mind during the drive. How was it possible to really decide between the two options, being so radically different from each other? I wondered. Still somewhat enamored with the big city, I tried to convince myself that I'd made the right choice.

I returned the car to the New York office the next business day after arriving home. I'd left no other pending cases in Greenville that I was aware of that would require another trip down South to testify again. I suspected that would be the final trip to the Magnolia State.

However, life being what it is, I received a telephone call a few months later from two of the stenographers who worked in the Jackson office. Barbara Little and Melissa Eatherly were traveling to Europe by way of John F. Kennedy Airport in New York. They were seeking help to find a room upon arrival in New York, as it was going to be their first time to the big city. I offered to help them find lodging and picked them up from the airport. It was good to see old friends and coworkers from Mississippi once again. And still I wondered, was this to be my final contact with the Jackson Division? I did get to know several agents in the New York office who had served at various times in the Jackson Division prior to my arrival there. And their complaints about it were similar to mine. But there would be no more trips to Mississippi, not for a while at least.

After working in New York for a couple of years, we did receive a visit from our Cleveland and Mississippi friends, Wayne and Joy Tichenor. It was their first trip to New York City. By that time in my life, the last thing I wanted to do was to travel to New York if I didn't have to for work. But to be a good host, we took our visitors to the city for the full tour. Of course, my wife always enjoyed trips to the city since she never had to tolerate the miserable commute, and there was always plenty of shopping to do.

It wouldn't be until we were living in Virginia and I was working at FBI headquarters in Washington, DC, that we would even contemplate a trip back to the Delta. Our original vacation plan was to take our two children to Knoxville, Tennessee, where the 1982 world's fair was being held. The fair's theme was "Energy Turns the World," and my wife thought it would be a great experience for our family. We also decided that we would spend some time at Opryland Park in Nashville, once we had enjoyed all the world's fair had to offer. And since we were going all the way to Nashville, why not consider stopping in Oxford, Mississippi, to visit our friends the Tichenors who extended the offer when they were with us in New York? Our first family vacation was beginning to become quite a trek. To extend the journey a bit further, we decided to reach out to Sally and Ken Ibsen in Greenville to see if they were interested in a visit, since we would be in Oxford, and Greenville was only another two and a half hours away. They extended the welcome mat to us as well, and we had our first extended family vacation planned. I'd never thought we would return to the Delta, but here we were on another journey across the Deep South.

The trip started well with our arrival at the world's fair for two days. Jason was nine and Brooke was almost six, both old enough to enjoy and remember the trip. However, the trip would become a lot more memorable for a more disturbing reason.

Shortly before arriving at the world's fair, my daughter noticed a couple of pimply pustules on her torso. Thinking it was only heat rash or some similar ailment, we continued on our excursion, enjoying all Knoxville had to offer at the fair. Her rash grew progressively worse, until we realized that she had come down with a full-blown case of the chicken pox. What a way to begin our epic journey. And what to do about it? Brooke wasn't feeling sick with the ailment, so we decided to continue on to Opryland in Nashville, hoping she'd soon be on the mend. And she seemed to be, not complaining too much as we enjoyed the classic amusement park.

We thought it best to contact the Tichenors and deliver the bad news that we wouldn't be able to make it to Oxford as a result of Brooke's condition. However, Joy said that her children had not had the disease, and if they were to get it, this would be as good a time as any. She insisted we visit them anyway, and she wouldn't take no for an answer. We reluctantly decided to continue the trip as a result of her insistence and because we were now so close to Oxford. However, before leaving for Opryland, Jason noticed a few pustules forming on his torso as well. He'd picked up the disease from his sister. So, after enjoying Opryland for a few days, we headed to Oxford with two ailing children in tow.

We enjoyed a several-day stay in Oxford, and Jason had improved enough to let him ride with us in the golf cart as Wayne and I played a round of golf. When we returned to the Tichenor residence, he was quite uncomfortable due to the sun he was exposed to on our golf outing. The good news was that our daughter Brooke was now almost over the worst of her symptoms. However, the Tichenor children wouldn't be far behind. We decided to call Sally and Ken Ibsen in Greenville and relay the bad news, saying we didn't want to infect the entire state of Mississippi now that Jason had come down with the disease. But like the Tichenors, they were insistent upon our visit, saying their daughter would need the disease at some time or another. Again, southern hospitality ruled the day, and we continued on our journey to Greenville.

Never having expected to return, this wasn't the way I wanted to do it if it was going to happen. But happen it did. We spent a few days with the Ibsens as Jason went from ailing to improving. We drove past our old house, the one Jason had no memory of, and toured the known areas of the Delta along with some of our old favorite haunts. Nothing had changed since we left in 1975; if anything, the place was even more depressing since more companies had left the area and unemployment continued to soar. More of the small shops along Main and Washington Streets had shut their doors. Seeing a lack of any rejuvenation in the town, I was glad we had made the move to New York and had left when we did.

After a few days, we left the hospitality of the Ibsens and began the long trip home. Fortunately both of the children had mostly recovered from their bout with chicken pox. Sadly, they probably infected most of Mississippi as both the Tichenor and Ibsen families eventually got a good dose of the disease. Once we returned home, I again wondered if I'd ever be back in the Delta, or if we would see our southern friends again.

In 1983, we moved from Virginia to Malvern, Pennsylvania, where I would finish my FBI career in the Philadelphia Division of the FBI. We contracted with a builder to erect our new home and were living with my parents back in Cheltenham. Late that summer, we received a call from the Ibsens saying that they'd like to come up for a visit. They arrived around the Labor Day weekend, and we returned the favor and hospitality they'd extended to us in Greenville a year earlier, this time without the communicable diseases. We took them to the Atlantic coast to try to help explain our rationale for leaving Greenville. I know home is where you've been born and raised, not necessarily where you hang your hat, and didn't think they'd ever leave Greenville. But I think they enjoyed their visit with us and had a better understanding as to why we left the Mississippi Delta. They would visit us again in 1989 for a weekend when Ken was nearby on a business trip. His wife flew up to meet him and spent a few days with us. It was the first time they'd seen our home in Malvern, as it was being built during their earlier trip.

Years continued to pass as we kept in contact with our friends by annual Christmas cards, always extending the invitation back and forth for a visit. Then, in early 1994, my son Jason decided he no longer enjoyed attending college at Lock Haven, Pennsylvania, and wanted to complete his college education in Mississippi. We decided to take an Amtrak train to Hattiesburg so he could visit the University of Southern Mississippi. I really didn't want to make the long drive again, down and back, so the train sounded like an interesting option. It took just as long to get there as driving would have, but at least it was more relaxing.

We rented a car in Hattiesburg upon arrival and found a comfortable motel. We visited the campus of the Golden Eagles, and he really liked it. I think he was more impressed by the fact that it was seventy degrees at the end of February and not piled deep with snow like Lock Haven. After a couple of days in Hattiesburg, and my first visit there as well, we drove north to Starkville to tour the campus of Mississippi State University. Jason seemed to like Southern Mississippi best, and when I offered to check out the University of Mississippi at Oxford, he said he'd already made up his mind to select Southern Mississippi.

Since we were now only less than a three-hour ride from Greenville, we'd made plans for a brief overnight stay with the Ibsens. Just a few weeks prior to our trip, the entire northern part of the state had experienced a severe ice storm, and as we traveled west on Highway 82, the downed telephone poles and wires made it look like a war zone. I'd never seen such destruction over as long a drive as we had.

We arrived in Greenville and took the usual trip past our old house. We enjoyed the hospitality of the Ibsens and were fortunate that their power had been restored. Unfortunately, with the piles of broken tree limbs everywhere and snapped utility poles, the town looked worse than ever before. Even a ride through Greenville failed to show any improvement in business activity or local enthusiasm for the place. It was still a rather depressing sight to behold. We left the following day to return to Hattiesburg and get the Amtrak train back to Philadelphia.

Jason decided to enroll at Southern Mississippi and was eventually accepted for his senior year. That summer, my wife, her mother, Jason, and our youngest son, Greg, traveled by van to Mississippi together to move Jason into his apartment. It was a long, tiring trip that I was glad I missed.

With Jason's college graduation in the spring of 1995, another family trip to Hattiesburg was in order. This time, we decided to travel by Amtrak again, thinking the train was the least stressful way to go. All things considered, the trip was a bit of an adventure and a fun way to travel, assuming one didn't require a good night's sleep. We arrived, rented a car, and attended Jason's graduation ceremonies. We stayed a couple of days and explored Hattiesburg as well as Gulfport and Biloxi on the Gulf Coast. I had my fill of crayfish and other southern delights before returning home on the train. We did not have time for a trip to Greenville this time. I thought perhaps we'd seen the last of Mississippi, but as usual, I was wrong again.

In September 2000, the Ibsens' daughter was getting married, and Donna and I were invited to the wedding in Greenville. No more train trips this time. We flew to Jackson and rented a car. We took the Natchez Trace Parkway, even though it was out of the way, because of its historic nature, passing through the tiny hamlets along the road in the southwestern part of the state. We stopped for a brief time in Natchez to look at the old antebellum homes still standing there. Our travel for the day ended in Vicksburg, where we decided to stay at a bed-and-breakfast for the night. Casino gambling on the riverfront had arrived at towns along the length of the Mississippi River, and Vicksburg was no exception.

After a night's stay and some shopping for antiques and Civil War artifacts, we headed north to Greenville, passing through Belzoni, one of my old stomping grounds. Interestingly, Belzoni seemed to have been built up a bit and now featured itself as the Catfish Capital of the World. Bully for them; they could certainly use some positive business advertising. That left me with a craving for some southern-fried catfish and hush puppies.

We continued on to Greenville and found our hotel located by the levee, just across from two new casinos. Greenville had begun to change at last as a result of new jobs from the casinos in town, located on Lake Ferguson. This hotel was new, as were several others. Our old honeymoon hotel, the Downtowner, had been torn down. It was beginning to look like Greenville was on its way to competing in the twenty-first century. Yet, as we toured through the town, it began to seem like the same old story. For every new restaurant that existed, an older, more homespun-type eat place was no longer in business. We stopped at a local bookstore and picked up a couple of books relating to the Delta. Years ago, there would have been very few, if any, of this style of book. It seemed like a few old roads had been extended and some new housing built to lengthen the corporate limit of the city. Our old street continued farther through what had been a cotton field, and newer homes and developments were popping up. Still, there seemed to be a lack of vitality to the place.

After a long weekend of reminiscing and celebrating with old friends, we returned home. I still felt a connection to the Delta, despite being away for twenty-five years, and I could not help but think how different our lives would be had we stayed there. I knew that Sally and Ken had a son who still wasn't married, and I thought to myself that we'd probably get one last wedding invitation to visit Greenville one more time.

Seven years later, my daughter was married, and the Ibsens flew up from Greenville to attend the special occasion. Following the wedding festivities, the Ibsens stayed with us for another few days, and we traveled and toured New York City together. The following year, we vacationed together in the Teton Range at Jackson Hole, Wyoming, and at Sun Valley, Idaho. There was still to be another trip to Greenville, however, spontaneous as it was, in 2014.

CHAPTER 21
Mississippi Musings

*Come and experience the spirit and mystique
of Greenville and Washington County,
where the culture and heritage of the past
still thrive in a timeless land.*

—Greenville / Washington County
Convention & Visitors Bureau

I was inspired to write this story about my experiences in the Mississippi Delta after first watching the film *The Help*. While my adventures were not quite as rash as those depicted in the film, my three years in the Delta did involve some of the hatred and some of the pain presented to us in the movie. I thought my experiences would be an extension of the film, coming as they were a few years later than the time frame depicted in *The Help*. I began to write this memoir in 2013, some fifty years after the beginnings of the civil rights marches in the Deep South. The fifty-year anniversary of the Mississippi Freedom Summer of 1964, the death of the three civil rights workers in Philadelphia, Mississippi, and of the signing of the Civil Rights Act of 1964 seemed to me to be an appropriate time to discuss my past and to examine how far we've come as a nation with regard to racial equality.

As I began the memoir, the stories flowed as the past memories came to mind. Mississippi was so foreign a place to me when I first arrived that I simply could not really comprehend all of its troubled history. And when it all comes right down to it, its violence broke out when the black man and woman simply asked for the same right to vote as white folks had, which was granted to them in the Constitution of the United States. It could have happened anywhere, but it happened in Mississippi. When I served the FBI in Greenville and in its surrounding Delta counties, the elected political figures, the county commissioners, and the sheriffs were all white. It seemed that this small group was so fearful of the black electorate removing them from office, prompted by the NAACP, that those blacks urging voter registration had been targeted for death. How tragic, and how foolish.

Before I completed my memoir, I wanted to return to the Delta for one more firsthand look at any changes that might have occurred since my last trip in 2000. It had been fourteen years since my last visit, and I wondered if any life or vitality had returned to the Delta area.

Prior to my departure, I called the Washington County Sheriff's Office in Greenville and asked to speak with Sheriff Milton M. Gaston. I knew the sheriff was an African-American, and I wanted to seek his perspective on the racial changes that had occurred in the Delta. I was directed by the operator to Gaston's administrative assistant and reached her answering machine. I identified myself as a retired FBI agent who had been assigned to the Greenville Resident Agency during the early 1970s and mentioned that I was doing some research for a book I was writing. I said that I would be in Greenville the following week, providing exact dates for my trip, and said I would like to interview the sheriff about changes in the area since I'd departed. I left both my cell telephone and home telephone numbers for a return call. I did not receive a return call prior to leaving on my venture but hoped I'd eventually get a cell call setting up a time to get together once I arrived.

My wife and I departed on our trip and worked our way slowly to the Mississippi Delta, stopping along the way in Charlottesville and Petersburg, Virginia. Petersburg was a quaint, old southern town that seemed to be somewhere between growing and collapsing. In many ways, it reminded me of the Greenville I was so familiar with in the past. For every new restaurant, there was a failed business. For every open shop, there was a closed one next to it. It became a stark reminder to me of the failed Reconstruction era in our nation's history.

We traveled on from there to Lumberton, North Carolina, to attend a book conference event known as Book 'Em NC. After the event, we took a tour of the original Lumberton town-square area. Much like Petersburg, we observed beautiful old homes lining the avenues that led into the town square. Upon arrival in the square, we passed the usual monument to the gallant Confederate soldiers and looked upon a well-kept, neat square of old storefronts. Sadly, the preponderance of the buildings were vacant, with only a few businesses now occupied by law offices and an occasional curio shop or bank. The center of town was virtually dead, yet had so much potential for restoration and new life. It was sad to see what had happened to Lumberton. Yet the outskirts of town were thriving with corporate-America stores, complete with all of the fast-food restaurants, Wal-Mart, and Lowe's. There were a few independent restaurants in the area, but for the most part, it was virtually corporate America at its best. I could only wonder if the charm of the old center of town would recover and compete with these corporate giants. It was very sad to see the changes, allegedly for the better.

Following our stay in Lumberton, we continued our travel toward Mississippi, stopping for lunch in Augusta, Georgia. Again, we were presented with an aging southern town appearing to be in the throes of not being able to survive. We didn't have much time to check out the area as we wanted to get to Birmingham, Alabama, for the night. While we prefer to stay at a local bed-and-breakfast to enjoy the culture of the places we visit, we stayed in a Comfort Inn in Birmingham that night.

The following day we made our way back into the Magnolia State. My first notable surprise came as we left Alabama and entered Mississippi on Highway 82, the highway that runs east and west straight across the state, which I was very familiar with in the past. Happily, the road was now a four-lane highway, far different from the two-lane road I'd traveled so many times before. And it was four lanes all the way to Greenville, which was quite a pleasant surprise, making travel so much easier. To add to that joy, the roadway was in excellent shape, in better condition that any of the roads we had previously traveled. We stopped in Starkville for a quick lunch. Starkville, a town supported in large part by Mississippi State University, seemed to be doing quite well from an economic viewpoint. The center of town was busy, and most stores and shops appeared open for business. Was this a harbinger of things to come in Greenville? I certainly hoped it would be.

After lunch, we began the final portion of our journey. As we headed west, the land flattened out as we neared the Delta. When we passed Greenwood, I marveled at the size of the plantations along the highway. Still looking desolate and vast, I'd never seen as much farmland for so great an area as I've seen in the Delta. It reminded me that the fertile soil brought in by the great river is the true lifeblood of Mississippi and its people. As I approached Indianola, I realized that there were many changes since the last time I'd visited. The town had grown in size, and corporate America had discovered the place at last. Perhaps that was a good thing for

Indianola; at least it looked to me to be thriving more so than I remembered in its past. We were only a half hour away from Greenville now, and I was really looking forward to what I might find.

Then finally, Greenville, Mississippi. We'd made it at last. Since our directions to the home of our friends the Ibsens directed us to turn, we did not get to see the downtown area until later the next day. Upon arrival, we were greeted by our host, Sally, and we unpacked from our journey. I let her know that I wanted to see as much of the Delta as I could in the next six days. I asked her about the possibility of speaking to the local Greenville police chief. She told me that he was an African-American, and that she didn't really know him or have any contact with him. I still had not received a telephone call from the sheriff, so I decided to wait on any law enforcement interviews.

That evening, the four of us went to supper at Doe's Eat Place. It had been quite some time since we last ate there, possibly even before we left Mississippi on transfer to New York. Fortunately, absolutely nothing had changed about the restaurant building or the food. The steaks, fried shrimp, tamales, and their simple specialty salad tasted as wonderful as ever. There's something unique about walking through the kitchen of the place where you are going to eat. Doe's is such an unusual eating place that it has been featured on Anthony Bourdain's television show.

The following day, we all piled into Ken's SUV, and he took us on the tour of the Delta I was so looking forward to prior to our arrival. We headed south on Highway 1, past a still-existing antebellum home that was actually for sale. I would love to own such a place, but reality sank in as we continued to journey past Leroy Percy State Park, the largest park in Mississippi. I remembered the park well as this was the place I stopped with Ken White-Spunner on one occasion to watch as alligators in a lake devoured a dead cow that had been fed to them by park officials. I'd never seen alligators feed prior to that time, and I watched in amazement as they tore into the flesh of the dead animal and spun their bodies rapidly to tear off a big hunk of tasty meat. I remember standing on the foot bridge with Ken, just above the carnage taking place below me, watching intently and hoping at the same time that the bridge wouldn't collapse into the lake below.

We continued past the park, traveling south toward Louise, Mississippi, where Ken pointed out the location of a bank that had been robbed, with a subsequent investigation conducted by me. It was amazing to me that he still recalled the event. We stopped in town and parked outside of the Lee Hong Company general store. The town looked very close to a ghost town, with most businesses shuttered up. Ken wanted to stop into the store to buy some of Mr. Lee's special marinade, called Hoover sauce (no connection to late FBI Director J. Edgar Hoover). Lee, a native of China, was only a year old when his family moved to Mississippi and his father opened his store. According to an article about the now-famous Hoover sauce by Chris Talbot in the *Cape Cod Times* (Associated Press, September 19, 2007), Louise, Mississippi, was described as a fading farm town of about three hundred people. To be honest, I would be surprised if there was anywhere close to that number on this day. We bought some Hoover sauce and had a nice conversation with Mr. Lee. He opened a can of boiled peanuts for us to share as we chatted. This store existed when I was working the territory, but I do not recall ever doing any shopping there.

Following our little experience at the general store, we headed to Belzoni, simply passing through after stopping at a Quick Mart for some soft drinks. I could see that the town had expanded, as there were more stores and business activity along the highway than ever before. Perhaps that was a good sign for the once-named Catfish Capital of the World. While I would have liked to drive through town, I didn't want to press the issue as we still had a full day planned, with a lot of driving yet to go.

We headed north on Highway 61, which, like Highway 82, had been enlarged into a four-lane highway, making the trip much more pleasurable. We worked our way onto Highway 49, heading north toward the Parchman penitentiary. As we traveled through the farmland, I was surprised to learn that many of the old cotton fields had been converted to corn fields. Ken explained that with the advent of the new biofuels, it became more profitable for the local planters to grow corn instead of cotton. Since this was early March, we didn't see any crops growing. However, we did see a lot of planters working on the soil to prepare for spring planting.

Our next destination was Clarksdale, Mississippi, well northeast of Greenville. Prior to my arrival in Greenville in 1972, Clarksdale had an FBI resident agency of its own. It was subsequently closed and consolidated into the Oxford Resident Agency. We stopped for lunch at the Ground Zero Blues Club, owned jointly by movie star Morgan Freeman and the mayor of Clarksdale, Bill Luckett. We met with Bill and his wife, Francine Gardner, a cousin of Sally Ibsen, for lunch at the blues club. I regretted that we did not have the time to stay until evening and listen to some of the local blues music. Clarksdale is often referred to as the home of blues music. The building was certainly quite old and unique, with graffiti of all sorts covering every available wall space inside. It was exactly what one would think of as a genuine honky-tonk in Mississippi.

After lunch, we began our return trip back to Greenville, driving south on Highway 61. We passed through Cleveland, which was built up much more than it had been when I served here, and it was encouraging to see how vibrant it appeared to be. Even the Clarksdale area was now boasting a population of near twenty thousand residents. Ken mentioned that many whites who lived in Greenville were beginning to move away to more distant towns like Clarksdale, Cleveland, and Leland. He thought this was why the towns seemed to have new life and growth to them. Late that afternoon, we returned to Greenville and settled down for the evening. Ken had to work the following day, so I made plans with the ladies to have lunch in Greenville and to drive around a bit to see what had changed.

The next morning, the three of us drove into the center of Greenville. I was surprised to see that the serpentine-shaped roadway through the center of town had been straightened out. During our stay in the seventies, the straight road was changed into a serpentine one, hoping to make Washington Street more attractive to shoppers. Apparently, it did not do the job, and it was eventually returned to its old, more practical shape. The downtown area of Greenville had not changed that much, although it seemed that more shops were closed than new ones opened. The only bookstore in town had closed, and now one had to travel an hour away to Greenwood just to visit a quality bookstore. The old barbershop and Jim's Café still stood in their original locations. I insisted on lunch at Jim's Café for old times' sake and enjoyed a wonderful plate of fried catfish. After lunch, my tourism ended as there was a two-to-one vote in favor of shopping. I did see that there were some new stores on the outskirts of town that hadn't been there before. Greenville did look livelier than Lumberton, North Carolina, at least in its old shopping district.

All of the old gambling establishments were still in business, and I learned that betting on sports events had not ended at all since my failed plans for a raid on them. Two of the casinos that were located over the levee adjacent to the downtown area were no longer operating. There was only one local casino, and it was located near the new Mississippi River bridge well south of town.

Our shopping trip took us to all the new corporate businesses, like Wal-Mart and CVS Pharmacy. There were now three McDonald's restaurants in town, where there had been none when we first arrived in 1972. The Greenville Lumber Company, builders of our first home, was no longer in business. In its place in a different location stood a Lowe's store. Greenville was beginning to look like all the other southern towns we'd visited in the past ten days or so. Old mom-and-pop stores were gone, replaced by national chain stores and chain restaurants. The southern charm of the small towns and thriving local merchants seemed to be almost as distant a memory as the Civil War. It was sad to see the old ways disappear, yet there seemed to be a bit more vitality to the region and more life on the streets. And that, for Greenville, was a good thing.

We stopped at our former church as Sally needed to pick up something. While there, we met with the interim pastor. A kind fellow, he was serving until they could find a permanent replacement for him. It was as though no one really wanted to take on the job. Sadly, the entrance doors were now alarmed and locked. It was simply a sign of the times that local crime knew no boundaries and would include theft from churches if they weren't locked up. I expected to hear that the church now had a significant black membership roll but was surprised to learn there were few black members. Apparently, the churches in Greenville remained predominantly segregated: black folks going to black churches, and white folks going to white churches. No one seemed to be able to explain why that continued to be how it was.

During two different evenings, we attended cultural events of a different sort. The first event occurred at Washington School, a private school in Greenville where Sally's granddaughter attended. The school was putting on a spring musical program, and all classes of the student body would be present. Upon arrival at the school, I would estimate about fifty children were in each class, from first through sixth grade, separated by class on the front stage. That number may not be totally accurate. However, I counted the African-American children who sat on the stage and counted exactly six. I may have missed one, but I doubt it. In some ways, it was encouraging to see that the school was integrated, despite there being so few African-Americans present. To be honest, I was surprised to see any at all. After the program ended, all the parents and students interacted with each other, and there seemed to be no bad blood between the races.

Another evening took us to a playhouse, converted from an old junior high school, to see a production of the play *Les Misérables*. The actors were local residents, and both the actors and audience were of mixed race. The white mayor of Greenville was there. However, I was advised that the previous mayor had been a woman, and the mayor before her a black male. It seemed that race was no longer a factor separating those who lived in the town.

The next day, Ken took us on a lengthier drive through Greenville at my request. We drove down the historically black, high-crime areas of Nelson and Clay Streets. The streets were empty of civilians, although it was before twelve noon. He took us past our old house, still in rather good condition, yet up for sheriff's sale. Many of the old neighborhoods south of Highway 82, which had been traditionally mostly white, were now predominately black. Ken estimated the black population in Greenville as close to 90 percent. He noted that it wasn't that more black folks were moving to Greenville, but it was a result of more whites moving out of Greenville to towns an hour away or to the Mississippi coast.

We took a short trip to Lake Village in Chicot County, Arkansas, and toured the homes located around a large lake that had formed from the Mississippi River. Many of the homes were quite beautiful, and every time I enquired about a cost, I would be off by hundreds of thousands of dollars. I knew that if I moved back to Mississippi or Arkansas, I could live like a king. Unfortunately, the humidity would be arriving shortly, along with the heat, and as bad as the winter of 2014 had been up north, that Mississippi heat and humidity of summer wasn't worth a beautiful, inexpensive vacation home.

We returned to Washington County and stopped at Warfield Point, walking up an observation tower for a good look at the mighty river. Markings on a painted billboard informed visitors of the record flood heights. I was reminded of the flood in 1974, when I could see the entire Marina restaurant above the levee in town, appearing as if it were sitting on the top of the levee. And that wasn't even the worst flood on record. We returned to town and traveled along the concrete levee, looking at the markers in place to show the previous flood heights. Much to my surprise, a new nickname for Greenville was painted on the river side of the levee. It read, "Welcome to Greenville—The Heart and Soul of the Delta." Perhaps the change was made to bring the historic nature of blues music into advertising for the town. Earlier references to Greenville as the Port City of the Delta or the Queen City of the Delta seemed to be passé at this time.

In the six days we'd spent in Greenville, I'd seen as much of the town and surrounding Delta as I'd hoped to see when we planned our trip. I was disappointed that the Washington County sheriff never returned my telephone call for an interview. I simply wanted to get a law enforcement perspective for an area I used to work from a black law enforcement officer, to see if my work forty years ago did something positive for the people of Mississippi. The area that I knew forty years ago had changed in some ways, and in some ways it hadn't changed at all. The racial makeup of the population was about the same, with perhaps a few more blacks in the city. The town had more attractions, even if they were the corporate giants and chain stores. At least there was some economic growth. The area was still and will likely always be a rural farming community. The racial tension that I remembered in the seventies seemed to have eased up quite a bit. Poverty still was evident in the rural areas, and I suspect jobs were still scarce. With farm mechanization, even jobs on the large plantations were limited as massive machines could now do all the work that used to be done by physical labor.

Perhaps the greatest change in Mississippi, a state with a population that is about 37 percent black, is that there are now more elected black officials than in any other state in the Union. I can give much credit to the FBI and to the gutsy civil rights workers who risked their lives to ensure equal voting rights for all.

Mississippi got a bad rap in the early 1960s, especially in the North, as a backward state that treated its black population with hatred and contempt. Perhaps that is true to some extent. But what is seldom stated is that blacks living in the North weren't treated any better than those who were living in the South. I remember living in my row home in Philadelphia, Pennsylvania, in the late 1950s, when things were so bad for the blacks in Mississippi. If a black family moved into a row home anywhere near or in a white neighborhood, the entire block of houses would slowly go up for sale as whites fled from the city to move to the suburbs. Any white homeowner who sold his home to a black person was accused of "breaking the block." The gracious, abolition-loving northerners would simply move away rather than live on a block with one black family. And we claim to be better than the people in the South? Our political districts up north were always gerrymandered to keep the black population isolated and impotent in their personal efforts to succeed and improve their way of living. The mayors in Philadelphia, Pennsylvania, were all white well into the 1970s. Our schools in the black communities were almost all black, and the white schools were mostly white. But it was important to integrate the schools in the South while seeming to ignore the situation at home.

I'm not sure if history can tell us exactly when the first effort was made by the black population to secure the rights and liberties afforded to them by the Constitution. One can look at the Turner Rebellion in 1830 as the start of the slave insurrections. But I rather think that the first effort to seek freedom and justice for the black race started with the first black person bound in chains and forced into slave labor. From that day on, until passage of the Thirteenth Amendment of the Constitution banning slavery and then the Fourteenth Amendment making all people equal under the law, did the hope of liberty begin to shine. Yet Reconstruction failed, and the sad plight of the black man continued for another one hundred years.

Now at last, for the past fifty years, positive changes are taking place. In 1972, I would have looked at any person even remotely suggesting that a black man would one day be president of the United States as a complete idiot. But we have indeed elected a black president. What statement could be any stronger a truth as to the progress made by the African-American / black community in the past two hundred years than that? There is still, and will sadly always be in the years to come, racial intolerance by the ignorant. But as the generations come and go, perhaps the troubled past will be put aside, and we of all colors can live together in peace.

Epilogue

*To understand the world, you must first
understand a place like Mississippi.*

Anonymous; attributed to William Faulkner

On July 10, 2014, a very significant event was held at the Jackson Division of the FBI. This was the fiftieth anniversary of the opening of the Jackson Division (July 10, 1964) by FBI Director J. Edgar Hoover, shortly after the three civil rights workers disappeared in Neshoba County. The anniversary celebration included several notables, including Mark F. Giuliano, deputy director of the FBI; William "Bill" Winter, a former Mississippi governor; Jim Hood, attorney general for Mississippi; Tony Yarber, the mayor of Jackson; and James Young, the mayor of Philadelphia, Mississippi, where the bodies of the slain civil rights workers were ultimately discovered. Despite the impressive cast of dignitaries present, including a taped video presentation from FBI Director James Comey played at the event, the one notable person who stood out above the rest was Myrlie Evers-Williams, widow of slain civil rights martyr Medgar Evers.

The prepared speeches were all full of praise for the FBI and its response to the national emergency occurring in Mississippi fifty years ago. Former special agent in charge Daniel McMullen served as master of ceremonies. Jackson Mayor Yarber welcomed the crowd on behalf of the 175,000 Jackson-area residents and offered his thanks for all those sacrifices in the past that enabled him to become mayor today. He singled out the FBI, whose entrance to Mississippi in 1964 ensured that it would take the leading role in bringing justice to all. He discussed his desire for a continued partnership between the FBI and the City of Jackson for the next fifty years, hoping all are counted and none are left out.

Sid Bonderson, legislative liaison to Governor Phil Bryant, then read a proclamation for the governor recognizing the FBI and its fifty years of service. He noted the successes in the work and civil liberties of the citizens of Mississippi in many different areas. He ended by proclaiming that week FBI Week in Mississippi.

Jim Hood, attorney general of Mississippi, provided commentary that law enforcement personnel have always been his heroes. Hood was the man who successfully retried the Mississippi Burning case in 2005, involving the three civil rights workers who were murdered in Neshoba

County. He noted that he appreciated all the work done by the FBI and the Department of Justice, and said that it was as a result of their labors that he was able to succeed with the prosecution of those responsible for the heinous crime.

Deputy Director Mark Giuliano discussed the murder of fourteen-year-old Emmett Till in 1955, the riots in 1962 regarding the entrance of James Meredith into the University of Mississippi, and the murders of NAACP officer Medgar Evers in 1963 and the three civil rights volunteers in 1964 who were slain in the period known as Freedom Summer. This was the tipping point when J. Edgar Hoover handpicked and appointed Roy K. Moore to lead the FBI effort in opening the Jackson Division. And more recently, Giuliano noted with pride, the FBI in Jackson has continued to work the civil rights cold cases where justice was delayed but not denied.

It was the presentation delivered by Myrlie Evers-Williams that stilled the crowd gathered for the ceremony. She opened her remarks by stating it was so important to remember the past and the names, known and unknown, of all who gave so much to make Mississippi and the United States what it is today. "We thank you, we appreciate you, all working to bring about a society of justice for us. Fifty-one years ago, we lost a man dearest to our hearts." She then continued, "The FBI was a name we feared and despised at that time, believing it to be an institution to keep people of color down, not a friend but a foe. I am proud to say I see the FBI as playing the role that they did, and I'm reaching a point in my heart where I can say 'friend.'"

She talked about the third trial held for the murder of her late husband. "There were two or three FBI agents sitting behind me in the courtroom. I recall vividly when the verdict of guilty was read, I felt the ghost of Mississippi escaped from my very being. My hope was that Mississippi could be the Mississippi that Medgar Evers believed it could be. I felt a hand on my shoulder—the hand of one of the FBI agents—and I felt a connection between that hand, the verdict, and the hope Medgar Evers believed in. Mississippi has hope—it will be all we hope and trust it will be. The FBI played such an important role in that." She then warned, "We cannot sleep on our laurels. I pray that all of us will be Americans under the Stars and Stripes."

A richly deserved standing ovation followed her presentation.

Former Mississippi governor William Winter followed Mrs. Evers-Williams's remarks, noting, "She has spoken for all of us, lived for all of us, and her martyred husband died for all of us." He said, "As a white man during the time, I felt imprisoned by a system I didn't think we could do anything about. But along came Medgar Evers. He freed the white people too." Then he added, "The 1964 murders set in motion the unleashing of the federal government to turn the tide against those who would destroy civilized society in our country. We were right on the edge of chaos in the country. We welcomed the coming to Mississippi of the FBI."

As the program ended, former SAC McMullen concluded his remarks by noting that "the FBI has changed to meet the current threats of the day, as has the Jackson Division. The Jackson office continues to stand for liberty and justice for all."

Some five months earlier, on February 21, 2014, the *New York Times* reported a disturbing incident at the University of Mississippi. Three college freshmen, all nineteen years old, were reported to have placed a noose around the neck of a statue honoring the college's first black student, James Meredith, who entered the college in 1962 amid riots that killed two people. The students apparently involved were all from Georgia. The report indicated that the vandalism might result in federal charges against the three students.

In an article by Jay Hathaway at Kinja.com on April 18, 2014, it was reported that the three students involved belonged to the Sigma Phi Epsilon fraternity. That fraternity had decided to close its chapter on campus following the incident. The article further stated that the college was pursuing disciplinary action against the three freshmen and that the FBI continued to investigate the matter. The Lafayette County district attorney said no state charges would be forthcoming because Mississippi's hate-crime laws only apply when there's a separate underlying crime. Since the statue wasn't damaged, the prosecutors are not pursuing vandalism charges.

This ugly incident and others like it throughout our country remind us of the words from Myrlie Evers-Williams when she said, "We cannot remain sitting on our laurels." Racism still exists, and only the passage of more time coupled with better education for all and vigorous prosecution when needed will likely be the answer to removing racism forever from our national psyche.

And one last comment...In the course of my research into writing this story, I learned that my old FBI resident agency in Greenville was closed by the Jackson office. In two press releases from the Jackson FBI in August 2012, it was reported that the Greenville and Tupelo resident agencies were being consolidated with the Oxford Resident Agency. The press release went on to say that "the consolidation will not reduce the number of FBI resources in the northern part of the state, within the state, or in the FBI Jackson Division. Any changes the FBI makes to the alignment of our resources, both personnel and otherwise, are for the purpose of allowing the FBI to better accomplish its mission."

If I've learned anything about my long and wonderful association with the FBI, there is much truth to the statement in the press release closing the two offices. New offices were subsequently opened in perhaps more troubled areas of the state. New national priorities for the FBI also clearly dictate solid reasons to change resources to better meet future challenges. It's apparent that the rural Mississippi Delta no longer contains an abundance of the new investigative priorities of today's FBI, including counterterrorism, counterintelligence, nuclear proliferation, and cybercrime matters. All civil rights cases will continue to be worked as energetically as they were in the past fifty years, and all federal criminal laws will still be enforced, only now from the Oxford Resident Agency, some two and a half hours away.

The actual reason for closing my old office may be lost in the bureaucratic red tape and "other reasons" common to all federal agencies. When talking with some retired special agents who worked and continue to reside in Mississippi, I learned that the Greenville office was closed because no one was willing to go there on assignment. That news certainly came as no surprise to me, having lived and worked there. What is somewhat disconcerting is that no one was transferred there in spite of their unwillingness to serve. I simply cannot imagine refusing a transfer in the FBI that I knew and loved. Like it or not, we either reported for duty or resigned from the bureau. Apparently, the Greenville office became known as a hardship assignment through the years and simply could not be staffed with appropriate personnel willing to volunteer and serve there. It seems that most of my Greenville colleagues knew it was a hardship assignment forty-two years ago. Yet we went and served, proudly for the most part. And hopefully, we made a positive difference and left the Delta in a better state than when we arrived on the job.

There will always be a special place in my heart for Greenville and the Mississippi Delta. It's where I began my life with my wife, raised my first child, and learned so much about the checkered past of the state. We made friends we've kept for more than forty years, and I look forward to returning for future visits. I hope I made a positive impact on the lives of many of Mississippi's citizens, along with my colleagues in the FBI. And for all of that, I remain proud of my service in the Delta.

Author's Note

One of the primary reasons I have now completed two books about my experiences in the FBI is that thinking back and reflecting on my career brings nothing but pleasant memories of important work and the wonderful men and women who aided me in the mission of the FBI. I have been truly blessed to have had such a marvelous career, and would still be working for the FBI if it weren't for the mandatory retirement age.

In the preparation of this book, I was fortunate to locate many articles in the *Delta Democrat-Times* that had been copied and archived by Ancestry.com, a wonderful research site. Without those publicly available news stories, some of the stories I related in my book may not have been allowed to be published.

I was also very fortunate to get more active with social media, particularly Facebook. In so doing, I was able to locate and renew old friendships with many of the FBI employees I worked with in the Jackson Division. I want to thank all the former special agents who allowed me to use their names in this story, making it more personal and accurate. I'd also like to thank former FBI support employees, especially Barbara Little and Melissa Eatherly, for their help in remembering some of the old cases. A big thank you goes out to Ray Mislock, a former partner in Greenville who provided some of the vintage photographs that appear in this memoir. A special note of thanks goes to John Neelley, my former supervisor in Greenville, who was able to help fill in names and events that occurred during my stay in the Delta. John has a wealth of stories of his own about the Mississippi Delta and should write a book himself. I must also thank my longtime Greenville friends, Sally and Ken Ibsen, for their ongoing friendship, for providing me with updated information on happenings in the Delta, and for being perfect hosts for my wife and me during all our trips back to Greenville.

As I was required to obtain permission from the FBI to publish this book, I'd like to thank the FBI Prepublication Review Unit for their assistance and subsequent authorization of this story. I'd also like to pay a special note of thanks to Mark Zaid, my attorney, who provided valuable legal assistance to me in the preparation of this manuscript.

All of my experiences as written in this memoir are as accurate as my memory and the local newspaper accounts recall the events. Most of the stories remain vivid in my mind, as the entire experience of living and working in the Mississippi Delta was truly unique to me. I want to thank my family for their support of my interest in writing, and my son Greg for his assistance in editing, working with the images, and his technical computer skills in assisting me in getting this manuscript to the publisher. I'd also like to pay tribute to all the folks at CreateSpace who helped me in getting this memoir published. Lastly, my loving thanks go to my wife Donna, who was cheerfully willing to accompany me on all my FBI career transfers without complaint.

Without a doubt, the hard work and perseverance of all FBI employees working in Mississippi since 1964 has made a huge impact on improving the lives of all Mississippians. Yet still today, racial problems continue to exist throughout this great nation. It is my hope that with time and future generations, the hatred and mistrust will slowly vanish from our national way of life, and all of us will share equally in the freedoms granted to us by our forefathers.

JWW

Appendix

Actual miscellaneous correspondence from FBI headquarters pertaining to the closing and subsequent reopening of the Jackson Division of the FBI in July 1964.

Cypress Shade

Office Memorandum · UNITED STATES GOVERNMENT

TO : THE DIRECTOR DATE: September 5, 1946

FROM : THE EXECUTIVE CONFERENCE

SUBJECT:

The Executive Conference of September 5, 1946, consisting of Messrs. Tolson, E. A. Tamm, Ladd, Rosen, Mohpan, Harbo, Tracy, Hendon and Glavin considered the advisability of closing the Jackson, Mississippi Office and reallocating the present Jackson Territory into the Memphis and New Orleans Division. For the Director's information, there is attached hereto a map of the state of Mississippi, that portion colored in green being the Northern District of Mississippi, that uncolored, the Southern District. The Jackson headquarters city is shown in the Southern District and all Resident Agencies are shown in the Northern District in the state.

PENDING CASES.

At the present time, there are 566 cases pending in the Jackson Division, of which number 101 are selective service cases.

The total cases pending 142 in the Northern Judicial District and 424 in the Southern Judicial District.

There are 6 Resident Agents in the Northern District and 7 Resident Agents in the Southern District.

The work in the state of Mississippi is so distributed that the work is handled out of the Resident Agencies, there being only 137 cases being handled by 6 Agents out of the Headquarters city of Jackson.

For the Director's information, the following is the spread of work by Resident Agents in the Judicial District in question:

NORTHERN JUDICIAL DISTRICT

Clarksdale -- 55 cases -- 2 Resident Agents

Tupelo -- 30 cases -- 1 Resident Agent

Columbus -- 24 cases -- 1 Resident Agent

Greenwood -- 33 cases -- 1 Resident Agent

MEMO FOR THE DIRECTOR -- Page -2-

SOUTHERN JUDICIAL DISTRICT

Greenville -- 36 cases -- 2 Resident Agents

Meridian -- 40 cases -- 1 Resident Agent

Natchez -- 29 cases -- 1 Resident Agent

Laurel -- 27 cases -- 1 Resident Agent

Pascagoula -- 27 cases -- 1 Resident Agent

Hattiesburg -- 41 cases -- 2 Resident Agents

Gulfport -- 87 cases -- 3 Resident Agents

For the Director's information, the Resident Agents at Gulfport and Pascagoula, which would be handled out of the New Orleans Office, are closer to New Orleans than they are to Jackson. The Clarksdale and Tupelo Resident Agents in the Northern Judicial District are just as close to Memphis as they are to Jackson.

The present pending work in the Memphis and New Orleans Division.

The Memphis Division at the present time has 555 pending cases and, if we are to include the Northern Judicial District of Mississippi, we would add 142 cases, making a total work load at Mississippi of 697 cases.

The New Orleans Division presently has 1,031 cases pending and, if we are to add most of the Southern Judicial District of Mississippi to the New Orleans Division, we would add 424 cases, making total case load of New Orleans 1,455 cases.

TRANSPORTATION.

All the territory in Mississippi could be just as well reached from Memphis and New Orleans as it is from Jackson. There are good first-class roads from Memphis and New Orleans to the various sections of the state where we have Resident Agents at the present time and from New Orleans to Jackson.

RENTAL AGREEMENT.

It will be recalled at the time we endeavored to renew our lease for space at Jackson, Mississippi, that we had a difficult

MEMO FOR THE DIRECTOR -- Page -3-

time in securing a renewal of the lease. The real estate men in the city of Jackson, due to certain activities of OPA and FBA, were entirely out of sympathy with the Federal Government and with the exception of the Bureau, refused to renew any lease for Federal Government service. They renewed our lease only after the Bureau had insisted that they do so. They did not give us any cancellation clause in the lease. Our annual rental is $11,022.50, and if the lessor at Jackson, Mississippi, was so inclined, he could hold us to the lease until the end of the year. Mr. Glavin pointed out to the Conference, however, that since the Commercial Real Estate Men in Jackson were anxious to get out of Government contracts, that they might be most happy to cancel our lease on 30 days notice at the present time, should we desire to close the Jackson Office.

The Conference unanimously recommends, therefore, that an effort be made to close the Jackson Office, and that the SAC at Jackson discuss with the lessor the possibility of our cancelling our lease and if we are successful in doing so, that immediate steps be made to close the Jackson Office within a period of 30 days and transfer the Jackson Territory to New Orleans and Memphis Divisions.

Respectfully submitted,
FOR THE CONFERENCE

Clyde Tolson

E. A. Tamm

Attachment

CC: Mr. Hendon
    Mr. Clegg

FBH/dmb

Appendix

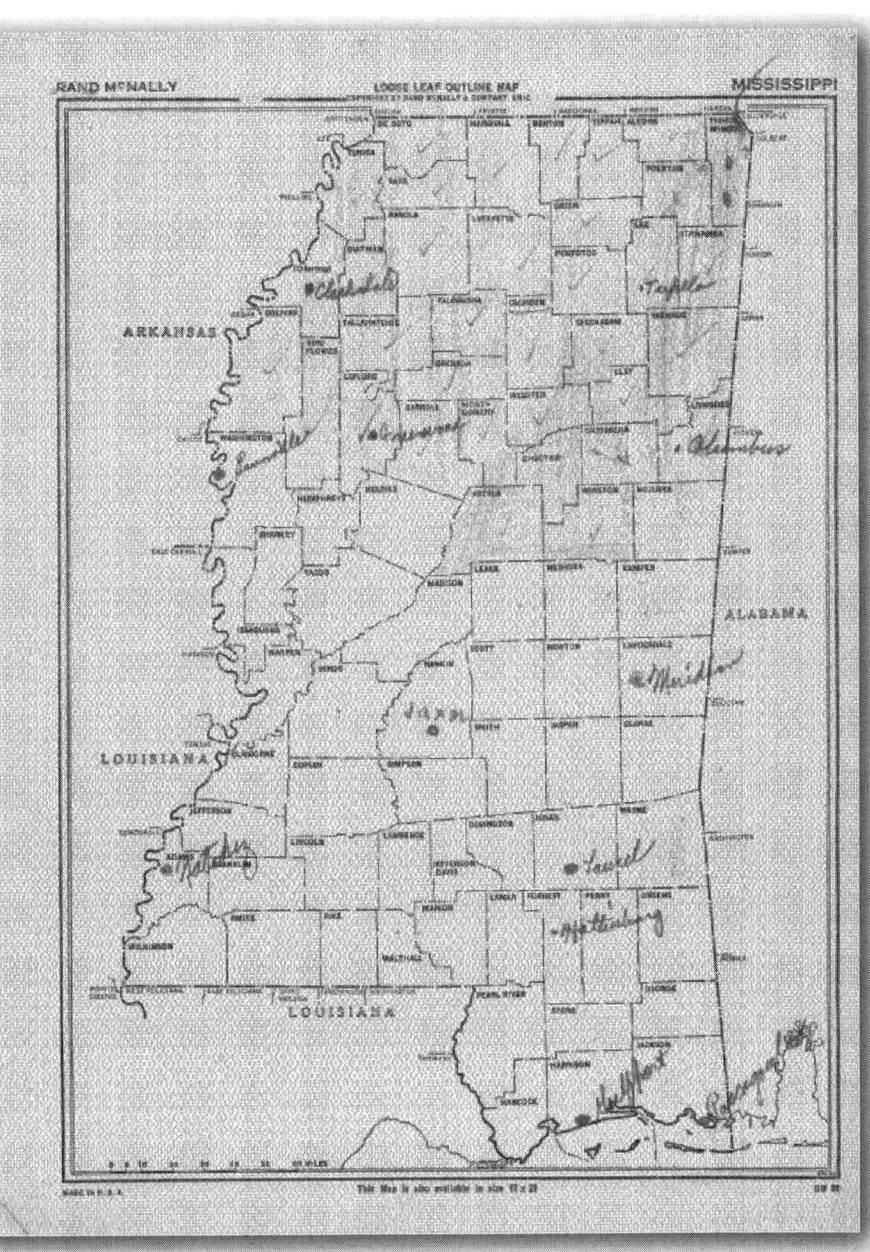

UNITED STATES GOVERNMENT
Memorandum

TO: MR. MOHR
DATE: June 30, 1964
FROM: N. P. CALLAHAN
SUBJECT: OPENING OF OFFICE
JACKSON, MISSISSIPPI
AVAILABILITY OF SPACE

SAC Dissly of Memphis, who is in Jackson looking over the availability of space suitable to house an office, telephonically advised this afternoon that a preliminary survey ascertained that the most suitable space is located in the First Federal Bank Building consisting of the Sixth Floor. This building is approximately two blocks from our present Resident Agency space which is located in the Post Office Building.

Dissly stated that the building manager for this building was not immediately available and he and the GSA representative from Atlanta have an appointment at 4:00 pm, CST, to see the manager to ascertain the exact amount of square footage on this floor (estimated at from 7,000 to 10,000 square feet) and ascertain how long it will take to ready it for occupancy. In this respect Dissly pointed out that the space as it now stands is entirely open with no rooms or partitions dividing it and the management would partition and lay it out to suit the needs of the new tenant.

SAC Dissly further advised that Mr. Capes, the GSA representative from Atlanta, has been going around this morning with Department Attorney Walter Sheridan to try to obtain space for he and two other staff members in Jackson and indicated that should the FBI open an office and give up the space our Resident Agency presently occupies in the Post Office Building, that this latter space would no doubt be made available to the Departmental Attorneys which would be desirable in that it would remove them from the same building that we would be located in. I told Dissly we definitely did not want to have the Departmental Attorneys on the same floor with us and preferably not in the same building with us; this should be borne in mind in his negotiations with GSA in obtaining any space we might need.

SAC Dissly stated that Mr. Capes had requested that Mr. C. Q. Smith of our headquarters be permitted to work with him in drawing up a layout the way we would want our office set up in order that he could utilize this in negotiations with the building manager in arriving at a lease figure for this space. Smith has handled similar assignments in connection with the openings of Tampa, Las Vegas and other offices and the relocation of other offices and pursuant to our discussion he will join Mr. Capes in Jackson tomorrow morning and work out this detail. It will be impressed upon the

NPC:jlk
1 - Mr. DeLoach
(6)

OVER...

Appendix

Memorandum for Mr. Mohr
RE: OPENING OF OFFICE, JACKSON, MISS.
   AVAILABILITY OF SPACE

building management the urgency with which we need to occupy this space in connection with any negotiations with them in order that they can accomplish the necessary layout work in the shortest possible time.

The Director may desire to give consideration to making some announcement to the President and/or the press with respect to our efforts to establish an office at Jackson since there is the possibility our efforts in locating space may become known locally and precipitate press inquiries concerning this.

The above is submitted for information. We will follow this matter extremely close to its consummation.

TELETYPE

12-03 PM   URGENT 7-10-64   MSL
TO ALL SACS   NY --4--
FROM DIRECTOR   1 P

    JACKSON, MISSISSIPPI, FIELD DIVISION OPENED TODAY WITH ROY K. MOORE AS SPECIAL AGENT IN CHARGE. IT WILL COVER THE ENTIRE STATE OF MISSISSIPPI. THE ADDRESS IS FIRST FEDERAL SAVINGS AND LOAN BUILDING STATE AND CAPITOL STREETS, JACKSON, MISSISSIPPI. POST OFFICE BOX ONE FOUR FIVE ZERO IS ASSIGNED THIS OFFICE. THE TELEPHONE NUMBERS ARE NINE FOUR EIGHT DASH FIVE FOUR TWO ONE, TWO TWO, AND TWO THREE. AREA CODE IS SIX ZERO ONE. YOU WILL BE ADVISED WHEN TELETYPE SERVICE IS INSTALLED AND CW RADIO FACILITIES ARE OPERATIONAL. ALL LEADS AND OTHER CORRESPONDENCE CONCERNING MISSISSIPPI ARE TO BE FORWARDED TO NEW ORLEANS AND MEMPHIS DIVISIONS AS IN PAST UNTIL JULY TWENTY FOUR, THEREAFTER TO THE JACKSON DIVISION.

END

JLW

FBI NEW YORK

About the Author

John W. Whiteside III enjoyed a thirty-year career in the FBI, serving in Cleveland and Akron, Ohio; Greenville, Mississippi; New York City, New York; FBI Headquarters at Washington, DC as a supervisor; and Philadelphia and Newtown Square, Pennsylvania. Prior to his retirement, he was a supervisor for three years in Philadelphia. He holds a BS in education from Temple University, Philadelphia, PA. After retiring from the FBI, Whiteside worked as a private investigator for a local West Chester company. Currently he provides counterintelligence consulting to the US government.

Author of the nonfiction *Fool's Mate: A True Story of Espionage at the National Security Agency* and *Cypress Shade*, a true crime FBI memoir, Whiteside currently lives in Chester County, Pennsylvania. He is married, with three children and two grandchildren.

Made in the USA
Middletown, DE
21 December 2015